KU-155-487

THE
WARRIOR
WITHIN

NITKI'S DAD

Copyright © 2022 Nitki's Dad
All rights reserved
First Edition

PAGE PUBLISHING
Conneaut Lake, PA

First originally published by Page Publishing 2022

Neither the United States Marine Corps, nor any
other component of the Department of Defense has
approved, endorsed, or authorized this book.

ISBN 979-8-88654-596-8 (pbk)
ISBN 978-1-6624-7649-5 (hc)
ISBN 978-1-6624-7648-8 (digital)

Printed in the United States of America

CONTENTS

CHAPTER 1

THE END OF THE BEGINNING

Your speed doesn't matter. Forward is forward.
—Unknown

S o much can be learned by hearing from those with experiences greater than our own—good and bad. We can also learn so much from those new to the world who see with open eyes and wonder, asking questions and watching them grow, learn, and even teach others just by their example. The indigenous peoples of this continent believe wholeheartedly in learning from elders and respecting them and their experiences. You don't have to follow someone's path to appreciate it or them. We can and will likely have company on our journey, and those individuals may walk with you and help you out. But no one can walk it for you.

In 2010 or 2011, some of my family were concerned, letting me know of my nephew's plans to join the US Marine Corps, and they wanted me to talk him out of it. Unfortunately, I had no intention of doing that because in addition to being a relative, he'd also be a brother. But this event was a starting point in the last decade or so of my life, which has been a significant journey—being tested on several fronts by people and things I never believed would hurt me or test me as they did. It's not about a military gung ho "kill, kill" mentality, although marines still breathing know how to do that when called for—brothers and sisters alike. If you don't believe me, threaten one of them, their family, home, or property, and you'll most likely see a side of something that you never want to see. The warrior spirit resides in all of us; and these events have shaped me—good to bad, wondrous to brutally painful, and most points in between that have knocked me down but given me the strength, courage, and determination to rise above them. I'm still here, and life is good and getting better. Even if these words are never seen by anyone other than myself or a significant other, putting pen to paper is liberating to a certain degree, and I am better because of it. The steps you take on the path you're walking will prepare you for the next ones you'll take on what I describe as a spiritual journey as a human being on this thing called life.

My eleven years on active duty were some of the best and worst I've ever had, but I found a set of principles and values that spoke truth to me and furthered my spiritual growth that began in my teens. I did want to understand why he wanted to join, hoping his reasoning was clear, not that he needed my approval or permission. This event was the beginning of my journey on a path I didn't realize I needed to walk. Had I known in advance of things to come, I probably would have passed on it or denied it just to avoid the pain. During the days of email chains, there was one that opened my eyes to the purpose of these struggles. A man observed a butterfly struggling to break free from its cocoon. He used his pocketknife to help free the butterfly from its cocoon, but when it emerged, it fell to the ground and would die a short time later. The purpose of the struggle was to force the water from its body into its wings, which would allow it to fulfill the purpose the Creator intended for it.

My nephew was moving up his ship date. I couldn't help but be concerned about how bad things might be for him, not caring if it was MCRD (Marine Corps Recruit Depot) San Diego or Parris Island. I'm not fond of bugs, and the Parris Island sand fleas would have been an issue for me. I attended MOS (military occupational specialty) school at Camp Del Mar aboard Marine Corps Base (MCB) Camp Pendleton, California, in the summer and fall of 1985. It was eye-opening, seeing the scars on those marines who graduated from Parris Island. I spoke to my nephew, Ken, about joining up and requesting the change and moving up his date, which would require him to attend PI instead of San Diego. I couldn't help but admire his strength and determination to start living his life sooner rather than later. My handwriting sucks. If I'm writing a letter more than half a page, I'll type it out so the individual doesn't need to decipher what the hell my cursive is supposed to be. I got ahold of the training schedule, which was similar to what I went through at MCRD San Diego, but the progress in training had advanced significantly since the mideighties. I admitted that I was uncertain what some items would entail but provided my best guess based on what I read on active and veteran marines' Facebook groups. Critical-thinking skills should be taught in all schools—not to tell the students what to think but how to think beyond what they see. Parents can also help tremendously in this area, and if we "ass-u-me" that everyone knows how to, we will only make an ass out of you and me.

> Knowing how to think *empowers you* far beyond those who know only what to think.
> (Neil DeGrasse Tyson)

I wrote once a week about my experiences during the same or similar week of training, sending it so that it would arrive a few days before the next week's training. It helped, letting me know that the drill instructors were impressed that he knew what "Mount Motherfucker" was on Marine Corps Base Camp Pendleton.

I attended his graduation at the end of March 2012, driving down from Charlotte, North Carolina, where I was living. His parents, who were divorced; his brother; his girlfriend at the time; and a few other family members drove down from Ohio to also attend. There has been a distance between myself and my oldest brother, Tom, his father, and a few other family members on my side of the tree, so we never really engaged in any discussion concerning typical family BS, *Jerry Springer* kind of material. During our visit but before the actual graduation ceremony, I came to learn that his father only wrote him once during his basic training. Years earlier, I recalled telling both nephews that "your father is a good man, but my brother is an asshole." They understood what I meant. We all have decisions to make about who we are and want to be. Every day, we are allowed to move in that direction. Even if we stumble or fall, that doesn't mean we are lost forever. No one is perfect, but some don't even make an effort or an attempt to try.

In mid-May, I drove from Charlotte to MCB Camp Lejeune to celebrate his completion of the School of Infantry training course that all marines are now required to complete after basic. I hit the road as soon as he was dismissed and getting ready for his flight so I could meet him and a few other marines at Charlotte/Douglas International Airport. At the same time, he waited for their flight out to "The Stumps," or its official name of MCB Twenty-Nine Palms, for his training as a data network specialist or its upgraded name of cyber network operator—potentially a great career opportunity in both the military and civilian sectors. In mid to late October, I flew out for his graduation from the MOS school in Twenty-Nine Palms, California, but the date changed. I had already bought the ticket, so I still went to see him for a few days. We would drive down to see my friend from high school, Rick, a brother (marine) who was now retired after twenty-five years of service as a military police officer in the corps and an amateur triathlete. Rick married his high school sweetheart, Lisa, when she turned eighteen; he was two or three years older. It was a three-hour road trip from Palm Springs to San Diego, but why not?

It was nice to see some of my old stomping grounds during my first few years of active duty. We drove by Marine Corps Air Station Tustin or what was left after the property was back in the hands of Orange County. The blimp hangars on Tustin were still there, and they are an impressive sight to see. The first command I was assigned to, HMH-462, was in one of them when they were back in the States and not deployed for six months to Marine Corps Air Station Futenma, Okinawa. I went on two six-month deployments with them over the three years I was stationed there before being transferred to inspector-instructor staff duty in Richmond, Virginia. Marine Corps Air Station El Toro met the same fate as Tustin, but we only drove by it, seeing it from I-5 as we headed south toward Rick's place in Escondido just north of San Diego. I wasn't trying to be something in his eyes that I wasn't, nor was I trying to relive my "glory" days. I was doing this to remind myself about honor and integrity and reflecting by sharing my experiences so that another might avoid the pitfalls or storms that life tends to throw at us. He would later achieve the rank of sergeant (E5) several months before his discharge four years later—six months earlier than when I reached the same.

Warriors aren't about death and destruction, even if their job is specifically combat-oriented and they train that way. All US Armed Forces members serve for various reasons, most of which are for the love of country and service to something greater than themselves—good reasons (most of them, others not so much). For some, in their mind, it may be their only chance to escape their current environment and improve their lives. Members of the military and veterans who served honorably should be respected because no matter the reason for joining, they did serve something greater than themselves for freedoms they weren't fully able to express or live while on active duty. Respect, like most things, is a two-way street. For those who have honorably served a cause more significant than themselves, they have earned respect. Many items may not be returned to you, even if given without condition, but this isn't about reciprocation. It depends on the individual and the situation, if there is one. At the forefront, ensure you respect yourself, or work on it, even though you may not be where you want to be.

> Words will always retain their power. Words are the means to meaning and, for those who listen, the enunciation of truth. And the truth is, there is something terribly wrong with this country, isn't there? (V from the movie *V for Vendetta*)

Powerful, thought-provoking, but this isn't primarily about the terrible wrongs with this or any other country but with us as human beings. Some may push your beliefs toward the better angels of our nature to the breaking point if you believe in them, but our response will either feed the fire or starve it of oxygen.

Aren't you tired of all the BS in our country, especially in the political arena, where some politicians are too busy trying to keep their jobs instead of doing the job? Some are no longer even attempting to focus on policy or have any substantive conversations with their constituents about the policy positions they advocated for and how they will help them. They dangle the flashy object in one hand while the other takes advantage of inside knowledge, schemes, and scams to increase their wealth, mostly at our expense. That should piss everyone off, as does the fact that they are allowed to lie, mislead, and misrepresent information on the House or Senate floor, committee hearings, or in their political advertising. Most people may have never heard of "there is always 10 percent" unless you've served in the military, but it's likely factual no matter if you have served in the military or not. It primarily served to describe individuals who were shit birds, never doing their job, never accountable or responsible for the things they said or did—basic screwups. And we know most politicians are more interested in power and keeping it by any means necessary than doing what is truly in the best interest of the citizens in this country.

If you're not doing your job, then someone else will have to; and while you need to count on one another in the military, it should be the standard in the civilian sector. There is also a percentage at the top end who are superior compared to us mere mortals. A sergeant (E5) who worked at one of the group command headquarters was married with two kids under the age of ten, pursuing his bachelor's and master's degree at the same time, and physically fit beyond belief. He was one of the top individuals in his field and still managed to help coach one of his kids' sports team. Later, as a manager in financial operations, I felt that it was my place to drive people up or out. Unions, are you listening? It was acceptable for those who didn't want career advancement, just wanting to do the job the best they could for the paycheck and live their lives. But I really "loved" those who would say, "That's not in my job description." My response? "I'll tell you what's in your job description." It only happened once, and then word spread. If you aren't helping the team, you are hurting them and, by extension, the department and the company and especially the customers we are providing a service or product to.

I'm not encouraging a revolution, at least not a political one, which could happen, and no, I am not promoting anything like the January 6 insurrection. For those who have read *Love and Respect: The Love She Most Desires, The Respect He Desperately Needs* by Dr. Eggerichs cover to cover, not just the introduction or first chapter like my ex did, the overall conclusion or ending will likely surprise and enlighten you, or at the very least, it should offer you the opportunity to expand on what you think you know. Over the years, when I've written letters of substance to loved ones or past employers, I felt like there were hands on my shoulders helping me write them to ensure I communicated what I wanted to so that the words would retain their power as the means to meaning. It could have also been a way to reaffirm my beliefs to individuals and the universe or even a way to tell this world's harmful and toxic energies that they won't break me. I admit that there were times that it did feel like I was broken but never beyond repair.

The legendary Johnny Cash fought for the rights of Native Americans and dedicated an entire album to them. He faced censorship and an angry backlash from the radio stations that refused to play any of the songs for speaking out. In retaliation, he bought a full-page ad of *Billboard* magazine, asking, "Where are your guts?" I needed to be brutally honest when confronting myself with what happened with Jill—a former love.

CHAPTER 2

JILL

*It's not the load that breaks you
down; it's the way you carry it.*
—Unknown

I own my story—from the hellish to the heavenly and all points in between. No matter what yours is, you must own it, which is nothing more than acknowledging the good and not so good, enjoying it, or using it to learn from it and grow. While not everyone's best is equal across the board, it should be easy to say that everyone wants the opportunity to live their best life. No matter your religion or spiritual beliefs, we are alive, even though some may not be living but merely existing. Life isn't the same for everyone, no matter how it's described or defined by the individual. A concept to consider is that "your life is a gift from the Creator. Your gift back to the Creator is what you do with your life," so shouldn't we strive to live our best life? If you don't feel right or feel lost, use the internet and social media. And search for things that will help you clear the clouds from your vision, improve your life, and help chip away and remove items that don't belong in your life. Some things prevent us from moving forward. Understand what those things may be, and then start chipping away at them. And you'll find that the weight you are carrying can be adjusted or dropped altogether.

We can be our own worst enemy when faced with a brutal truth because of a *freak* taking up residence in our minds, whispering in our ears to avoid the issues or finding the strength and courage to face them. Drugs and alcohol may be the easiest to identify, but many other self-destructive behaviors happen without our informed consent or even understanding why. In the book *Promise Me, Dad* by Joe Biden, I've wondered if the injuries his son, Hunter, suffered early on as a child made him more susceptible to the addiction or destructive behavior that he has experienced on his journey to date. No matter how many times you have been asked to change, told by another, or said "never again" to yourself, it's unlikely going to register or change you until you are ready, which may or may not be an active choice you make. Without a doubt, reflecting on the past is a must, but that doesn't mean you should live there. The phrase "hindsight is twenty-twenty" emphasizes people's clarity about past decisions instead of the uncertainty before making the decision. A few sayings or memes I've come across have highlighted this and reminded me not to get stuck in the past.

> Even though there are days I wish I could change some things that happened in the past, there's a reason the rearview mirror is so small and the windshield is so big. Where you're headed is much more important than what you've left behind. (Unknown)

> Who you are becoming is more important than who've you been. (Unknown)

> If you want to touch the past, touch a rock. If you want to touch the present, touch a flower. If you want to touch the future, touch a life. (Unknown)

For most, it's only through a struggle, hardship, or heartache that allows for authentic learning and growth to emerge from the cocoon, freeing yourself from the prison you've locked yourself in. During the early days of the internet and before social media, chain emails were popular. One that hit home for me and helped clear my perspective and perception about the struggles one goes through was a man observing a butterfly trying to emerge from its cocoon, which I included in the first chapter.

In the spring of '98, I met Jill, who was seven years older than me, but that is just a number. Having an athletic build, albeit not as in shape as she was during her basketball days in school and college, she was "my kind of beautiful"—not just her physical appearance but because of her energy, smile, light in her eyes, humor, both her quiet reserve and ability to stand her ground. A middle school gym teacher by profession, she had been previously married with one teenage son of whom she had primary custody. Her family owned and operated a farm in Johnston County, North Carolina, which she and her son would work during the summer months; and it was backbreaking work, to say the least, to hand-cut the flowers off the tobacco plants before they bloomed. She preferred Jill over her given name because it was too close to her mother's name, and using Jill alleviated confusion. It was remarkable when I discovered that her real first and middle names were the same as my younger sister's. After that serendipitous moment, I told her she shouldn't keep her Social Security card on the fridge but in a file or safe. Jill was beautiful—a country girl with a rock and roll heart, a beautiful and inviting smile, a great sense of humor, and captivating eyes that you could just get lost in. And it all captured me. We didn't date long initially, maybe six months, but that is all on me.

In the fall of '98, the position I was working in at a full-service brokerage firm in downtown Raleigh was a year away from being relocated to the corporate operational headquarters in Charlotte. I immediately began to worry, almost panic even. I had gotten out of the corps in '96 and knew what I could do and was capable of if given a chance, but I had no college degree. And society was telling people it was a must to have opportunities in the job market.

In February of '96, I was discharged and went home to Ohio to recover from the BS I had been through for the last year while on active duty. An argument with my father prompted me to move to Homestead, Florida, in May, where my extended family was living. Two months later, I needed to get a job and get moving on building a life as a civilian. Unemployment wasn't an option since I left Ohio, and the money I had received from being in a car accident while on active duty was running low. I interviewed with a temp agency, and the second job I interviewed for brought me on, which lasted about eight weeks. And then I was hired permanently as an administrative assistant. I checked with my supervisor, who agreed with the recommended changes to make things more efficient and streamlined. I started improving the front-office processes, creating efficiencies, and streamlining responsibilities. I produced an Excel spreadsheet report with graphs showing key performance indicators for our OSJ (Office of Supervisory Jurisdiction) office. A few months later, I added the entire North Carolina and South Carolina region. A year later, an audit of the financial company by the Office of the Comptroller of the Currency (OCC), a federal agency under the Department of the Treasury, did not go well. The OCC threatened to shut the doors after an audit revealed a significant problem.

The company had six months to come up with and implement a solution that fixed this. A decision was pending on who would be taking on the new role when the national sales manager visited our office a few months later. I wasn't initially considered for the job as they seemed to want either our compliance officer or supervisory principal to take on the responsibilities. The national sales manager promoted me virtually on the spot after observing and speaking with me, listening to the improvements made to the front-office responsibilities and production reports, including my philosophy and approach to things. An item I would later find and purchase from a store called Successories that had what would become my mantra was a "rock" with the following: Every Job Is a Self-Portrait of the Person Who Did It—Autograph Your Work with Excellence. My new position would require series 7, 63, and 24 securities licenses, more for the information than the actual responsibilities. I was trying to study during the summer while Jill and I were dating, but my heart and head just weren't into it. I just wanted to enjoy being with her. Her son was about fifteen at the time with typical teenage stuff. He didn't like me kicking his butt playing basketball. Still, I told him the best way to get better is through practice and competing against those who are better, which is both a motivation and learning opportunity to see if you wanted to improve your game or were in it for the show. We found baseball as a great connecting point also. I played from age six through my sophomore year in high school. The political BS at the high school level was just not worth it to continue playing for the school, so I stuck to the summer recreational leagues.

A few months into the new job—late October or November, I believe—real progress was being made at every OSJ office. An internal audit showed significant improvements that exceeded expectations. Unfortunately, our manager said that discussions were ongoing to bring the entire process back to the operations processing center in Charlotte. Some managers needed people to manage or wanted more power to justify their positions and salaries. So I began to stress about the future, which led me to withdraw from Jill. When she called about a month after I became distant, asking what was going on, I couldn't convey anything about my fears to her. I didn't know how, and they had absolutely nothing to do with her. I know I hurt her, and that is one scar that will always remain as a reminder about what I would have to come to terms with later. And it is set in my foundation *never* to let it, or anything remotely close to it, ever happen again. When you hear "It's me, not you," your eyes roll, and you call BS. But this one was mine—lock, stock, and barrel. At the end of January '99, I finally passed the series 7 exam just after getting the news about the relocation plans for my job.

Early February, I received a certificate of appreciation recognition award signed by the national sales manager for my achievements in taking the lead to help the other coordinators in the OSJ offices build out a sustainable and repeatable process. A month later, I passed the series 63. A sigh of relief came over me as I now felt I had something tangible for future employment. It also became clear that I needed to reach out to Jill and apologize for what I had done by distancing myself. I sent her a card for Mother's Day, apologizing, hoping she'd understand what I wasn't able to convey back then and forgive me. Much later, I would discover more of a deeper issue that would come to light, but that was a few years off from being realized. And I had no earthly idea what it was. We reconnected shortly after and began seeing each other over the summer without calling it dating. I passed series 24 about a month before the official layoff date of October 1. There wasn't anything at the company available or even in the Raleigh area in financial administration or operations, and I had zero interest in sales. A newly created online brokerage firm was expanding in Charlotte, and that is where I headed. I was initially hired as an operations associate, but one of only two had their securities licenses. So I was in high demand. Three months later, I was promoted to operations manager of the account approval team, whose initial responsibilities were to review and process all the online applications. We would add mail-in applications and margin (credit) approvals to the team's duties in behalf of the firm as more of them became licensed. I began writing our standard operating procedures, which we used as our training and resource manual. With the team's input and review, it became the "law of the land," even being handed over to the Equifax representative by our compliance director, who had asked me for my permission since I wrote it.

Jill had come to see me a few times, even mentioning that she had looked into teaching positions in the area. I attended her mother's funeral, sitting with her and her son. I made excuses, reasons for not being able to come to see her, and the changes she'd made to her mom's house, which was now hers. It was right next door to her house. February 9, 2003, Jill passed away suddenly, and I didn't become aware of her passing until late May, which hit me hard. It still does at times for the loss obviously and that of her son's, being at his wedding and the grandchildren she'd never come to know. *Regret sucks!* I called Jill on Friday, February 7, and she told me about injuring herself, sleeping in the recliner the night before, and not moving all day. I thought about driving up from Charlotte for the weekend but never conveyed this to her, and she didn't ask or imply that she wanted me to. In reality, I was thinking of moving back to Raleigh to see if we could try again, but I'd come to learn later that it was me running away, avoiding what others could see in me after I met and began dating Adrienne in November. I did ask her to get up every few hours to work through it, take aspirin or any other pain medication, and use a heating pad, if she wasn't already, to help her recover.

When she got up on Sunday evening, a blood clot went from her knee to her lungs, and she passed a few hours later. I hadn't seen her on AOL to chat and no response to the emails I sent or forwarded. I think when the first one bounced back as undeliverable or whatever it said, I called her number, and it was no longer in service. I searched online for her address for a phone number at that address. Her cousins were now living in her old place. I called, and they told me of her passing and gave me Matt's number, her son. I called him immediately, then left a message for him to call. When he did, I asked him to meet that weekend as I drove up to find out what happened. He was in his first year of college in Lumberton, North Carolina, and I can't recall if he was living at home and commuting or had an apartment and was home for the weekend she passed because she had hurt herself. I didn't want him to relive it beyond the basics, and his father helped him with her estate. We met at a bar and had dinner. I think he told me of the events; and my regret became more profound, immediately regretting not calling on Monday, February 10, to check. A dream where she seemed to be screaming or crying in pain woke me up. I proceeded to tell him about our meeting through the personals, with my message saying something similar to "Looking for a country girl with a rock and roll heart, who, like me, is old enough to know better but still too damn young to care."

I told him about things we would do when we got together— shoot pool, movies, music, etc.—but not every detail as there are some things no child, no matter their age, wants to hear about, and having sex with their mother is one of them. There was one incident early on in the relationship—the first time I spent the night. Jill had mentioned she hadn't told her son yet that we were being intimate and was worried about him, so I slept on the couch. She was pissed the following day because I didn't sleep with her, and I reminded her of what she had said. And she then told her son that we would be sleeping in the same bed together. He was okay with it—problem solved. Another story was when she and a girlfriend needed a girls' night out, and they wanted to crash at my place—no problem. But this wasn't going to be one of the old cliché fantasies of being with two women. I understand the visual aspect that is appealing to men. The male sex organ is on the outside, so we are more visually aroused, while the female organ is internal, and being stimulated internally is more likely needed, at least initially. They arrived at my place around midnight after drinking, feeling good but not intoxicated, and I wish they would have called for me to pick them up instead of driving. Jill wanted to go swimming and was wearing her bikini under her clothes. The pool for my apartment complex was next to my apartment, located in the back of the property. We went swimming and attempted to get busy, but the water wasn't helpful, no matter how much we wanted. After returning to the apartment, we had fun. Her girlfriend was asleep on the futon, but I don't think we woke her up.

He told me he found the journal she kept and that she had written quite a lot about me in it. My eyes widened at the thought of what she may have written in it—not for anything embarrassing but the guilt of knowing that I hurt her. And I couldn't combine that with the regret I had felt since hearing the news. Unbearable, it would have been, overwhelming me, releasing the uncontrollable flood works, and it had zero to do with being a marine or some other kind of macho BS. The two things he offered up were that she did love me and felt at home with me and that I was the best lover she ever had. I didn't ask for any more significant details or read her journal but would have if he had offered me the opportunity. I took some comfort in knowing that I did make her happy. She had a picture of us together watching one of his baseball games next to her bed. He gave me a copy of it, and I have it in the collage of pictures in my hallway. He recalled an event where his impatience caused her to be upset with him. Patience has been a weakness of mine, but that wasn't the case here. August 14, 1998, we had tickets to see Aerosmith but rescheduled for October 1. Unfortunately, a volleyball game would be rescheduled and on the same date. She coached the school's girls' volleyball team. She was upset, but it wasn't like she could not show up. No rescheduling was allowed, and if they didn't play, they'd forfeit. Not sure if it had any tournament or playoff implications or not, but that wouldn't have mattered.

I only wanted to ensure she got to see the performance of "I Don't Want to Miss a Thing" and hold her as she wished. She got tired of "Can't we leave yet?" from her son, so she told or asked me to take him and that she'd meet us there once the games were over and equipment put away. I had broken down, and having bought a cell phone at some point earlier that summer, I called her to get updates on her arrival and where we were. Short story long, she got there in time to see the performance of the song, but we weren't able to find each other before or during them playing it. One of the last things I told Matt during all of this reminiscing was being startled awake sometime around 3:00 a.m. on February 10 by what appeared and felt like Jill crying out in pain. When I heard the news of her passing months later, I became overwhelmed with guilt for not calling that morning after my dream. I questioned was it my fault for what happened to her because I was thinking about moving back to Raleigh. I've come to learn and accept that it wasn't my fault. When we've accomplished our purpose for being here, we return home. That doesn't mean that things happen that shorten life, which is tragic. Helping others could extend our reasoning for being here, not because it's part of our life lessons but rather to impact another life. Perhaps that is why most refer to it as a mystery.

I told Matt that I loved his mom and realized that some issue or concern had prevented me from proposing to her and that I needed to figure out and come to terms with things that may be keeping me prisoner in a prison of my own making.

CHAPTER 3

My Own Prison

Don't speak negatively about yourself,
even as a joke. Your body doesn't know
the difference. Words are energy and cast
spells; that's why it's called spelling.
—Bruce Lee

The song "My Own Prison" by Creed on the album of the same name brought the message home for me. I never wanted to experience the kind of pain and regret from Jill's passing ever again, nothing even remotely close to anything similar to it, and I knew I had the power within me to figure this out. Whatever it took, I knew it wouldn't happen overnight, nor would it be easy. I began a brutally honest assessment to reflect on everything from my earliest memories to my current point in time. I started with the one primary question that I wanted, needed an answer for—what held me back from proposing and marrying Jill? Some follow-up questions would also need to be answered to ensure I wasn't running away or avoiding things. If I was, why and what was the impact on me; my life; my relationships; or my physical, mental, emotional, or spiritual health?

Was I wearing blinders because they were comfortable? Or maybe I was just in denial—you know it's not just a river in Egypt.

A line from the movie *Hope Floats* that speaks about spending the rest of your life trying to overcome your childhood is tongue-in-cheek, but there is substance there. The worst part of our past is if we come up with excuses or justifications to avoid the heart of the issue. Resolve any internal conflict. Forgive those, or even ask for forgiveness. "Let go, let God" doesn't mean giving it all to the Creator to solve; you still have to do your part and help the higher spiritual being out. It's understandable why you wouldn't want to think about any of the negative, but how do you know it's not affecting your current life in some small way? What you may ultimately find and resolve could be positive because you learned, grew, and brought it into your wheelhouse, owning it so you could move forward without the baggage of it weighing you down—only a one-time process unless there are more significant psychology issues at play, where a professional's help is needed. *Success* means different things to different people, but don't all parents want their children to be more successful than they are or were? It's not always about money, but at the foundation, to be able to live your life and not merely exist in it should be a part of any description or definition of success. No, I'm not suggesting everyone can sing or win *American Idol* or be a big-time movie star. Still, everyone has the opportunity to be whatever they choose to be, which, for most, takes hard work, dedication, and practice. And through all that, you may find a life that isn't what you dreamed, but it is what you love, creating a new dream that you are living. Some might consider Simon Cowell as cruel. But perhaps he is just brutally honest with the contestants. The reason may be to test the mettle and resolve to see if the contestant can take in the criticism, work harder to overcome any deficiencies, and try again, or maybe it just isn't the right time for them. But they still have promise. Look at the character Paul Walker played in *Varsity Blues*, where the character found their calling only after being injured and derailing his college hopes. Those events may need to happen, even if it's not in an exact way, and they are or can be instrumental in finding your true calling or purpose.

I would have to be brutally honest with myself for any actual, meaningful, and lasting change to prevent that kind of pain or anything even remotely close to it from happening again. The truth is a bitter pill to swallow, especially when confronting the reflection in the mirror, but only real eyes realize real lies. If we can't or aren't willing to be brutally honest and come to terms with it, excuses and justifications are likely to continue to be made, and so begins the cycle of repeating the same or similar mistakes. These may not be all the events and observations that have shaped my life until the summer of 2003, but they are the ones that stand out the most. It is what it is, with whatever lesson or learning I took from it. While most of it may initially appear negative, it's all in how we carry it and move forward. I was able to drop the negative aspects of those that were and move forward in a positive direction, and that is all that matters. Nothing happened overnight, nor should it, unless it's something pretty easy and solvable. The first thing I did was reach out to all family and friends that I knew via email or phone, asking them to confirm their contact information and ensure they had mine listed in an actual phone book, and I briefly explained why I was asking. In today's technology-driven ways, it's not a bad idea to also have the information written down as a backup. Adrienne was the first email response I received. We hadn't spoken much, if at all, since we stopped seeing each other, not even on Yahoo! Messenger; but a few weeks after an incident occurred at her house, which was hard to believe, she invited me to shoot pool with her and her team on Thursday nights around the end of June.

I questioned the memories, events, or observations to determine if there were any unresolved issues that might be negatively impacting my life in any way. Were there deeper issues at play that I might need to seek professional help for? I'd joke with myself by asking if I should just cut to the chase and get myself committed. The memories, events, or observations range from silly to "what the F was I thinking." In each—good, bad, or in between—there was likely something to be learned, and eventually, it was. And they have shaped my life in one form or another, even the silly ones that you can't help but look back on, laugh, and roll your eyes. Throughout this writing, other memories or events have had some impact on me. Most, if not all, are from my youth until the time I shipped out for basic in late February 1985, but revelations or understandings finally made sense or hit home as two powerful things ultimately did help me. I was having lunch with Adrienne's mom, Myrna, on May 1, 2021. After seeing the Michelangelo Sistine Chapel exhibit in town is when I realized one. The other brought me full circle. I began to understand why I felt a distance between myself and some of my siblings, including my heritage. Life, like a picture, can be developed from the negatives. In this development, as it pertains to life, we can also build on the positives.

By June 2003, I had been out of the corps since February '96, just shy of eleven years, divorced twice while in the corps, harassed at my last unit because I fought for custody of a child who wasn't biologically mine, and other events that I'll get into later. So the scars, bars, or observations, looking out and looking in, were part of me creating my prison. But "the names have been changed to protect the innocent," and *innocent* is a relative term. Still, it's not relevant to the underlying item, and I am not interested in some back-and-forth on this, although some names are correct because they are no longer with us physically. The key to the process was identifying the issue, looking at it under a microscope, breaking it down, and checking to see if it was still currently an issue, not that they were before. Still, some elements will always remain with me as I learned and grew from them, mainly my resolve to ensure they will no longer control or impact my life in a negative or self-destructive way.

The six earliest memories I recall were before we moved to a new house in a new subdivision in Oregon in the late summer of '73. It was still in Lucas County, and that would be when I was six. I asked one or both of my parents about the colors of the traffic signals because I would see them on the walk home from kindergarten at McKinley Elementary School and didn't know what each one meant. I would meet my oldest brother, Tom, outside DeVilbiss High School, and we'd walk home together. I think we walked home every day, maybe also walking to school, too, but not sure; and I would think a six-year-old walking alone, even back then, may not be a wise thing to let happen. It was only about two and a half blocks to the house, so it's possible. There was always a police officer in the middle of the intersection directing traffic, and the next day, the light was green. And I was off, running across several lanes of traffic but through the crosswalk, not weaving in between cars. The officer caught me just as I stepped on the other side of the sidewalk and asked why I did that. My reply was "Green meant to go, red to stop, and yellow to slow down. And the light was green, so I went." Yes, Captain Obvious, I misunderstood the answer—thank you for clearing that up. As punishment, I had to go back to the elementary school side of the street and then cross the road to the other side three times when the pedestrian lights indicated, which the officer explained. I was mad and upset as I got the wrong answer for the question I was asking about, and on top of that, my glued picture of George Washington that the teacher gave me a gold star for got ruined because it was lightly raining. Once done with my punishment, I thought I waited for Tom outside the high school. Still, he had already left; so I ran home—cold, scared, feeling alone, and crying the entire way because I got in trouble. I didn't fully understand why, and my brother wasn't there to explain. I wouldn't say anything once I arrived home.

Sometime that summer, my younger brother, Mike, and I were walking around the neighborhood, seeing if any of our friends wanted to play; and we were eating dog biscuits out of the box, which we didn't know weren't for humans. My dad loved our German shepherd named Rusty but suspected that my mom intentionally left the gate open, and he escaped before we moved. Anyway, I recall the biscuits tasting okay. And I guess it had to do with being the two youngest in the family at the time, and getting snacks or treats with four older siblings was next to impossible. So when we found them, we indulged. Yes, we got laughed at the first house by friends who were closer to our age as they said they were for dogs, not humans. And we've never done that again—at least I haven't.

That same summer, I recall falling off the small ledge on the side of our aboveground swimming pool because I had fallen asleep and tried to roll over—ouch. Sometime later in the summer, I had thought of how fun it was watching rocks make big splashes, so I began to pick up the flat stones around the pool. They were about a half to one inch thick and six or more inches in diameter. Not sure how many I actually tossed into the pool—at least five and probably more. Safe to say that my father was not very happy about it as I watched him in the pool trying to find all the rocks—not sure if I had an actual choice or not. The water was dirty, and he was trying to locate them with his feet. No damage to the pool liner thankfully, or my story may have likely ended right there. I never did anything like that again.

The next one, in the same summer, was about kissing the girl who lived on the same street. She was a year older. Kissing is all that was done and not like anything passionate or with tongues or open mouths. It may have just been one time, but it seems like it happened on more than one occasion. And I also walked onto the rooftop porch to see her as she and her girlfriend were sunbathing and, yes, with swimsuits on. The kissing was always in her closet, sitting on the floor so that no one would see us.

The last of the six was some strange drama crap. I was lying in the front yard, hoping the teenage girl walking down the sidewalk heading toward our house would "revive me." I don't think she walked by, but if she had, she likely thought I was enjoying the sunshine and the smell of fresh-cut grass. I had no earthly idea what I was thinking or why I would want a stranger to rescue me. I didn't know if in kissing the neighbor or the incident above, I was mimicking adults or from what I saw on TV. Was I an old soul who had a problem in a previous life that carried over? Whatever it was that had me acting like that at such a young age, I'll never know. Still, it's not an issue these days, even though I would learn through this process that my ability to handle or deal with rejection or someone I liked "losing that loving feeling" toward me would need some understanding.

I was in first grade at Star Elementary at the time, and in the evening, I wasn't feeling good. And after I said it, up came everything from dinner, and it was in the family room. I'm not sure the stain on the carpet ever came out fully or not. I think it happened on a Thursday or just before we started a vacation for the holidays. I only missed a total of three days of school in my twelve years, and this was the only time because I was sick. One was when I was traveling back from visiting my extended family in Liverpool, New York, in the spring of '82, and the other was Senior Skip Day. I never participated in any of the other "skip days" before. But I was graduating early and leaving for basic training, so why the hell not? I didn't get sick, but I would feel that tingle every April and October. And a cold sore would appear like clockwork. Somehow, I got the impression that they were preventing me from getting sick. The first one at age seven was the worst because I had no idea what the hell it was, and picking and scratching made it worse and created a scab about the size of a quarter. Campho-Phenique was the only thing around at that time. In junior high, a science teacher recommended camphor spirits and zinc oxide ointment—neither worked. Eventually, medication would take care of the problem; and even though I still get that "cold sore tingle" every once in a while, they never get beyond a small pea-size sore. With other ointments available, they don't appear or last for more than a couple of days, if at all.

I was getting ready to go into third grade; and that Fourth of July, we went downtown for the fireworks, although we stayed on the east side of the river. I recall a huge thunderstorm building in from the west. When the lightning flashed, you could see a blue bubble over the skyline that just seemed like evil. The fireworks were over, and I pulled my mother or father to get to the car faster. A few hours later, we were yanked out of bed and taken to the basement. The patio furniture was wet because they had just brought it in from outside. The first tornado siren I recall hearing was a few years later; a tornado touched down near Wheeling and Seaman Roads. We heard a few minutes later on the radio that Elvis had died. Thunderstorms freaked me out until after I joined the Marines. I was home on leave during one spring, not sure of the year; but I remember watching from the front porch a thunderstorm that was coming in—some thunder and lightning but nothing that would rattle your teeth. And then it moved on, which was pretty soothing as I remember.

In third grade, I began having horrific nightmares, waking up screaming and drenched in sweat. The nightmares involved me drowning in a lake or pond too far from the shore, gasping for air, and for whatever reason, numbers were all around me. My parents let me sleep between them a few times, hoping they would stop. Still, eventually, I would be taken out of school a few times to talk with a therapist or psychologist. It didn't take more than a few meetings with her to resolve, which had to do with math and trouble with the multiplication tables and division. During one of the sessions where my parents were meeting with her, my younger sister, Jillian, and I explored the offices and found a room with a Ping-Pong table with one side up, so I began to play. We had a pool table and a home-made Ping-Pong table in the basement, and I loved playing both. As I understood it, my father went to go and see my math teacher at some point to see if she was the cause or not. She wasn't, and when I saw Roz from the movie *Monsters, Inc.*, it became a laughable reminder of my third-grade math teacher. What I would eventually come to love was math. In the fall of '79, I was at Fassett Junior High School. I was asked or chosen—can't remember—to participate in The Greater Toledo Council of Teachers of Mathematics's yearly event, which involved a math exam on a Saturday at the University of Toledo. In '80, I placed 574 out of 769; and in '81, I placed 311 out of 719. My freshman year, I didn't participate because I played sports the entire year.

In the fifth grade, we had our first and only health class on sex education. It shouldn't be a surprise to anyone that most boys aren't very mature at that age. I'm sure there are some ladies who, from experience, think age is irrelevant as some males have never been or will be mature. But armed with new information, none of us were brave enough to ask the teacher any follow-up questions. I asked my mom when I got home, and my oldest brother happened to be there. So I wondered, *How does a woman get pregnant from a man peeing inside her?*—or something like that. Their response was just laughter, with no follow-up or asking me what I meant so they could understand what I was trying to ask. I sure as hell wasn't going to bring it up again, and you could forget about me asking questions surrounding sex with anyone in my family.

In the fifth- or sixth-grade years, I was in Cub Scouts, and there was an overnight weekend trip to a camp in the area, coming home on Sunday morning. An initiation made no sense whatsoever; the Cub Scout would kneel before an older Scout with a hand on their knee. The older Scout would tell the Cub, "You have something on that doesn't belong," so the child would struggle to think what it was before being provided the first clue: clothing. And it would continue until the boy was down to his underwear, and then something else happened. But I have no idea what because when it was my turn after I lost my shirt and socks, another Scout did something that scared me to death. It wasn't sexual, and I think it involved ice. But I only remember screaming. My initiation was over. The next Scout was blindfolded and made to stand on a plank lifted off the ground. His was different because he already knew the initial initiation trick.

I have no earthly idea what the purpose was to any of this, but I couldn't sleep that night. And the following day, Sunday, I didn't think I needed to go to church because we had a service at the camp on Saturday. I went upstairs to sleep. My father was pissed that I wasn't ready and was making the family late to Mass, so we had to go to the later service at St. Clement's. Now, being late for the church was the family mantra. The only way we made it early or on time to services would be if we were already or going to be fifteen minutes late to eleven thirty. We'd head to a church that had a Mass at noon. The running joke was that we'd be late for our funerals. He was so pissed that he told me that I couldn't sit with or near the family. So I walked ahead a bit faster, went in, and sat down in the first seat I found in the back. The rest of the family walked to the front pews. A few minutes after Communion was done but before the service was officially over, I got up from the bench, knelt in the aisle, did the sign of the cross, walked to the car, and got in the back seat. Later that afternoon, to deflect from something, Mike would proclaim that I didn't stay in the church. My father then grilled me about the man who needed an ambulance. There wasn't, but my father had no reason to lie to me, right? So I responded with answers I thought he wanted to hear. Because my answers were incorrect, I had to go to church again with my oldest brother at 5:00 p.m. I considered later that what he did was pretty cruel, considering, and I never engaged with my parents on any level unless I was asked or responding to something.

We sat near one of his friends from high school during the service, and I had to sneeze and did so. I was embarrassed because snot came out, some hitting the floor and the rest dangling from my nose. For the next thirty years or so, when I would sneeze, I'd hold my nose because I didn't want a repeat. When Adrienne heard the whistling sound effect of air passing through my eardrums as a result, she pointed out the damage I could do, and I eventually stopped doing it most of the time. Years later, I was on leave at the extended family home outside Raleigh and attended Easter services with them. I couldn't breathe from the moment I walked in; it was psychological but having a physical reaction. I kept my composure, but it was the last time I attended a church regularly until sometime in 2013 or 2014. Maybe someday I'll go again, but for me, the church isn't a place I need to go to worship or speak to God. It's for people—a place for the community. A line in the movie *Stigmata* really brought it home for me.

> The kingdom of God is within you and all
> around you. It is not within buildings of wood
> or stone. Split a piece of wood, and you will
> find me. Look beneath a stone, and I am there.
> (Gospel of Thomas)

I had seen on a Facebook meme with a quote attributed to Quanah Parker, Comanche, which read, "We do not go into ceremony to talk about God. We go into ceremony to talk with God." I began further discovering that my faith or spirituality aligned more with the indigenous peoples of this country. I'm sure there are similarities between it and all religions of the world.

In the same time frame of the fifth or sixth grade, after the health class incident on sex education, the most embarrassing and shameful feeling I have ever felt happened—at least that's how I felt. I had clothes on; but a female, who was a few years younger, didn't or was partially undressed—not sure why. We were sitting on a bed, but nothing happened. Nothing penetrated anything—no mouth to mouth or on any body part, no skin-to-skin touching—and we were both laughing. The door unexpectedly opened, and I felt an immediate and overpowering feeling of shame and embarrassment, which I didn't understand why at the time. But it was enough. I am grateful that nothing more serious happened because I wouldn't have been able to bear it. I never wanted to feel anything even remotely close to that ever again. At such a young age, I had no one to talk to about it—why I felt embarrassed and ashamed—or, more importantly, to explain what was wrong or bad about it. Adrienne would be the only one I would ever mention this to, which was after I knew I would propose and before I did. I needed her to know all my skeletons—everything about me—and the events that had the most profound impact on me, who I was, and why.

I wanted to live my life with honor and integrity, not necessarily perfect but without fear of judgment being passed against me when I knelt and reviewed my life to ensure I had learned the lessons I was sent here to learn. I reached out to the woman sometime after I finished the "brutally honest" process because I was aware of her struggles with her relationships with men. She didn't remember anything about the incident and knew her relationship issues were because the man she was in love with, who had professed his love for her, wouldn't leave his wife. She tried to break away from him several times, but he would visit her at work and act like he was there to pick something up for his side business. Or he'd call or stop by her place relentlessly until she caved. I didn't need to, but I forgave myself long ago for any shame or embarrassment I felt at the time for not knowing what was wrong about it and having no guilt for the woman's struggles with men. I'm not sure if it's like this all over the world; but talking about sex, or issues surrounding it in general, seems to be a struggle for most. What I would come to realize about love and what I wanted or needed from my significant other is for them to be willing to fight through all the demons in hell and the devil himself to be with me instead of coming up with bullshit excuses as to why they couldn't or wouldn't. I don't want to be needed, at least not in a dependent kind of way. I needed to be wanted, desired in the most positive of ways, as we all likely do. Yes, Captain Obvious, I am aware of the appearance of hypocrisy here considering what I did to Jill, but remember, this was after the brutally honest assessment that I began after finding out about her passing. This process would evolve me into a better person—someone I could look in the mirror and be proud of. It's hard to look at the reflection in the mirror and see the truth, especially when you didn't know what it was or have avoided it like the plague up until that point.

I began playing sports as soon as I was eligible to participate in them. I started with T-ball in the summer of '74 through the summer before my senior year—football and basketball on teams for the schools and baseball in the summer recreational league. My parents pissed me off during basketball season in my fifth- or sixth-grade year. I was wearing old tennis shoes with significant holes in them during the winter and still trying to play basketball in them and on a basketball floor that wasn't wood but old tile; even with a good pair of shoes and traction, you were going to slide. I know money was tight, but the shoes they'd buy were from the discount stores. I begged for new ones, but for whatever reason, it would be sometime in the spring when I'd get new ones. It was more than the embarrassment of it all; it left me with a feeling that I didn't matter.

In the summer of '79, a female friend a year ahead of me invited me to swim at her girlfriend's house. Sometime within thirty minutes of swimming, laughing, and cutting up, both approached me laughing and attempted to remove my swimming trunks, and they nearly got them off. It scared the ever-living shit out of me. I got out of the pool, hopped on my old banana-seat bike, and sped home like the devil himself was behind me. I never mentioned it to anyone at home out of fear of being laughed at by friends who would all try to come across as macho or some other kind of BS. I never looked back or thought of it again, even in the fall of '80 when the female friend and I "dated" for a short time. I wasn't even remotely mature enough to understand what dating meant; all I knew was that we liked each other. I wanted to feel something other than the loneliness of being alone in a crowded house, sometimes walking on eggshells out of fear of my father being in a mood and getting in trouble and kicked off whatever sports team I might be on at the time. She was on the freshman basketball cheerleading squad, and I'd go to the games. It didn't last more than a month or two, but we remained friends.

Saturday morning in the spring of '82, my father yelled for me to get out of bed and come downstairs. I was still waking up as he asked me what the notice from the school indicating that I could potentially fail a class was about. I told him it was no longer a concern as I had already improved my grades in the two weeks since the teacher informed me about it, which was up to a *B* now. I attempted to explain this, but he slapped me across the face before explaining why it was no longer accurate. If it had been a closed fist, which he never did, it would have knocked me out. After the stun wore off, my response was something to the effect of "Oh hell no!" and took off out of the house, running up to the junior high football field and sitting in the bleachers. I had a shirt on and shorts but was barefoot, and I probably ran faster than I ever had in any track meet before or after. My older brother who had graduated in '79, Mark, would eventually show up about five to ten minutes later. I proceeded to tell him that the notice was no longer an issue or accurate because I had been working hard for the last two weeks to bring it up and did, and if he had any concerns, he could confirm by calling the school or teacher on Monday. I don't know if he ever did, but this hurt more than his belt ever did. I went back home about an hour later, and my father steered clear of me, and I of him. I think he realized he had gone too far but never let on, and he never apologized about anything.

My freshman year was eventful in virtually every aspect. I was the starting left guard on the football team and made the basketball team, not as a starter, but I made it. Of course, it's also possible the coach had a soft spot because Mark also played for him, and he had a hell of a lot more talent than I did. I ran the individual mile, one-mile relay, and the half-mile (880), which was my race in track. My best run time was two minutes and twelve seconds against the third best in the state, I think, or Northwest Ohio, beating him by a few strides. Cindy was a seventh grader with an eighties hairstyle and a great smile that struck home and was so easy to talk with. I think we "dated," but I can't honestly recall. And neither did she when I asked recently. I began earning money by watching some neighborhood kids down the street on Friday nights while their mom bowled and their dad worked at night. In December, I met Jerry, who had just moved into the area. He would become my brother from another mother over the summer as I was "adopted" as a member of his family, which would become my extended family. During lunch, we'd crack up with our friends. I was friends with everyone no matter how they were referred to by others—jock, burnout, social, nerds, etc.

I previously met Rick while running eighth-grade track. He ran for Eisenhower Junior High School—our "rival." He convinced me to hitch a ride on the eighth-grade track team's bus going to the high school for a track meet, and he wanted to introduce me to someone. Both freshman teams had the day off, so I wasn't missing any practice. I hitched a ride and sat in the first open seat next to Casey, who was friends with Sara, a neighbor who lived on the same street I did. Both were in the eighth grade. We all joked on the way there and back, met Rick and the girl, and had fun—but no sparks or pursuit beyond knowing each other. I got a call the next day saying that Casey was interested. We spoke at school and on the phone a time or two before we started "dating." This was a soap opera, not because of any drama but because of the back-and-forth time frame. It lasted for about a week initially. A day or two later, we were back together for about four or five days before a day break and then back for one, maybe two days. She invited me over to her house on the first Saturday after we met, and I saw Jerry and asked him, "What are you doing here?"

He said, "I live here."

Casey wasn't my first love. That was a girl that lived up the street from me when I was in sixth grade—puppy love but still felt great. Casey was the first that I kissed. Even though I didn't have a real clue how to kiss, there was a natural feeling behind it. I would struggle with a kind of rejection, feeling like a lost puppy dog even though the "relationship" had just run its course. The struggle was that I had no idea how to comprehend or process the emotions, and there was no one I felt comfortable speaking to about it. I got a bit jealous, maybe even a little creepy, when she began seeing another guy from another school, which lasted not much longer than our time together did. Her family had moved a few times in the last few years because of her dad's work at nuclear power stations, which made getting close to people hard, so I know it wasn't all on me. Still, it probably wasn't until my second visit with them near Syracuse at the end of summer after my sophomore year that I'd changed in that I was no longer creepy or jealous. I'd apologize years later for any creepiness that may have been present during that time, but she let me know she didn't remember me acting that way or, at the very least, that it left no scar tissue or issues on her part.

I had my first physical fight with someone in my freshman year's late winter or early spring. It was the beginning of building up my resolve, courage, and strength to stand up for myself, and it was before I would give my younger brother the ass whooping he deserved from the bullying and constant torment I received from him over the last three years or so. A classmate was getting on my last nerve for some reason and wouldn't let up or go away. It may also have been a combination of him provoking me and making fun of or harassing a girl who was my friend and sat next to me in art class. Don't laugh; it was a required elective. No matter the reason, I had enough and challenged him, and he agreed to fight. But it would have to be near his house after school since he'd have no way to get home after school if it wasn't. I walked to school, and yes, I did walk through the snow when it snowed. I sat with mutual friends who rode the same bus, interested in seeing how this would play out. Once we got off the bus and it left, I allowed him to back down or apologize. He wouldn't, so I stepped in and proceeded to throw and land multiple punches to his face and maybe one or two to the gut. It lasted about ten to fifteen seconds. He gave up—the end.

I ran the three miles home with light snow falling and saw Joe, an older brother in his senior year, running down one of the main streets about a half mile from the house. I told him about the fight but no one else. Mike, the "golden child" as my other siblings and I would refer to him, could do nothing wrong in our mother's eyes and get away with pretty much everything unless my father found out. He was the only one with red hair. My mother had blond hair, and my father black—interesting, huh?

During my years in school, I had a habit of silently mouthing the last few words of what I had just stated out loud, and people would ask why, which I had no idea. Mike would tease me about it, and one of his favorite things to call me was "Bubble Butt," along with other things. And I just let it roll off, or so I thought. I was able to get the family dog to playfully attack him on command, which would turn his attention away from me. The rest of my family witnessed his tormenting and bullying, and neither said or did anything to stop him. I would come to realize later that my father just wanted me to fight back. Of course, I had to learn this through osmosis right—nothing new. I was confused because I thought we were supposed to turn the other cheek as Christians. At least that's how I thought it was supposed to be after nine freaking years of catechism classes and making my confirmation that year. For the record, I agree with each of the gifts of the Holy Spirit received through confirmation, except the last one (wisdom, understanding, knowledge, fortitude or courage, counsel, piety or love, and fear of the Lord). I love the description and explanation of the relationship between the three personas of the Creator (Father, Son, and Holy Spirit), understanding above all else that they are love. As such, I do not fear the Creator, his Son, or the Holy Spirit. I also don't want to disappoint them or those loved ones who have passed before me; so when I kneel before them, reviewing my life, I hope that I can stand tall in defense of the things I have said and done in the life I have lived.

It would be the year after I got my driver's license before I began to appreciate or like going to church, not because I no longer had to but because it was now my choice as to when or what service, Saturday or Sunday, I could go to and drive myself. I only then began to appreciate the readings and homily, finding the connection between it and what I had been through the previous week—nothing earth-shattering, just a small connection. So one afternoon, Mike was starting in on me, and I had enough and told him to stop or I would kick his ass. He kept it up. Second warning, same response.

There would be no third warning. I said, "Let's go outside." Our oldest brother followed us to the front porch, and I proceeded to beat the shit out of him as soon as the storm door closed. I started hitting him on both sides of his mouth and stomach for about two to three minutes, never letting up. When I first connected to his jaw with a right and his cheek with a left, his eyes got big, and I suspect he realized I was serious. I continued for a minute or two until he said he had enough. I told him if he ever or said or did anything to piss me off again, I wouldn't stop until the cops arrived and put me in handcuffs. I never had a problem with him again.

On Friday nights during my freshman year, I began babysitting three kids in the neighborhood. The summer before my sophomore year, I cut grass for about two months with a neighbor's boyfriend and his older brother, a Vietnam vet marine. In the spring, I wanted a bike—a twelve-speed road bike—and I saw the picture of it in the Sears or Montgomery Ward's catalog. Costing $120, my father agreed to pay for half if I could come up with the other half. He had got laid off in May or June, and we made ourselves scarce when he was home because he would come up with all sorts of crap for us to do to keep himself busy. I'm not sure; but when I said I had half, he said he couldn't pay for his half for it and that if I wanted it, I would have to pay for it myself. I had the money, and we drove to Sears to pick it up in the box. And I assembled it when we got home. I began riding it everywhere, including to see a neighbor's cousin who I had recently met and who lived near the University of Toledo.

In my sophomore year, it was time to order class rings. That year I ran cross-country but passed on trying out for the JV basketball team. There was just too much better talent, so I chose to play on a team in the intermural league, which I also did in my junior year. I did play on the JV baseball team. The cost was going to be $400 for the ring; and once again, my father said, "If you get half, I'll pay the other." I earned more than what I needed, and when I asked, he again said he couldn't. So that meant if I wanted a class ring, I'd have to pay for it all myself. So I did. Two things that pissed me about this is that I dated a girl in the winter and gave her my class ring to wear as a necklace. That was what the girls did when they were dating someone, or they would wrap enough yarn around so that they could wear it on their hand. When my father found out, he said I had to get it back. I was pissed because it was mine. I paid the entire cost of it, and it wasn't like she was going to keep it if we stopped seeing each other. I got it back, and we continued seeing each other for a few months after. The other happened the following year. My father made the same deal with my younger brother, but my father ended up paying the entire cost of his class ring. It was then that I began to feel that I couldn't trust my father's word.

During my sophomore and junior years, I coached a basketball team of fifth and sixth graders at my old elementary school, and it was one of the best things I ever did. I loved everything about it, especially seeing the kids learn, gain confidence from improving their abilities, and have fun as a team. One of the kids I was still babysitting for could hit shots from a three-point range on each side of the basket. We went to the playoffs each year, and I can't recall if we won. But we did against the only coach I truly wanted to beat. Not sure what it was about him. He was an adult with his kids that I was in school with. All I knew was that I just wanted to win those games each year. On the last game of the season or playoffs in my junior year, I had to miss the game; and a backup coach, someone who also knew the kids, coached them. They played well but not with as much energy probably because I wasn't there for them. I was at work at the Pizza Inn, and the manager had called a mandatory meeting for the same time as the game just to announce that she was going to become the restaurant owner and run it as a franchise store. I got to the game a few minutes after it ended and kicked myself for a month because I felt I let the kids down. I began to develop a sense of wanting to ensure I never put myself in a position in my life, especially my career, that put the job over doing what I knew, in every fiber of my being, was right and for the right reasons.

A major life-altering event happened in February of my junior year. The following two to three months would be the worst thing I had ever gone through since, although a few competed for first. I was dating Kristen, who was a year younger, and it was great! I thankfully blame her for my "addiction" to Burger King's original chicken sandwiches. Her parents still seemed to be very much in love, and they were funny, especially her mom. Her father was a marine, not sure if he served in Vietnam or not. Her siblings were mostly out on their own but still close. We had plans to go to the variety show at the high school on a Saturday night in February. I'd pick her up after I got off work. My parents played cards at their friend's house, and I had the number if anything happened. I called her, but she was at her sister's near the Medical College of Ohio in the southern part of Toledo and seemed distant on the phone. I got directions, verified them on the map, and headed that way after speaking to her. She was upset at something but wouldn't tell me over the phone. We talked when I got there. All was okay. She was upset because she had a dream about another guy or something like that. An hour after I got there, I left to go home.

It was raining, and I was headed north on the Anthony Wayne Trail approaching South Avenue. My mind wasn't on the road but on what we had been discussing. I noticed the red lights at the intersection and the cars already in it and immediately slammed the brakes and turned the wheel, hitting a light pole. It was better than T-boning a car—but oh shit, I knew my life was over. And I was upset as the cops showed up and started asking questions about drinking. I explained that my father was going to kill me or beat me close to it. Once I got to the police station, I called my father at the number he gave me and told him what happened but forgot which precinct I was at because I didn't know, and he didn't ask. They got home and proceeded to call virtually every police department in the area looking for me. After about two hours, I called and had the operator break into the call to tell him where I was. He and my oldest brother got there around 2:00 or 3:00 a.m. I heard them come in the door, and I got up from sitting on the floor. I had my driver's license in hand and tried to give it to him. He looked away—no question or concern if I was okay or what happened, straight to the desk to get the information about where the car was, what condition it was in, what caused the accident, and a copy of the ticket.

On January 1 in Ohio, the mandatory insurance law became effective, where every vehicle was now required to carry liability insurance. As I understood it, hospitals were losing money for the cost of medical care for those injured in accidents or something like that. My father didn't like being told or forced to do anything. I can't imagine many people do. He insisted that he'd pay the homeowner's insurance and property taxes directly to the insurance or city or county offices. He absolutely wouldn't allow them to be part of the mortgage payment. For whatever reason, the bank allowed it, or maybe it wasn't mandatory then. The next day, I was getting ready to leave for work at the Pizza Hut off Woodville Road, and it was over three miles on my bike, which I had ridden several times in the snow and slush to get there. My father told me that I had to quit, which I wanted to challenge but knew if I did, I'd end up against the wall or my body's imprint would be. I called my manager, who also happened to be my mom's nephew, and let him know, and from that point on, I was alone in a house full of people—my parents, oldest brother, younger brother, younger sister, and the dog. The dog would be the *only* one who would acknowledge me or that I existed for the next three months.

I became a pariah as no one was going to do anything to chance to upset our father. No one was going to chance to have our father get pissed with them because they talked to me. I seem to recall hearing something years later that, at the time, he thought I was on drugs and accused Kristen of it, but I don't know if he ever approached her or her parents. Sometime in that first week, my father began feeling chest pains and went to the hospital, but it was stress- or anxiety-related, not any heart condition. He was stressed because he didn't have the required insurance as mandated by the new law. The charge was driving too fast for conditions, but I have no idea what actually happened in court—a fine maybe, which I could understand I'd have to pay for. But it wouldn't have been the entire amount I had saved up, which I think was around $600. He may have had to pay a fine as the owner for not having the required insurance, but I never knew.

College for me was no longer in my immediate future. I understand that my father had informed the judge that I used the car without his permission or knowledge, which wasn't exactly true. I had permission to use the car for work and to go to the high school after but not where I went. Safe to assume that wasn't disclosed and was probably why I wasn't in court. I couldn't be called to the stand or speak about what happened if I wasn't there. Within that first week or so, the car was brought back home and put on the basketball court for the entire neighborhood to see, and every day I went to school or went outside, it was a constant reminder as if the treatment by those in the house wasn't bad enough. I couldn't get a job and wasn't babysitting since it was only in the fall that I did. A smarter person would have dived into books or something else to keep the mind engaged and occupied, but depression from solitude would worsen. My oldest brother was living in the house, but the next two weren't. Mark was living in Columbus; and Joe was in the Marine Corps, stationed at MCAS El Toro, California. My oldest sister, Marie, was in her apartment in East Toledo.

Sometime in early March, suicide had entered my mind on more than a few occasions, daily or every few days, but it never moved beyond the thought. I wasn't doing that. I'd pack some clothes and leave before doing that. They could figure it out later. My extended family was living near Syracuse, New York, and I hadn't called or spoken to them in a while. And I don't think I told them because they might have called my parents out of concern and maybe even offered to let me live with them for a semester of school. I knew I could sure as hell use one of "Mom C's" hugs! I vaguely recall that Sara, the neighbor from down the street who was also part of the extended family, would live with them for a semester. Sometime around the end of March and the beginning of April, Candy, a neighbor who lived on another street a short distance from the house, said hi and smiled at me in the school hallway. She was beautiful, with a great smile that made you melt. I looked up, smiled back, and said hi, and we talked for a few minutes. I asked if she'd be okay with me calling her sometimes, and she was. A few days later, I called and would every few days for about two months in the early evenings or the afternoon over the weekend if I hadn't spoken to her at school. I don't know why I didn't walk over to her house to see if she wanted to go for a walk to talk. Oh well, I don't believe I ever let on about what was going on at home or how I was feeling because when I heard her voice on the phone or in school, everything else just seemed to drift away.

Sometime in late April, a recruiting card for the Marine Corps addressed to me arrived. I'd be eighteen in the fall and would have to register for the draft. I set up an appointment and then came in and took the ASVAB test. The job I'd be pursuing was unit diary clerk, an administration job responsible for entering pay and service record book-related information into the system, reconciling it against mainframe reports. They offered a bonus, an East or West Coast choice for the first duty station, and guaranteed promotion to corporal (E4) within a year of active duty. Joe was already a corporal (Cpl.-E4), and he loved the electrical work he was doing. And I recall him building the new living room TV in two days while he was home on leave. Not sure if my dad also helped. I remember only him. My extended family was going to be moving again. Arizona was looking to be the destination. On June 8, 1984, my recruiter spoke to my parents because I wanted to join. I am not sure if my mom stayed for the conversation. I wasn't eighteen yet, so my father needed to sign before I did. He did. The determination and desire on my face were crystal clear, and I never said anything or led on about the home environment since the accident as part of my decision. After the recruiter left, he went up to the track at the junior high to run, which was after 9:00 p.m. He wasn't in shape to do that, but I think he realized that he screwed up by keeping the car in plain sight for as long as he did.

During one of Mark's visits in May, he asked, "What the fuck is that car still doing here?" but within two weeks of me signing on the dotted line, it was gone. I went to Detroit a few weeks later to have all the exams and—I think—even to take another ASVAB test. Before shipping out and signing the final papers, the bonus had increased, but everything else remained the same. I chose the West Coast option because it would only be a five- to six-hour drive to an area close to Phoenix, where my extended family was likely to be. I told them sometime in July about it; and by then, their destination would be Raleigh, North Carolina, and not Arizona. I don't think I ever told my extended family about what I endured or thought of doing to myself because of the treatment after the accident, and I apologize if I didn't. And yes, I'd expect to be "spoken" to, even now;

but that would be out of love and empathy, not anger, just as it would have been back then. That same summer, 104.7 FM was having a contest—the 104.7 FM Fox of the day, week, or month. I wrote a two-page letter about what I had been through and that it was Candy who brought me back from the edge without knowing any of the details that had me there. They messed up pronouncing my last name on the radio, but that's because of how I sign the first letter of my last name. She called and let me know, thanking me after a dozen roses with baby's breath were delivered. She showed me a picture of her next to them. And we've recently connected on Facebook, and she sent me a copy. I printed it and added it to the picture collage in my hallway. She is still just as beautiful, and her smile hasn't changed. It still melts you from the inside out.

I played baseball that summer, and wouldn't you know it, we had a game on July 7 against the same coach I wanted to win against when I coached the basketball team. The problem though, my first concert, Def Leppard's Pyromania Tour, was going to at the sports arena, and I was going! My coaches tried their best to guilt me because I was just that damn good, but I said, "Pray for a rainout then" or something similar because I would be at the concert. I admit I didn't want to miss the game, so I was hoping for a rainout, but unfortunately, there wasn't a cloud in the sky nor was there likely to be. Music would be instrumental for me from the moment I heard "Photograph" and even more so during later trials.

My senior year was a cakewalk, only needing one class to reach the number of credits to graduate. I was leaving at the end of February for recruit training. In January, I would be a camp counselor at the YMCA Storer Camps for a group of kids from the same elementary school I attended. I went when I was in the sixth grade and loved the entire week. Unfortunately, the schools were closed because of the snow, but the counselors were already there. They eventually canceled the trip for the kids after the second or third day; but my classmates and I stayed for the entire week, going cross-country skiing every day, enjoying the times and experiences.

The staff heard I was going into the Marines at the end of February and wouldn't be attending school anymore after the semester ended. They approached me to see if I'd be interested in coming back to be a counselor for a group of eighth graders from a Toledo school in early February. I said yes. I can't remember the name of the cabin I was the counselor for, but one of the cabins for the girls was the Appleseed Cabin and near ours. The two girls' counselors were beautiful. I connected with the brunette. The other counselor was blond, but she also had a boyfriend. So friends we could be. When we returned to the city, we spoke on the phone several times, and she invited me to a country club for an event, which included dinner. I can't remember if her parents or the blond's parents were members, but it didn't matter. I didn't have a suit but dressed like I was going to a wedding, actually borrowing a sweater from my younger brother, who was all into fashion or the name tag. I had a great time, and the energy was just tremendous. And the thought of her helped me get through boot camp when I felt alone—no letters received from home. I wrote more than a few times but not every week, but I never heard back.

In the letter I sent before I graduated, I said I would call her in the late afternoon or early evening after my graduation, which I did, but her mom said she was sorry she couldn't be there to answer when I called. I stopped by when I got home on leave to learn that she had a boyfriend. I wasn't crushed or even hurt by it. It felt liberating. I gave her one of my graduation photos with a note written on the back, which I think said something like the thought of her and what we shared before helped me get through the tough times in boot camp. I wished her well and left with a smile on my face and rock and roll in my heart. A few years later, I received a letter from Jen, one of the girls in the Appleseed Cabin. We wrote back and forth a few times, and I had the impression that she was troubled somehow. But I don't recall if she ever went into detail. Even though I was married, I remember thinking I should take her to her senior prom. Everyone would be in awe of her showing up with a marine in their dress blues. It seemed that might help her get through whatever she was going through, but it never came up. And we eventually lost touch.

Don't ever be ashamed of the scars life has
left you with. A scar means the hurt is over, and

the wound is closed. It means you conquered the pain, learned a lesson, grew stronger, and moved forward. A scar is the tattoo of a triumph to be proud of. Don't allow your scars to hold you hostage. Don't allow them to make you live your life in fear. You can't make the scars in your life disappear, but you can change the way you see them. You can start seeing your scars as a sign of strength and pain. *Yes*, they still are tender as they heal, and some may even try to revisit them to bring you down. But their efforts will only show who they are, not who you are. (Unknown)

I'm not ashamed or embarrassed by any scar or event in my life. Recruit training was just the start of me breaking free from things that no longer served me, especially those things that helped create "my own prison." I wanted it to last longer than eleven years, but I got what I needed and wanted. Later I would learn that my guardian angels were working on getting me out.

CHAPTER 4

ELEVEN YEARS

Demonstrate to the world there is "No Better
Friend, No Worse Enemy" than a US Marine.
—General James Mattis

February 25, 1985, to February 13, 1996, is ten years, eleven months, and twenty days; so it isn't exactly eleven years. Considering what I went through in those years, especially the last few, I've more than earned the right to round up. "Eleven Years" is a better chapter title than the actual time.

The yellow footprints are where each recruit begins the journey, hearing the sheers, feeling and seeing your hair fall away, and then going through a series of things that would keep us awake for two days before being able to sleep. Well, damn, I'm not in Ohio anymore. It cements you in the knowledge that you are at the beginning of a life-altering event that breaks away the individual civilian to building you up to becoming a United States marine. No disrespect to the other branches of the armed forces, but it's the earning of the title of "marine" that you carry with you for the rest of your life, no matter the experiences during your time on active duty or in the reserves.

And this is how it began for me, and it continues to shape me still to this day. Within the first week, an initial physical fitness test (PFT) consisted of a timed one-and-a-half-mile run, pull-ups, and sit-ups in a minute. I ran faster than anyone else with a nine-minute-and-thirty-second run time, but I'd become slower between then and the final PFT because running in formation didn't let me run like I was used to doing. A classmate said my running was like an antelope because of the power of my long strides. I probably would have been faster if I had shortened the strides, but it was gold when I got that runner's high. The three moments that struck home for me during those twelve weeks were shooting rifle expert, boxing in the smoker, and stepping back from advancement because of the potential effect of negatively impacting the platoon's score for the final drill.

At the beginning of the third phase, the smoker was a boxing match. Only a few participated in the ring, and they asked for people with boxing or fighting experience. I told the story of kicking my brothers' butt on the house's front porch. My smoker's name was the "Religious Ripper" as I was the Catholic lay reader for the platoon. I distributed Communion during the last week or two as the training we went through met the church's requirements. I've since attended church on occasion but never took part in the Communion as a lay reader and giving others the body of Christ (bread) or his blood (wine). We had to wear large boxing gloves, twenty ounces or something heavier. The gloves were almost cartoonish in nature as they seemed to be three times the size of standard boxing gloves. We had head and groin protection, but that didn't stop me from getting a nosebleed—a problem since elementary school. An uppercut fell short of the mark as my opponent came in too close before my glove came up, and it landed a hit below his waist—oops. After being stunned and a thirty-second delay, we resumed. He'd eventually end up on the canvas just before the end of the third round, but it wasn't a knockout. My drill instructors were pleased, especially Senior, who was there with his family in civilian attire.

The last moment of substance before graduation was when one of the squad leaders had broken a rule or code in the few days before the final drill. I replaced him, which required me to call out commands to my squad if the drill card that Senior received called for it. I practiced with the guide and other squad leaders on Saturday and Sunday and then with the entire platoon on Monday. Still, I couldn't pick up and execute what I needed to, and I didn't want it to negatively impact the platoon's score on the final drill. I doubt I would have had a problem if I had been a squad leader since the beginning of the third phase, but this was only a few days away. Out of several tries with the entire platoon, I only managed to hit the mark once. Monday evening, I requested permission to speak to the senior drill instructor and did so with another DI in the office. My difficulties in picking up and executing what I needed to in such a short time were obvious. I asked for the fired squad leader to be put back as squad leader and disciplined in another way to give the platoon the best chance for success on the final drill. They did that, and we either won or came in second.

My senior drill instructor received orders to Marine Barracks, Washington, D.C. as a member of the Silent Drill Platoon, which is something remarkable in itself. There is nothing like seeing them perform—impressive, to say the least, and motivating as hell to watch. The gunnery sergeant, his grandfather, had been the commandant of the Marine Corps years earlier. It was nothing like that for the staff sergeant, but he was as tough as anyone I had ever met while I served. And his sarcastic humor would have you busting a gut laughing but while trying not to show it. The corporal had less than three years on active duty and had just graduated from DI school, which was remarkable. He was promoted to sergeant after our graduation, I believe, early on when he picked up the next platoon. I was technically a private first class (PFC-E2) from day 1, but I wouldn't wear the rank until the day of graduation, which was when we officially earned the title of "marine." Current marines earn the title a few days before graduation after completing the crucible.

In the two weeks before graduation, it was getting real that we were going to graduate. We completed all the final requirements and the physical fitness test and turned in our weapons to the armory, and we finally saw civilians again. Our training on Fridays and over the weekend was out of the main areas, so we never got the chance to see any. And being in Southern California in May, it was probably best that we didn't. We saw women dressed as they were—oh my god—and still a week before our graduation. And I thought hearing the airplanes take off and constantly land from the airport next to the depot was difficult to bear. Visitor's day was that Sunday before graduation the following Friday, where family and friends could visit us for several hours. My brother, who was at MCAS El Toro, drove down with a few of his friends. We went bowling, ate, and I shared the highlights as they remembered their own. He was there to see me graduate the following Sunday and took me to where he was living in Orange County, which was with another marine and his wife, while I waited for my flight out of LAX. I scheduled my flight out of Los Angeles because that would be about the same distance to San Diego, and I wasn't leaving until around midnight, which would allow me to sleep on the plane and get to Detroit first thing in the morning. When I got home, I crashed on the couch. Not sure why, but my older brother was still living there. And he or someone else had heard me in my sleep saying "Sir, yes, sir" several times. Not necessarily a nightmare, but it was what it was.

My return flight was to San Diego. My brother couldn't pick me up, and I had no right to ask him to. But I reported in only minutes before midnight, so it was a wake-up call. We were about ready to begin our school training a few weeks later, but several reservists had shown up. And because there were stricter requirements for how long they could be on active duty, we got bumped to the next class, which started in the fall. I learned how to cut grass "the Marine Corps way" that summer—or dirt because the grass isn't likely growing during the summer, not in Southern California. During my free time, I'd go running with a few others who were there. One day during lunch, it was well into the nineties, and we ran anyway. I went to sick call the next day because my groin was hurting. I had surgery the following day to repair a right inguinal hernia, recuperated in the hospital for a few days, and then went back at it but took a few weeks off from running. In August, I received my promotion to lance corporal (LCpl-E3).

My first duty station would be at Marine Corps Air Station Tustin with HMH-462, the "Screw Crew"—a CH-53 Super Stallion helicopter squadron deployed to Okinawa, Japan, for six months after a year in the States. My brother would mention years later that he should have tried to get me assigned to his unit at El Toro, which I would have enjoyed, but I probably would have also gotten on his nerves. I had a "Hawkeye" problem, Alan Alda's character on *MASH*. I loved my job, but there were some times when my passion for the job would temporarily blind me to the authority within the chain of command. Nothing ever disrespectful or anything close to a violation that would require disciplinary action, but I'm sure I aggravated a few because I challenged doing things the same way when there was room for improvement. I, without a doubt, respected and was fiercely loyal to my entire chain of command—earned multiple times over. And their leadership and advice were instrumental in me removing any weight from my shoulders about being concerned for my family and the struggles they were experiencing. There were others in the command who needed improvement on their tact and leadership abilities, but most never impacted my peers or me.

Sometime during the first deployment, which began in June of '86, two things happened. One was embarrassing, which forced me to grow up more and become more accountable and responsible for my words and actions. The other would be the creation of a reputation of sorts. When I got promoted to corporal (Cpl.-E4), an error on my military ID added two years to my birthday, and I never corrected it, at least not until after I was twenty-one. On Friday and Saturday nights, my friends and I would head to the club just down the street from Tustin's main gate, The Barn—a club upstairs with a great live band and a restaurant on the main floor. And yes, it was in the shape of a barn. Fridays were unofficial "Secretary's Night," and Saturday was just a blast. We decided to celebrate being on its downhill side and headed to the enlisted club behind our barracks halfway through the first deployment.

A few beers in, and someone suggested a drinking challenge. I didn't think much of it because I had drunk like a fish on the weekends before the deployment; but when we switched to Long Island iced teas and then doubled shots of Bacardi 151 rum, well, suffice to say the night didn't end well, at least what I couldn't remember about it but was reminded of a few days later. A girls' band from the Philippines did music sets for about thirty minutes each with a fifteen- to twenty-minute break in between. They did four, but I only remembered three of them and was told that I got up and tried to dance with them and almost got into a fight after stumbling onto some other marines. And those I was with were letting me go and laughing their asses off. I had to be carried and dragged up the hill back to our barracks because I was out. I woke up the following day for work, and I was hungover but heard the knock on my cubicle by one of the marines I worked with who had carried me back and was checking on me. I had missed the small trash can that they put near me. He told me to sleep till noon, and he'd tell our admin chief that I went to medical. I got up at noon, showered but still hungover, and got into work, where I confessed my sin to my admin chief. While he did laugh and understood, my punishment would be to clean the office after everyone left, stripping the floors, waxing and buffing them, which took me about six hours into the late evening—lesson learned. Never mix beer and alcohol ever again, and know your limit, pretty much swearing off hard liquor. But I still occasionally will drink some; my favorite drink is a frozen Kahlúa mudslide.

Now, as crazy as that was, it wasn't the embarrassing part that would take me two days to discover, and I showered each day. I noticed my groin area had been shaved clean. A Polaroid of two of my fellow marines standing with shit-eating grins over me was funny when I think back on it but not at the time. I was embarrassed and overreacted and destroyed the picture and "threatened" them, which was just a lashing-out response. The only other event that was stupid and fun at the same time was when marines were stuck in the barracks because of a typhoon and nothing to keep themselves busy. A typhoon was passing the island off the coast with winds over eighty miles per hour. Well, standing up and running seventy-five feet between the barracks in such weather is a challenge—stupid, yes. When we are young, we all do silly and stupid things, which is understandable, or there wouldn't be any old and wise people.

The reputation came from a first lieutenant, who had tried to berate me in front of the entire office; I have no idea what the hell the issue was. It rolled off my shoulders and didn't faze me. A month later, he received a "no pay due" notice, meaning he wasn't getting paid for the next payday. He was upset—who wouldn't be? But he was trying to blame me, accusing me of doing something, but I had nothing to do with it. I confirmed with my admin chief and sergeant major that I didn't have anything to do with it and needed to do the research and report my findings back to them. The officer had taken too large of an advance for a temporary additional duty trip six months earlier. Had he stayed for the entire time, it wouldn't have been an issue, but he owed the government money. Emergency paperwork was completed, delivered the same day to the disbursing office, and paid the next day, but he'd still have to have a portion taken out until it was paid back in full. Word quickly spread about what happened, and someone had said that you don't piss off the marine who controls your pay, which was a significant exaggeration.

Still, people started responding quicker when I called and needed information from them, which I appreciated because I could get impatient trying to get things done. I hated waiting on someone else to finish whatever I was trying to accomplish, but that was my issue, not theirs. At the end of the deployment, which was just before Christmas, we were boarding the flight back to the States at Kadena Air Force Base, and the plane could fit four hundred-plus passengers. We had around two hundred or so. The CO opened up the additional spaces to those traveling Space-A, which was free and first come, first served. Even though no one wanted to wait another three hours to board them, it was the right thing to do on every level. I earned several awards and recognitions in the performance of my duties during my time in the unit, one of which was for my participation in the command's administration and maintenance inspection drill team. As the most recent graduate from boot camp, I was able to help the platoon leader by bringing them up-to-date on the drill commands as I recalled them.

Somewhere either before the first deployment or just after, I was flying home and met a single mother living in Taft, California, traveling to Tennessee. After takeoff, I offered Toni my cassette player and headphones to relax as much as possible to enjoy the flight; her son was asleep. Being a single parent is challenging enough, but she took classes toward a degree and volunteered at a city or county office. I don't recall if the state required it because she was receiving assistance or it was her desire to give back, but it didn't matter because it was something I admired and respected. Mechanical issues would require the plane to land in Kansas City, and we had different final destinations. But I got her address and phone number. We kept in touch. I even traveled up to see her and her son, but it was friendship, not an intimate relationship. I have a picture of her in the photo collage in my hallway.

My second deployment in January to June of '88 was uneventful for me, but the command lost a plane and the seven on board, one happened to be one of two brothers in the unit. The office and I were doing great work and passed a group inspection with flying colors. In the summer before, I reconnected with Kristen, my former girlfriend, and I got home a few times before the next deployment. And she even flew out to spend a few days with me. In the fall before the deployment, I played softball with a group of civilians, who lived near my apartment, and had twisted my ankle, injuring it pretty significantly. Still, I loved playing softball, so I kept playing. I went to the base medical facility, but it wasn't a full-service facility. So I picked up my medical records and went to Long Beach Naval Hospital the following day, October 1. After my fiberglass cast was dry, things started to move, and the pillar in front of me cracked. I wasn't entirely sure what was going on until the female petty officer, who put my cast on, grabbed me from under the table and pulled me to her.

Oh, it's an earthquake, my first—cool, I thought but never said. She held on to me for dear life, shaking and visibly upset for about twenty minutes after it stopped, which was understandable. I reassured her we'd be fine. Later that evening, it would take me a few attempts to get off the waterbed and under the table in my apartment during an aftershock.

It was sometime after that I experienced another and was outside walking—no place to hide or way to get there with the ground under your feet moving. Feeling helpless would be an understatement.

In the fall of '88, I transferred to the Inspector-Instructor Staff, Hotel Battery, Third Battalion, Fourth Marine Regiment, Fourth Marine Division in Richmond, Virginia, as one of several active-duty marines training the reserve unit. My extended family was living in Raleigh; and I met my first wife, Ruth, who was a friend of my sister Casey's, in the summer before I transferred. And she had also come out to California just after my orders were confirmed. Unfortunately, we would marry in '89 and divorce in '92, and I'd jump right from the frying pan and into the fire. It was the best of times for my military career and the worst of times for my personal life—but lessons learned, especially about yourself when you are abused and have finally had enough. I was responsible for training two reservists who were also unit diary clerks but hadn't been allowed to learn their jobs. The administration chief, a gunnery sergeant, was an asshat of the tallest order, as was the worthless piece of shit I was replacing as he had checked out long before being discharged. An inspection from the Marine Corps Disbursement On-Site Examination Team (MCDOSET)—the motherload of inspections, especially for the administration staff—took place in four months. The work to be reviewed wasn't primarily mine, so I got pretty pissed when I dug into everything and found no records of the transactions entered and reports reconciled—absolutely nothing. It was beyond me how this was allowed to happen, but I got to work. The inspectors were impressed with what I had accomplished in such a short time. We passed with pretty high marks, even though they dinged us for a few things that didn't have a financial error associated with it, except one. I was due a family separation allowance for one day, which was $2 because I got married in Raleigh, and we didn't return to Richmond until the next day. I disagreed with this "error," but they had to come up with something.

In the late summer of '89, Ruth would quit working as a bank teller to begin a training program that would allow advancement in her career, so I worked a part-time job to help offset the income loss.

The local pizza place worked well, and I stopped after she completed the training program and returned to full-time work. A few months later, I decided to start delivering pizzas under the premise of saving for a house. Still, it was because we were in this cycle that repeated every six to eight weeks, where she would intentionally try to push my buttons, acting like a bitch. She had problems with endometriosis, but that was only part of it. Virtually every weekday night, she'd come home from work and immediately take a bath, smoking a cigarette while we talked, which wasn't a conversation; it was me listening to her. Then she'd get on her "grandma pajamas." We'd eat dinner, watch TV, and then go to bed. Sex was so mechanical—one position, no foreplay, no exploring, not even kissing. I tried to get her to change things up by going to a movie, a club, a concert—hell, anything—even taking a walk around the pond in our apartment complex before the sun would go down. We were in our midtwenties and were behaving like we were retired and waiting on death. It was suffocating.

I worked hard, was promoted to sergeant (E5), and received several awards and recognitions in the performance of my duties from each level within my chain of command. Created documents and streamlined processes were instrumental in my success and the I&I staff's rating of "Ready" from a mobilization operational readiness test. I shared the documents and procedures with those in similar roles at the battalion and regiment levels because this wasn't about me; it was about the success of all. My first sergeant spoke highly of how I trained the two reservists, who had the same MOS I had, as the example to follow, primarily having them do the job on drill weekends with me supervising, training, and mentoring. I knew one of the reservists because he was one of the reservists who had bumped me that summer when I was in school at Camp Pendleton. The first sergeant had also given me the best advice early on when I approached him with a question, and his response was, "Don't come to me with a problem unless you have a potential solution in mind." It is still some of the best, if not the best, advice I ever received as to how to approach things and has helped me achieve success in my career since.

I bought a new car—a white 1990 Dodge Daytona with custom pinstripes and a two-door hatchback with everything I wanted—as a reward to myself for all that I had achieved to date, also for reenlisting for another six years on my father's birthday in late 1990. I had it a month, maybe two, before the wife crashed it because she was showboating on a trip to Raleigh with Casey in the passenger seat. It took two and a half months to repair, and she had the nerve to ask me to drive it as soon as I walked into the apartment after driving it back from Raleigh.

"Not only *no but hell no.* You have your car."

And then out of spite, she went and bought a new car a few days later. Things came to a blow two months before I reported to Marine Corps Air Station Cherry Point, North Carolina, in the fall of '91. I played softball each year in Richmond, and she was finally going to be there to watch one of my games. But her stepbrother called, and instead of saying she'd call him after the game, she just carried on as if I no longer mattered. So I left for the game. She never showed up, at least not until it got late and the guys and I were having a few beers at the club on the Defense General Supply Center Base a couple of miles from the house to celebrate the season. I met Lynn, a younger woman, earlier in the day as she had just graduated from the US Coast Guard basic training and was working at the reserve center to extend her time in the area to see her brother. He was getting ready to complete army basic training. She looked like Erika Elaniak when she was in *Under Siege*, which hadn't come out yet. She was at the game and began flirting with me even though I was married, which felt good to have someone take an active interest.

Around 11:00 p.m., the wife showed up at the bar on base, pissed off because I was not home yet. Thankfully she didn't walk in ten minutes earlier because Lynn had been sitting on my lap. When we got home, she proceeded to rip and break pictures from the walls, break dishes, yell, and spout some bizarre bullshit, using the beer bottle she was drinking from as a prop for her performance. She never drank beer. I stood there until I couldn't anymore. I had enough and grabbed her with both hands around the throat but didn't choke her.

I pushed her against the wall and lifted her a few inches off the floor, forcing her on her tiptoes.

A second later, I removed my hands and backed away and told her, "This isn't me. I'm not doing this. I'm not going to jail or ruin my career over you. I want a divorce."

She began to cry and, a few days later, moved in with a female coworker. A week later, a marine on the staff was getting married, and I brought Lynn. We'd spend the weekend together and would end up jumping from the frying pan and into the fire. In my eyes, it was just a fling, even after the trip I took out to see her over Labor Day weekend in San Francisco as she was attending her MOS school in Petaluma. Sometime in October, before I officially transferred, the soon-to-be ex-wife asked me to come to her place so she could apologize. I went. She admitted what she had done and discovered her issues, which I had previously tried to discuss, but she wouldn't hear any of it. She then indicated that in a therapy session, she recalled a memory of her stepfather fondling her breasts when she was around sixteen. He was a retired army lieutenant colonel in his sixties at the time, passing away in the fall before we married. Her breasts were much more than a handful, even after the breast reduction ceremony she had at fifteen, I think. Short story long, it was "revenge sex," not mean or insulting—just was what it was. She would remarry in a year, have a child, and, as far as I know, is living her best life. Nothing but best wishes for her and her family.

I arrived at MCAS Cherry Point, North Carolina, and within a month, I'd receive the Navy Achievement Medal for my performance, dedication, and professionalism while a member of the I&I staff. My extended family was in Raleigh, which is why I chose Cherry Point, but it didn't take long before I began to feel that I should have tried to go back out of California. There was just something about the base and commands that were off—too much political and hypocritical bullshit that was, in my opinion, in direct contradiction in keeping with the highest standards and esprit de corps.

Lynn and I kept in contact, writing and calling each other, and in November, she told me that she was pregnant and that I was the father. I was happily stunned, considering a sperm count test two years earlier, which the tech admitted to messing up, indicating a low count, so I never really knew for certain and wouldn't until almost twenty years later. She transferred to the coast guard station near Morehead City, North Carolina, through some phone calls to those who controlled assignments. A few hours after picking her up on that first night, she told me she had been raped and began crying. There was love and chemistry there—or so I thought—and I told her I'd raise the child as my own. And I asked her again if she still wanted to get married. When "Mom C" had asked me three times in a row if I loved the ex-wife before we married, I never said yes and would indicate something in the affirmative as I danced around it. When she asked me about Lynn, it was a 100 percent yes—frying pan fire. We married as soon as I got the final divorce papers because her pregnancy was difficult and delivery could happen anytime. I would transfer a month later from my current command because I wouldn't sign an acknowledgment that I could deploy. The difficulties during her pregnancy continued, and I wasn't going to leave her alone. So I was transferred to a training unit that would later merge with an actual squadron with a training unit under its umbrella. I'd take care of her and the stepson from the moment I got home until I had to go into work the next morning as she was exhausted and never really "recovered" from the pregnancy. The stepson would be in base day care starting in September, and I'd go over during my lunch hour and spend twenty to thirty minutes with him.

After the new year, Lynn wasn't happy with work because she wasn't being trained at anything specific and wanted out. So she applied for a discharge under "false" pretenses, and I would later learn that she had "forged" her parents' signature and my father's on letters indicating that they wouldn't be able to care for the stepson in the event both of us were deployed. The reality was that she wasn't happy being married, being a mother, or having adultlike responsibilities. It was over before we'd officially split in July '93, which happened after the stepson and I returned from a trip to Florida with my brother Jim from my extended family who was on break from training with the CIA, the Culinary Institute of America, out of Hyde Park, New York. I would later discover that she had gone away for the weekend with another marine who we both knew, although he was more friendly with her as it turned out. We tried marriage counseling for a session or two, but it wasn't going to help. But I kept up with the counselor because I wanted to do all that I could to avoid going through anything like this ever again. The counselor suggested I read *Don Quixote*, and I tried. But after the first chapter, I knew the rest of the story, which I explained at our next session and asked about his reasoning for reading it. He remarked that I needed to look at the relationship with my father as it pertains to my mother, and sure enough, that was an eye-opening moment.

I would refer to what I suffered from as a "knight in shining armor" complex, and it stemmed from my father promising my mother the world as part of their courtship. And later on, he tried to buy her those fancy things almost as if it was a *Keeping Up with the Joneses* kind of thing. My brothers and I would fall into this pattern, at one point or another, when it came to the women in our romantic lives. We tried to show what good providers we were to earn their love and affection, which was probably more detrimental to the relationship than anything. It was our parents' relationship or pattern, and I know there was love there. But there was also some anger or bitterness in things not working out the way each of them had hoped. The Havelock Police pulled me over with Lynn and the stepson in the car a few weeks before the Florida trip. They brought me into their cruiser to "talk." They gave me an inside story about an incident that had happened a week earlier, where she accused another marine of rape before she stabbed him in the leg—more lies from her. And I had enough, so it was just the stepson and I going to Florida. The police never said or suggested anything; but sitting in the cruiser, listening to them, there just seemed to be a feeling like they would actually like a murder investigation to shake things up. My command forced me to move back into the barracks, and about a week after I returned from the Florida trip, her parents packed her and the stepson up and returned to Virginia. My name was listed on his birth certificate because we were married when he was born; and that was the law in North Carolina unless the birth father's identity was known, which it was. But she proclaimed otherwise. I wanted to be a part of his life; so I fought to have, at the very least, visitation rights. It took me over a year between North Carolina and Virginia courts before Virginia granted me custody because North Carolina already had, and they had jurisdiction. The week I had him, I'd be on the rifle range, so it was very early days. And thankfully the wife of a marine that I worked with would watch him.

After several congressional inquiries and endless harassing phone calls to my chain of command, I still wasn't going to drop my custody claim. Social Services visited me about two days after I got him and would dismiss the accusation that I could not provide for him, which pissed them off, forcing them to become more desperate in what they were willing to do or say. If I didn't stop fighting for custody after all the congressional inquiries and endless harassing phone calls to my chain of command, I'm not sure what made them think I ever would. They finally came to a North Carolina court, and the judge ordered me to give him back, pending a hearing in a few weeks. They took him to the police station; it became clear that every allegation or accusation under the sun would be thrown at me, from physical to sexual abuse to whatever else they could drum up. Using the "abusive marine" stigma as much as they could get away with wasn't something I would not put him through. I withdrew my custody claim after speaking with the base counselor and my lawyer.

The saving grace moment came when I would give him back to Lynn. We were standing at my car, her parents about twenty feet away near theirs, and I told the stepson that he needed to go with Mommy. He said no and grabbed my leg tight. It warmed me up on the inside, not because of the obvious FU to her and her parents but because the positive impact I had on him in only his first year of life was enough to carry him through his second. I hadn't been able to see or talk to him since the separation, and I only hoped that it would further carry him on until he became an adult and that we could reconnect.

Within a few months, I had learned that the sheltie we had was killed by a car a week after they left. It would be when I reconnected with the stepson twenty years later that I would learn that at the age of four, he was beaten by his mother's boyfriend, suffering a traumatic brain injury and a cracked skull, which led to a minor stroke, and he was in a coma for thirty days. Her parents had sole custody a few years later. I tried to help him several times since we reconnected, but the last straw for me was when he pressured his boyfriend to press assault charges against me when I evicted him from my home. And they were trying to remove items that didn't belong to him. The purpose of this was to create a situation. I haven't seen or talked to him in several years and have no desire, want, or need to.

I began to focus my energies on my career. I was headed down the career path but needed to get back in shape, but I had become aware that my command had other plans. They weren't happy that I fought for custody of a child who wasn't biologically mine, that I had orders to attend a senior admin school and would immediately transfer to Marine Corps Air Station Futenma. Hence, the bullshit was about to begin. A funny thing happened, which I think scared them about "my powers." A master gunnery sergeant (MGySgt-E9), who was the senior enlisted member of the training command, had orders to Hawaii, but the new unit code didn't appear on any report. But it was on the system; and no doubt, they suspected I had done something, which I had not. Headquarters Marine Corps in Washington, DC, was the only command authorized to enter such information. Anyway, they were about as subtle as Barney Fife with what they were trying to do. I had received a copy of my official microfiche that included the letter sent requesting them. The reason the command was seeking them was that "they were investigating me for disciplinary action"—news to me and my gunnery sergeant, the admin chief whom I respected and was fiercely loyal to because she had more than earned it. She had been a drill instructor at Parris Island and wasn't the in-your-face, gung ho type, at least now she wasn't. But her integrity, professionalism, and leadership commanded respect. She would be transferred to another command just before my last surgery because I suspect she had spoken to the two senior enlisted marines and wouldn't go along with what they were planning. There was suspicion that the master sergeant (M.Sgt.-E8) who signed the letter had an inappropriate relationship with a female marine. The latter was a student in the command, so it had its own *Jerry Springer*-type drama.

With the stress, anxiety, and just overall shit show with the first and second ex-wives, my weight became an issue as I was close to exceeding the limits, if not dancing back and forth over it. I had injured the big toe on my foot while on the second deployment to Japan. I didn't realize that it had me slightly adjusting my foot before it would hit the ground when I ran; and over time, running five miles a day during the workweek, it took its toll. We discovered in the first x-ray that a calcium deposit had formed in the joint of my left big toe. Surgery a few months after the stepson was born didn't entirely remove it, and another would develop. Second surgery months later was to remove the cartilage and fuse the joint with a screw, which would be taken out a few months later. Several months of running didn't help as the joint separated. I had already been "passed over" once for promotion to staff sergeant (S.Sgt.-E6), so I only had one more opportunity before I'd be "forced" out due to service limitations. The command officially placed me on the weight-control program, and I lost what I needed to. Still, a few months later, they did it again and convened an administration board to potentially reduce me in rank, proclaiming, "I lacked the self-discipline to control my weight." I could not lose the weight I needed, which was only about two pounds, so they began the discharge process for failure to conform to weight standards. The process usually took about three months, four tops. Since I didn't have to continue the training program anymore, I focused on getting everything I needed before being discharged, specifically another surgery on my left ankle and foot. The x-ray showed the joint separated again, and a bone spur had formed in the ankle. This time, the screw would stay in regardless. Surgery was scheduled and then performed in late August on a Friday. I would have thirty days of medical leave to recover. Still, the command would not approve it, which I found out after climbing to the second floor of the hangar to the admin office; and the new admin chief, who had been there less than two weeks, informed me after I got up from falling and landing on my ass, which felt like someone cutting my legs out from under me. I was still groggy from the anesthesia.

So no medical leave initially, and I needed to return to work Monday morning. A coworker and close friend picked me up after the surgery and would take me to the ER on base because the blood on the bandage from my ankle was bright red and getting bigger. Short story long, all the stitches on the ankle and inside had broken. The doctor repaired the damage, and it was pretty cool to see him work. My foot was still numb, so it didn't faze me. I stayed with my coworker and his family over the weekend; his wife was the one who watched the stepson when I had him. Monday morning, I'd be on my way to Camp LeJeune, where the surgeon was. He had already seen the ER report, and he had spoken to the commands flight surgeon about the denial of leave before I got there. He was pissed because the new flight surgeon, with less than six months in, acknowledged that he wasn't aware of what precisely the operation entailed. The podiatrist wrote it all in my medical records. No doubt the two old farts from the Muppets—the master sergeant and master gunnery sergeant—told him not to approve it. Upon my return, the command authorized the thirty days of leave. It wasn't medical leave but restricted leave or restricted medical leave, which isn't a thing, and no one explained what it meant or about any specific restrictions. It listed my barracks room and phone number. The Friday before my leave expired, I had a follow-up appointment and was given the all clear—but no running or strenuous aerobic activity for another forty-five days. When I returned to the base, I packed a bag and headed to Raleigh to see my brother Jerry from my extended family and his wife, who had recently started his own family, spending the weekend with them. On Sunday, his brother-in-law, John, and I went up to the store in his older sports car that he was restoring. I noticed after we left that the driver's seat had a lap belt, but there wasn't anything for the passenger side. And less than a minute later, *bang!*—a car had hit us from the right and on the passenger-side front wheel. I ate the dashboard, fracturing my right cheekbone, with a cut on my eyebrow. Thankfully my glasses came off, so no damage to the rest of the face. And John had hit his head on the steering wheel and began to bleed onto his face. I grabbed a towel or piece of cloth and applied pressure until the ambulance arrived. I gave someone Jerry's phone number to let them know, and he came about the same time the ambulance did.

After getting back to Jerry's, I called my command and let them know what happened and that I had an appointment with a lawyer the next day and wouldn't be back returning from leave. Once the discharge process started, I began working in the avionics training department, being "relieved" of my administrative role within the command. My new boss had called to confirm I was where I said I was and approved the extra day. The medical leave isn't deducted from what you officially earn, so there was no need to order me back to the base. And if they had and something were to happen, they would be held liable. A day or so after my return, I discovered that I wouldn't be paid on payday because the command had reported me as UA—unauthorized absence—and brought charges against me for it. Funny-, they didn't include anything about disobeying orders or whatever the restrictions were for my medical leave. I consulted with a lawyer at the JAG office. I had a choice to accept nonjudicial punishment or request a court-martial. He confirmed that there was no such thing as restrictive or restricted leave, medical or otherwise. I did my research to see if they had attempted to contact me during my medical leave period. They didn't, or at least they didn't follow proper procedures in doing so. My phone records showed no incoming calls. The official duty logbook for the barracks, avionics department, and squadron showed no indication that anyone was looking for me or had attempted to contact me. Each had a marine operating the post twenty-four hours a day, seven days a week and was required to indicate all activity. If a visitor wanted to see me, they were to first report to the marine on duty and let them know who they were and the purpose for a visit, and all of it would be required to log in to the official duty logbook. Even if a call asked the same, it would still need to be indicated in the logbook because the marine would be away from his appointed place of duty and needed to account for it all. It was a cover-your-ass kind of thing contained within the barracks' regulations and the same thing for the marines on duty in the avionics section and squadron.

I copied the three logbooks for the entire thirty days I was on leave. There was not a single entry that anyone was looking for me, and no one visited the barracks or requested to see me or called me in which the marine on duty would go to my room to let me know of a phone call. When the master sergeant asked me what it would be, NJP or a court-martial, I said, "Court-martial me." It was the only way to ensure that the logbooks, podiatrist statement, and other evidence would be entered and considered by someone outside my current chain of command. They never dropped the charges but never pursued the court-martial. Nor would they correct the error in reporting me UA. I could have cleared it up by showing my medical records, which I should have done, but by then, I already had another problem as the reason they wanted me to remain on base became clear. The administration review board approved my rank reduction from sergeant (Sgt.-E5) to corporal (Cpl.-E4). I was pissed. They were intentionally and deliberately trying to push me into doing something so they could go after me. This kind of command behavior happens more than you'd think, at least it used to. I can't speak for now, but like with any civilian job, it comes down to the actual character of the individual or lack of one.

I didn't take the bait and went to work on my appeal. I obtained copies of the training records, including weigh-ins of myself and three other marines who were overweight. A chief warrant officer 4 (CWO4-W4) was close to his twenty years on active duty or already had them and could retire. A staff sergeant (S.Sgt.-E6) who was allowed to take advantage of an early separation program, receiving an actual severance package for his fifteen years of active-duty service, was offered as part of the reduction of the US Military in the nineties. The third marine was a lance corporal (L.Cpl.-E3) who was a student within the command. While all four of us were over our weight limit, I was the only one who was put on the weight-control program or punished in any way for it, *and* I was the closest to coming off the program altogether. I only had another two pounds or so to lose, but the others were all over ten pounds. And the officer was more than twenty pounds over. The CWO4 had been relieved of his duties, which meant the fitness reports for the five of us sergeants had to be corrected, but the hypocritical BS was that mine was the only one to be redone. I completed my appeal quickly and sent it up the chain of command, where I included everything, documentation and all. It would be early in February '96 when a decision would be made on the appeal of my reduction. I couldn't be discharged while it was pending, and by then, I was so fucking done and just wanted out. There are certain truths for those serving the military—like sometimes, more often than not, the job comes before family, and it's understood and accepted to a certain degree. Still, I never embraced the "suck," in military jargon, which means consciously accepting or appreciating something extremely unpleasant but unavoidable. I would never buy or tolerate dishonorable and hypocritical bullshit behavior just because someone had to prove that they were in charge. Honor, courage, and integrity are more than just words to me.

Around the same time, I received word from the lawyer handling my accident claim against the insurance carrier that my share of the settlement would be roughly $26,800. I guess I impressed the insurance agent who met me with my lawyer to discuss a settlement offer. I had pictures of my face and close-ups of the injuries taken, and they knew I was pending discharge. When asked if I ever thought of modeling, I may have embellished a little but did say that I'm open to anything. There was also some nerve damage to my right cheek, which wasn't going to heal fully. With the settlement, I'd be able to pay off my chapter 11 bankruptcy I had filed in '94 and was making monthly payments to repay my debts. I'd still have more than $12,000 leftover with zero debt. I could have been free of debt had I filed a chapter 7 bankruptcy, but they were my debts—in my name. My last name is the only real thing my father could ever leave me with, and how I treated it would be my gift back to him because for me, being known as a man who gave his word and stood by it was invaluable. Hypocrisy is the practice of claiming to have moral standards or beliefs to which one's behavior does not conform, which is not who I am.

Trust is earned when actions meet words.
(Chris Butler)

Once something is broken, even if repaired, it will never be the same again.

But what is happiness except for the simple harmony between a man and the life he leads?
(Albert Camus)

An indigenous people's belief is "Your life is a gift from the Creator. Your gift back to the Creator is what you do with your life."

I received an honorable discharge. Officially it's a general discharge under honorable conditions, but I didn't care. Get me out. My discharge and insurance check claim dates were the same days, and I made no secret about it but ensured those who screwed me over were aware. The staff sergeant, the admin chief who had written a derogatory statement about me for the reduction board package, was present in the administration office. She proclaimed things about my performance that never happened and gave the impression that she had observed my performance for several weeks when it had been less than two. After handing over my military ID, I received my discharge paperwork.

I said loud enough for the entire office to hear, "Staff Sergeant [and her name], you should consider getting legal representation as you, along with others, can expect to be served with a lawsuit within a few months." I walked out, drove to the McDonald's on base to change out of my camouflage utilities and into civilian clothes, which I had done just the opposite of when I first reported to the air station. I proceeded to the bank, got the check, deposited it into my account, received an official bank check to pay off the bankruptcy, and then hit the road for Raleigh, North Carolina, to spend some time with Jerry, his wife, and his infant son.

After ten years, eleven months, and twenty days, I was no longer on active duty; and it would be nice to take time to relax, decompress, and try to recover from all of it. A few days there, something seemed to be calling me to visit Charlotte, North Carolina, as if it's where I and my future would be, so I went for the weekend with a cousin of Jerry's who I was dating. A couple of weeks after returning to Raleigh, I headed home to Ohio to see my parents and siblings and try to recover and build a life I wouldn't need a vacation from.

CHAPTER 5

My Immediate Family

I have friends who are family and unfortunately family who aren't really friends.

—Me

I wasn't going to deny this any longer, nor was I going to expend the energy on trying to bridge whatever gap there is. I tried for years to do that, and it was exhausting. I'd live my life as best I could. They had my number and address, but I didn't hold back on any of them in a sixteen-page letter sent to each of them and a sister-in-law after something I had wanted to do for all of us was hijacked and screwed up, not even coming close to the desired intent. It became the boiling point that ignited my last straw. Everything had to do with the things that happened after our father's passing, and while a few things were disappointing to realize after I tried to resolve them, it wouldn't be anything I'd lose any sleep over. I do not occupy any moral or ethical high ground that requires acknowledgment or praise from anyone. I want to be informed, want to be able to have an honest conversation of substance that goes beyond the talking points. I ask this of everyone I know in my life—friend, family, or even an acquaintance. Suppose at any time in any discussion, I am wrong, incorrect in my understanding or perception. In that case, I expect the other person to bring me up-to-date to have information from their point of view. I'll add that to my own and see if it adjusts my thinking. If your eyes are the windows to your soul, there is no one better to show you the reflection in the mirror than those closest to you, be it family or friend. Even a coworker, a peer, or even a stranger on the street can be the one who brings the message or teaches you without knowing you need to be taught. Nothing any of them ever did hurt me to the degree that I was angry with them, maybe disappointed, but we all have our paths to walk and crosses to bear. Ultimately though, when your actions speak for you, don't interrupt.

Over the last decade, I'd pen what I will call impassioned letters—two to family, not including my stepsister, and one to Ade. I wrote a fourth one at the beginning of May 2021 to someone I had never met or was likely to meet, but what I experienced was so powerful that I just had to put it down on paper. Each of these letters offered me a moment to reflect and reaffirm my beliefs, expectations, and desire to live my life. From oldest to youngest, my siblings are my stepsister, Ann; oldest brother, Tom; oldest sister, Marie; next brother, Mark; next brother, Joe; younger brother, Mike; and youngest sister, Jillian. I love my family, but I don't necessarily like all of them. It's a mutual feeling, perhaps, but that's on them to correct me if anything I have said was incorrect. And do it in a letter because in person tends to become volatile as talking to some of them is like talking to a brick wall or speaking in a foreign language. We are cordial when together for a holiday, special event, or family reunion, but it's just not as warm and fuzzy as other families are or appear to be. We have each learned different things from our parents that have shaped our lives, perhaps even selectively picking and choosing the things we wanted, which may or may not have been what we needed.

Opinions are like assholes; and while I can or may be critical of some of the decisions they may have made, it really wouldn't be right or fair until and unless I've walked in their shoes, experiencing the same thing. Since I can't do that, I can't say for sure that I would have made different choices. I would however pounce on any false or misleading proclamation that "It's what our father or parents would have wanted or done."

"Really? Then please provide me with an example or similar situation that leads you to believe that our father or mother would have wanted or done whatever you are proclaiming they would have." This would be my typical response to their statement. Silence is all that would be heard from them when challenged. I admit, my perception or understanding could be off. I'm not perfect. I can be wrong at times; and I just hope I don't let emotions remove my ability to think and reason, which no doubt they can, no matter who you are.

> Don't do something permanently stupid just
> because you are temporarily upset. (Unknown)

Or if they attempted some abstract reading of some of the teachings in the Bible, they'd receive the same questions. Both of those would set me off because they were lying to themselves and others, using excuses or justifications to rationalize away the words they spoke or actions they took or didn't take. I try to keep my opinions to myself until and unless I'm specifically asked for it, which I hoped is an informed opinion, especially when discussing the politics in this country.

Throughout my first enlistment, I would send birthday or holiday cards to family and friends, calling them on their birthdays, even from Japan on my dime, which I started to do after realizing that it was unfair to continue to call collect. Sometime after my second deployment, I stopped sending cards and calling to see who would remember my birthday by sending a card or calling to wish me a happy one or just to catch up. I know everyone is busy, and it slips the mind. But it would become the first step I'd take to begin backing away from being the peacemaker in the family. I would hear endlessly from a sibling each time we spoke about the issues in their life, which now included kids and a spouse. It was time to change the broken record. It was worse when I visited because it would go on for hours. My ears couldn't take any more, so my enabling days were over.

My father was never physically abusive, although some of the ass whoopings we received could be questionable or over the line by today's standards. No bruises or broken skin—damn, they hurt. When he was stressed or something was upsetting him, you walked on eggshells. Some of us would try to outsmart him by forcing him to lift our entire body weight as he wanted to spank us, but he began telling us to bend over and touch our toes, which hurt more. Thankfully, I didn't get more than I did because my younger brother was a train wreck, and no matter what I would do, he would have done something worse already or would shortly after. There wasn't a lot of dinner conversation, or after dinner, he'd be in the living room, reading the paper for an hour or so, and then watch TV or read a book. He hated liars more than anything else, which he often said but never fully resonated with me until my first summer in the Corps. I joined the delayed entry program in '84 and received a bill from the utility company demanding $1,700 a short time later for the light pole I hit. My mother was aware and told me to take care of it without letting my father know—a big mistake—but I didn't know that yet. I spoke to my recruiter, and the issue had the remote possibility of delaying or canceling my ship date, which wasn't an option. I'd go to the utility companies' offices and sign a promissory note to pay the bill over time.

My oldest brother was home when I showed my mother a copy of the note, and he blew a gasket. Still, my mother told him that she wouldn't chance our father experiencing stress-, anger-, or anxiety-related issues that he did shortly after my accident. My older sister agreed to let them send the letters to me at the address of her apartment. In June of '85, I made my first payment, and in July my second. Late July, I think my father found out, finding a letter addressed to me from the utility company or something like that. He was pissed, and Marie took the brunt of it in front of her fiancé and my mother.

Her fiancé told my mother, "You know the truth. Why don't you tell him?"

But she never spoke up and may have even denied it. My father asked me over the phone directly for the truth, and I told him. He told me not to send any more payments, and I didn't. Years later, I'd find out that he had gone to the utility company, telling them that I was a minor when I signed, etc., and never to contact me again.

My father was my sounding board during the difficulties in my custody fight for the stepson. He went through similar emotions during his custody fight. I'd hear later from others that he was worried I'd be pushed too far and would kill someone or very close to it, ending up in jail or the brig. His father forced him to marry a woman he had gotten pregnant, which ended his college pursuit because he needed a job. It was unfortunate because he was only a couple of credits short of earning his degree. The marriage didn't last long, and he didn't go back to complete his degree as he had married my mother and my older brother was already on the way due in November. Their anniversary was in January, but in reality, it was April. You do the math and figure out the time line. One of my earliest memories was at the old house on the couch with police on the porch, my mother telling them that he was coming home and that they could talk to him, my father. I'm not sure, but I think Ann's mother was there to pick her up early. Stories from my aunt and uncle, who knew the details, indicated that he would stop paying child support for a month or two and force his ex-wife to take him to court at which time he'd pay up just before the court date. Not positive, but I think my mom would continue on a warpath until eventually, he stopped having contact with his daughter. Jealousy was something not seen much in her, but it was there. My siblings would reconnect with Ann years later, but our father told them not to include him in anything or promise anything. And yes, my mom was still furious and vocal about it all. Ann is a remarkable person, very devoted to and living her faith as she sees it. She homeschooled her five children for most of their education, I think, and she even credits my mother for teaching her the things she did through her example, which I presume meant taking care of a home and family. But I'm not entirely sure.

While at home for a month during December '93 after a custody hearing in Virginia, the judge was retiring and didn't want his decision overruled, so he punted to the next judge a few months later. My mother started in about Lynn, calling her a slut, whore—everything awful under the sun. My father was watching TV, cat in his lap, and I listened, acknowledging her but not agreeing with her even if I thought some of the same things.

Once she stopped, I replied, "Mom, I understand that you're upset, but let me be clear. If I do get any custody or visitation and we are home and you speak like that about his mother in front of him, you will never see either of us again."

My father never said a word to me about it. Still, I suspect he was proud of me for saying what I did in the tone I did as he was so tired of my mother's toxic and hostile behavior to the spouses or girlfriends of my siblings. It's why no one visited anymore, at least not in groups.

Mike would join the navy in the early nineties, and the ship he would be on was in the combat zone for a period during Desert Shield and Desert Storm or in the short time after. A year or so later, I spoke to my father and found out that Mike would get discharged before his contract was up. He suspected he wasn't being told the truth about it from my older sister. My brother hadn't called in several weeks or months, so he was worried. My older sister knew the truth but would tell him that it was medical or some other kind of side step. My father suspected he was being lied to, and the only military graduation they would be able to attend was his in San Diego. Money was too tight for mine or my older brother's. When I heard the stress, worry, and anxiety in his voice, which was subtle but clear, I said I'd check into it. I called my sister first, but she gave me the same bullshit, which I knew wasn't right. You think she knew I was smarter than that. Using my rank, I began making phone calls, reaching his command in Guam. They told me he was in the process of being discharged from active duty. He was in the brig at Treasure Island, California, pending his discharge—bad conduct or dishonorable, not sure which. No other specifics were related. I called and got him on the phone; he gave me some specifics but probably not all. I told him about Dad and that he had two hours to call him and let him know he was okay and would be home soon. I encouraged him to tell the truth about what was happening but only cared about putting our father at ease. He received a waiver for his drug use before being accepted, and being busted for it while on active duty was stupid beyond stupid. He would have been eligible to join the VFW, the Veterans of Foreign Wars organization, if he had kept clean and gotten out at the end of his enlistment.

It is an excellent organization with perks, but that was no longer an option unless he appealed the discharge once he was home, which I encouraged him to submit. I called my sister; I told her I knew the truth and gave Mike two hours to call Dad to put his mind at ease or else I would. She yelled at me and told me not to tell our father, but I responded, "Fuck that. Our father is worried about one of his children and rightfully so, and the only reason why is because he suspected you knew the truth and were lying about it. Had you just kept your mouth shut and said basic things like "He's doing well, enjoying the experience," etc. but not much more than that, especially that he was being discharged and would explain things when he got home, then none of this would have been necessary. He is our father. What the fuck is wrong with you!" I hung up. I don't think two hours passed before I called my father, letting him know. Hell, I don't think I waited fifteen minutes, but he thanked me. And his worrying was over, but he was angry at being lied to and disappointed in what my younger brother had done. My younger brother never called.

I know my father loved me, even though I don't recall him saying it until I was about to board my return flight to California in '87. At his request, I purchased a gift that he could give my mom for her birthday, a lighted wall-piece of the Brooklyn Bridge with small pinholes for the streetlights, and on the suspension cables, the lights could be turned on and off. After saying he loved me, I was stunned because I thought I misheard him, but he repeated it. And I said I loved him too. I was probably told multiple times over the years, but I never recalled hearing it before then. And I know he showed it in his way. In the summer of '94, I was on leave, and Marie asked me to clean the cement slab where their barn had once stood. Mike was supposed to do it, but he only did a small portion. And the dumpster the insurance company was paying for was about to start costing them. I went over early in the morning, cranked up my car radio, and got to work. It took me most of the day. Two days later, I wasn't feeling good and went to lie down. A few hours later, I was burning up. I took my temperature and then went downstairs to tell my dad that I needed to go to the ER because my temperature was 103.7. He got up immediately, and we headed to St Vincent's. While waiting for the spinal tap, he was talking, somewhat joking about something to keep either himself, me, or both of us from worrying about whatever the problem was. Excellent, I had pneumonia from inhaling the burned wood and pig shit from the barn; I guess the bandana wasn't as helpful as I thought it would be. A few days later, I was good to go. So yes, without question, I know my father loved me; he just may not have been able to show it in the way I needed or wanted him to. Sometime after his passing, my mother sent me some pictures, and one of them was of him holding me, looking at me and me at him. It was probably when I was around two months old as the Christmas tree was in the background, which is up in my collage in the hallway.

A few months after my discharge, we would argue because he looked through my checkbook, questioning who and why I was making payments to someone. It was a payday lending company. I'd give them a $125 postdated check for my next payday and would receive cash in return, minus whatever their fee was, which would help carry me over as I was still paying on the bankruptcy and hadn't received the insurance money. I stopped that cycle a month or two before my discharge. I packed my car, left a few things in my younger sister's garage, and headed to Homestead, Florida, where "Mom and Dad C" lived. Casey was nearby with her husband and infant child. Jim was in Lake Worth with his girlfriend, whom he was marrying in a few weeks. A few weeks before the argument, my younger brother called for help; he'd been arrested for a DUI again.

I had the money and told him the only way I would help him is if he swore to pay me back in full as soon as possible; my mom and I were on the phone with him. Unknown at the time, my father was also listening. As I got ready to leave, he confronted us. Not indicating he was in jail, my mother told my father that I was just going to see Mike for the weekend. Short story long, he told her not to lie to him and had been listening on another phone. He tried to convey and convince me not to help him because he wouldn't keep his word, etc. A few years early, an uncle on my father's side had died of prostate cancer, and he became reflective about family and being there for one another. Most of the siblings were not getting along, and he told us to get past whatever it was and stay close as a family.

I heard him then, took it to heart, and replied, "My brother has asked me to help him. I understand what he's done, lying and disrespecting everyone. He hasn't lied or disrespected me, and what does it say about me if I pass judgment without allowing him the opportunity to pass or fail? I hope he doesn't, but he will never have an opportunity to do so ever again if he does. My brother asked me for help, and I am going to help my brother!"

He was pissed when I left, but I would hear a few years after his passing that he was proud of my stance for the sake of family. In retrospect, I should have used the situation of his discharge as reason enough, but he came through, not paying me back in full. I got most of the money over the weekend after taking him home just north of Cincinnati, but he'd still owe me $60. I could have chalked it up to lesson learned, but his wallet was on the dresser when he was home for our father's funeral after the new year. I looked, noticed $80, and took the $60 he owed me. When he noticed money missing, he asked if I had taken it.

"You're damn right I did. You promised to pay me back in full and weren't going to, or else you would have done it at some point in the last six months. So I took the $60 that you owed me. Got a problem with that?"

He replied that he was glad I did it because he would never have paid me back. He and I haven't spoken in more than twenty years. It's unlikely we will ever unless it's in cordial conversation at a family event, which could have been at our mother's funeral twenty-two years later. He never showed up for it, some bullshit excuse about not being able to handle it. But he was the "golden child," so whatever.

As an adult, conversations with your parents, even critical ones, should be attempted and not in a disrespectful or demeaning manner. There is a way to stand your ground and be respectful to them, even if you aren't necessarily feeling it at that time. It is hard to confront or challenge your parents when their words and actions don't appear to be in harmony with each other or contradict what they taught you growing up. It could be a generational thing, but their path is different from yours. And what is right for them may not be what is right for you.

> The soul is dyed the color of its thoughts. Think only on those things that are in line with your principles and can bear the light of day. The content of your character is your choice. Day by day, what you do is who you become. Your integrity is your destiny—it is the light that guides your way. (Heraclitus, Greek poet and philosopher)

The quote above is at the bottom of "The Light of Integrity" framed picture hanging next to my front door. It's a reminder, a way to keep myself in check, on track, and focused on those values that are universally true. I am comfortable in my skin. But I am by no means perfect, nor would I ever claim to be. Jokingly, I will say that "I am better than most," which tends to bring up a smile to the listener's face as funny, but I say it more for the smile than wanting or needing reassurance or confirmation from anyone that it's true. In truth, I only need to be better today than I was yesterday. Even though I may fall short on occasion, it's a journey, not a destination.

> Watch your thoughts; they become words. Watch your words; they become actions. Watch your actions; they become habits. Watch your habits; they become your character. Watch your character; it becomes your destiny. (Unknown)

A XIV Dalai Lama quote is "Give the ones you love wings to fly, roots to come back and reasons to stay."

"The Roots of Character" is a framed picture depicting the quote below and shows the roots of a tree.

> Those who preserve their integrity remain unshaken by the storms of daily life. They do not stir like leaves on a tree or follow the herd where it runs. In their mind remains the ideal attitude and conduct of living. This is not something given to them by others. It is their root. It is a strength that exists deep within them. (Anonymous Native American)

Shouldn't our roots continue to be fed in understanding, deciding, refining, living up to, and expanding on the values parents try to teach and instill in their children? I think it is or, at the very least, honoring your father and mother should include not just living up to the values and principles they taught you but improving, expanding, and strengthening them. It may be something you'll have to think or pray about if you do not believe so.

My father would mellow as he got older, and had he lived longer than he did, I am sure I would talk to him more about some of the things that troubled me before. I'm not sure he'd want to revisit some of the punishments that are now hilarious, but it would have been telling to see how he would respond. One of those hilarious punishments would be recounted sometime after his passing, and it involved and levied on my three older siblings before they hit double digits. So I wasn't even a thought yet. Joe, who was two or three, spilled some sugar, and the three oldest were supposed to be watching him. They had to count the sugar granules that spilled, and our father wasn't hovering over them as they counted. But at some point, my oldest brother asked the other two something to the effect of "Why are you counting? He isn't going to know how many there are."

They continued, but they weren't counting. I honestly can't recall any hilarious punishments I witnessed. I did not believe a story about him being upset because my mother wouldn't let him help wash the cloth diapers, which happened in the sixties. I called bull-shit. There is no way my father would ever, but multiple people confirmed the story. And I reflected on my first year with the stepson and how I would care for him once I got home, giving Lynn a break. I never minded, so it was possible and probable that he did.

All losses of life are painful, some more than others. The argument my father and I had a few months after my discharge left us strained and unwilling or unable to speak directly to each other; we were probably more alike in some areas than either would admit or acknowledge. I moved to Raleigh after being in Florida for two months and needed a job. I love everyone in the extended family, but I wasn't a fan of the heat and humidity. I stayed with "Mom C's" sister, Jo, and her husband and three older kids in Garner, which was cramped, but we made it work. I helped out financially as needed and would get my apartment as soon as I could afford it, which took about five months. I had the money enough money in three, but a new barely used washer and dryer would fall into my lap, too good of a deal to pass up. I made a disability claim to the Veterans Administration after my discharge and had the physical evaluation two months later. I came home in the fall to get the things I left with my younger sister, and unfortunately, my father and I put her in the middle on the issue of a phone bill as the go-between because we couldn't talk to each other. She had enough at some point, which I apologized for, and then went over to see my father and try to mend fences. I had faxed my senator from Ohio several times directly from the computer in an attempt to get my last command to respond to the points I made in the appeal of my grade reduction. I hoped there still might be a chance to have my rank restored and receive the severance package. I had used the wrong format when faxing the document directly from the computer, so it took longer to fax. We'd speak for a few minutes, bringing him up-to-date on the new job, etc., and I offered to write a check to him or pay it directly to the telephone company. We went upstairs to my old bedroom that he had turned into an office, and he gave me a check from the VA for almost $500. Six of my eleven disability claims were approved, but only my ankle injuries would be percentage-rated. The doctor who was examining the cranial nerve damage on the right side of my face from the accident to see if was legitimate was skeptical. A slight droopiness, like I had a minor stroke, was pretty obvious. Still, the doctor didn't believe me, or he was trying to gauge the extent of the damage. So he proceeded to use a sewing needle on the left side of my face, and as soon as he touched the skin, the nerves in my face twitched every time. When he did that on the right side, it didn't, and he checked multiple areas. Not giving up, he proceeded to puncture the skin several times. After small amounts of blood started to appear, he was taken aback and remarked that maybe he had gone too far. I responded maybe as I wiped the blood away. Anyway, I thought it was funny, and I told my father about the story and then offered to sign over the entire check from the VA to him for the phone bill and from my collect calls from Japan, but he didn't want that. I cashed it and handed him the money owed.

He would pass the following January from a stroke. I spoke to my mother after the doctors initially examined him. He was alive; and the doctors were, as I understood it, optimistic. Sunday night or Monday morning, I got the call that he had another more severe stroke and came home. I got a ticket but missed the flight and took the next available flight to Detroit. I got in around 7:00 to 8:00 p.m. and at the hospital an hour later. The doctors were going to disconnect life support to kick-start his brain function, which if it didn't work, nothing would. We each had a few minutes alone with him, as much as you can be alone, and it took about thirty minutes. By 11:00 p.m., he was gone—still tough to relive for many reasons, but to lose him…

His physical presence was the rock that kept my siblings and me in line, to a degree, calling out BS and not allowing petty things to get in the way of the bigger picture. Perfect, he wasn't; no one is. But the strength of his character and principle is part of my being, differing slightly. His is missed beyond the words, to say at the very least. I recall hearing stories about how he'd push the envelope when doing his taxes, bending the code as far as he could before it cracked. He had been audited twice but never found to be in violation of anything. Unfortunately, karma would need to resolve outstanding issues between our mother and my siblings fully. Years earlier, I got the tattoo I wanted after being told that the family dog, Duke, had died two days earlier. Had I known he was sick, I would have made the trip to see him, and my father knew I would. But he didn't want me to know for some reason. A year earlier, I had noticed a growth on Duke's right side, mole-like but raised and the size of a nickel, maybe quarter. I asked my father what it was. He didn't know, and I suggested getting him to the vet. And his reply was "Why? It isn't bothering him." He'd finally take Duke to the vet a year later; it was cancer and was in over 60 percent of his body. How much longer is standard when you get such news? And the vet was surprised he had lasted this long, but it could be anytime, hours to days. The vet offered to put him down, but my father took him home. He died two days later on my father's birthday. I know it ate him up, even though he'd never admit it. While talking with my brother recently about things growing up and what it was like in our house, I concluded that "we learn what we observe" as talking or discussing feelings, fears, or concerns wasn't dinner conversation or something there was a comfort in approaching.

Two months after he passed, my siblings went to a psychic, also a friend or acquaintance of Joe's wife. Her gift was that she could hear your guardian angels and would record the sessions because there would be things that we'd listen to but wouldn't recognize or understand until a later date.

While I was on active duty, I saw her as I attempted to understand the struggle I was going through, why, and what could alleviate it. I would listen to one of the tapes years later and heard her clearly say that my guardian angels were working on getting me out of the Corps because it was or would no longer serve my higher purpose. Two months after my father passed, I suddenly woke up and knew someone was in my apartment. It was small, so it didn't take me long to look in every corner or crevice. I calmed down as no one was there, but the feeling of someone being there was powerful. I thought and said out loud, "It's okay, Dad. I'm fine. I'll be okay, no need to worry." He left a few moments later, and I was able to go right back to sleep. Later, I'd hear from one of my brother's reading about how my father's guardian angels had been debating letting him stay or bringing him home. His guardian angels knew, as we all did, that had he lived, it would have killed his spirit long before his body because of where the stroke was. I'd also hear from that reading that he was worried about me. Not sure if there was any mention of him visiting or not, but that had already happened. Me telling someone about it may have prompted the conversation.

> Do not take life too seriously. You will never
> get out of it alive. (Elbert Hubbard)

Depending on your definition of *life* or *living*, is it better to be living or just existing? When I looked at this, I thought back on the Terri Schiavo case. I would ask myself what it means to be alive and living versus existing and going through the motions. I'm busy living and preparing for what is ahead as best I can, no matter what may be on the horizon or beyond. If I am ever in a vegetative state and there is no medical or realistic hope for me to recover, give it no more than thirty days and let me go. It will be part of my will, which I need to complete, but I also need to document current possessions for insurance purposes and use that to ask family and friends which items they'd want. It doesn't mean they will get it, but it gives me an idea of what will remind them of me and hopefully bring a smile to their face. No one is getting out of life alive, and the only thing I can take with me is what I have packed inside my heart, which I plan on stuffing with as much love and light as possible between now and then.

My mother was simple and probably complicated in other ways. However, I never really learned about her upbringing or side of the family. I knew I had an aunt on her side and uncles, but I only recall ever meeting the aunt and her family. I worked for her nephew before the accident, but he never really spoke to his side of the family tree. She wasn't in your face about it, but she was a woman of faith—firm in her belief. But I would come to question at least a portion of it. She prayed, but that was about it. She seemed to be waiting on the Creator to deliver her prayers. I would think, *How about helping out a bit and taking at least a few steps toward whatever it was you were praying for?* I am sure that her upbringing was difficult; I recall some-one in her family having trouble with alcohol but don't know who. She had a brother, maybe more than one, and a sister in her family dynamic. She was friendly and well-liked in the neighborhood.

Because my younger brother is all over the place, I'd try and keep my nose clean where and whenever I could; but in those times, she wouldn't tell my father everything that happened. Not that there were daily or weekly events, but no doubt it saved more than a few punishments. I don't have many of the same stories on her side as I do for my father, but it is what it is. She would suffer from mental health issues, which started a few years before my father passed, which con-cerned him; and after, it would worsen when she wasn't taking her medication. Along with several neighborhood kids, I would hang out on the street corner in front of the house during my youth under the streetlight or on the basketball court, which had another streetlight shining on it. On late summer nights, they knew where we were. My mother liked to go dancing with my father, and on one summer night, we had permission while they were out to go swimming at one of the neighbors. Sometime after midnight, she walks over in the dress she had worn for their night out dancing, barefoot, shoes in hand. Not sure if she had a beer in hand or not, but she had been drinking, not drunk or unable to function but funny as hell the entire time she was there standing on the platform talking to all of us. We were all laughing loud. She'd also gone to most of my baseball games before I could drive or when my younger sister had a softball game and me a baseball game. My father attended two, maybe three, over ten years because he was worried that his being there would make us nervous. It only made me nervous because it was so rare for him to show up. I'm sure if he were there more, it wouldn't have been an issue, and we may have benefited from it.

We weren't as close as I may have liked, and I never called Mr. and Mrs. C "Mom and Dad C" in the presence of my parents. They'd never understand. One time, I got in trouble, which I think was because I had a pack of cigarettes. My mom smoked for years, so sometime in the summer between my sophomore and junior year, I had plans to go to Cedar Point with the extended family. But I wasn't allowed to go because of the cigarettes. My mother, not my father, was punishing me, and she brought this up while Mrs. C was in the entryway to pick me up. My mom was hoping she'd join in the beratement, but she wasn't having any part of it. I never blamed or accused my mother of abandoning me after my accident, but it is how I felt, at least for a time. I'd ask her years later how she felt about my "punishment" and why she didn't speak up or try to intervene. She indicated that the punishment or treatment would only have gotten worse if she had intervened or spoken up to my father or disagreed with it. I wasn't sure how it could have, but I knew she was more right than wrong.

When she'd ask me if I wanted anything of his after his passing, I wanted his black onyx ring with a raised gold eagle that he got from Franklin Mint or the Bradford Exchange. We both had an appreciation for eagles and what they represented, and we both liked the hymn "On Eagle's Wings." It's the symbol for strength, honor, courage, and integrity, to name a few. Advice from an eagle—let your spirit soar. See the big picture. Cherish freedom. Honor the earth and sky. Keep your goals in sight. Bald is beautiful. Fly high! After my father's passing, I began calling my mom every two weeks, and we'd talk for at least thirty minutes each time. I didn't ask about the ring until she brought it up and would then come up with a reason or excuse not to send it. After about six months of that, I told her I no longer wanted it, which is probably why the length of our phone conversations began to decrease. I said I had my tattoo, and I knew who my father was and didn't need anything physical to remind me of him. Hurt and pissed off but never letting her know that, I just let it go. My mother's manipulation has been the cause of some issues the rest of us faced. As much as she didn't want conflict in the house, a good deal of it resulted from her; I am not sure if she knew or could admit to any of it. Over the years, I've observed that we learn what we observe and would see or hear about children wanting attention, even if it was negative; at least that was something. I am uncertain if my mother's issues were related to seeking attention or one of her parents or siblings having an issue with alcohol. We never really knew her side of the family, and the stories I did hear about would be bits and pieces. Not being closer to her family was because my father paid the taxes on her parents' estate before distributing it to her siblings, and they were unhappy about it. But my father didn't trust them to pay the taxes from their distributions or something like that.

My parents began participating in the foster parents program, which I believe started in the summer before my sophomore year. Still, they were only beginning, so they tested the waters by only occasionally having a child stay over the weekend to give the actual foster parents a break. Someone I knew by name at school and was in the same grade as me stayed with us for a few days, even a weekend or two during the summer. I may have even suggested it. My brother and I were up at the junior high playing baseball when he showed up and said my father wanted me to come home so I could refill the gas can for the lawn mower. I didn't, at least not immediately, and when I got home, shit hit the fan. I was yelled at, was grounded, and couldn't see the extended family in New York before my junior year. I was pissed and said that it wasn't fair, reminding him of his own words about how we should treat any foster child and that it was as though he was already a member of the family, so why couldn't he go and get the gas can refilled? My mother had somewhat agreed with me as my younger brother and sister were just stone-cold silent but all in the family room. He thought and then acknowledged that he should have sent him instead, but he never said I was right or even apologized. That was the nearest I ever came to anything of an apology. In order to go on my trip, I'd have to write a two-page paper explaining either why I was wrong not to come home or how I shouldn't have disrespected him or that it wasn't honoring my parents' commandment or something like that. I wrote the paper, but it wasn't what he wanted. And my anger flowed at what I felt was hypocrisy, but I wrote it like a lawyer preparing my closing remarks. I got to go on my trip; and sometime during my enlistment or after my discharge, he offered to send me to law school and pay for it, which I briefly considered. But it wasn't for me. I've wondered on occasion what would have happened had I taken him up on the offer, but he wasn't in a position to pay for it.

They didn't have a foster child living with them until after I joined the marines. I recall being home before my first deployment and meeting this little boy and hearing the absolute horror stories of what this little boy younger than five had been through at the hands of his grandparents. When I returned to California, I saw a counselor at the family center and told him I was concerned about the situation and why. Social services visited them, and my father suspected I had said something to someone. But he never said anything to me. A year later, I was home, and the little boy was still there. But it was a night-and-day difference in how this child was. Not anywhere close to normal, but he wasn't "Chucky" anymore. My father's methods were unconventional, but you couldn't deny the results. My mother had grown more than attached to the boy, and when the state wanted to get him off their payrolls, they put him up for adoption with a couple who had no earthly idea of what was in store for them. No doubt the trust the child had built up with my parents, especially my mother, was now destroyed.

The relationship between my mother and younger sister would be a difficult one, but to my younger sister's credit, she didn't let it stop her from being the one who took charge of most things for several years after our father's passing. My younger brother had moved in with the family I babysat for during his senior year. My father commented years earlier that he saw the devil in Mike's eyes after a playful wrestling match in the kitchen turned ugly. My mother's hurt from losing the first foster child would weigh heavy on her for the rest of her life, and she blamed my father, who had no control over the decision. The state wouldn't allow my parents to adopt the child and just wanted to save money on the foster-care costs. I know my mother kept in contact with him from time to time, but the kid never had much of a chance after he was adopted because it just seemed that the adoptive parents had no earthly idea or training on what to do or how severe his abuse had been. I don't think the state wanted them to know out of fear of them backing away, but I could be wrong about that. In the early to midnineties, my mother had mental health issues and was admitted to the hospital. It lasted a few weeks to a month, and I know my father was worried. I knew he loved her and wanted to give her the life he promised, but it would never have been enough. She'd be on medication pretty much for the rest of her life, which she would take if someone were there watching her take it.

Once I moved away from Ohio in '96, I'd only return for the occasional visits. During a time of volatility in the family, I had started asking my mother if she would be happier in Florida, where I think her brother lived, or later after I married Adrienne if she'd consider moving in with us. But she wanted to stay in the home she had raised her family in since the early seventies. A decade after my father's passing, she'd be moved out of the house and into an apartment, which wasn't what she wanted. Tom, Marie, and Jillian moved her out of the house after they first evicted Mark for reasons that are right out of a *Jerry Springer* episode. They began dividing up the booty, and one of the items we had in the family room was a large framed picture of *Jesus Praying in the Garden of Gethsemane*, as I think it was titled, and would end up with my oldest or youngest brother. I was pissed off after I heard who got what, etc., not because I wanted anything but because of the ghoulish nature of it—expensive china cabinet to this person, solid oak bedroom furniture to that person. Younger brother got the pool table, and no one knows what happened to all of our father's old tools, which had "disappeared" years earlier. Adrienne found the same picture, or one just like it, online and ordered a much smaller size. We had it framed and sent directly to my mother in the apartment. After her passing, I'd get it back and give it to my nephew and his wife.

My younger sister would give power of attorney to my older sister a few years later at my older sister's request, proclaiming that she "wanted to take care of her mother." Yeah, what a crock. But besides knowing Marie as I do, I have no concrete information to support my assessment. A few years later, my mother moved into a retirement home, but the rest of my siblings weren't aware of the move until the day it happened or just after. She had been on the waiting list for a few years before then, and my mother made friends whom she'd eat and visit with. She'd be in a wheelchair permanently now because of problems from not rehabilitating her hip. In late September of '19 everyone was now taking an active interest in our mother because her health was about to deteriorate. I visited her several times when I was in the area, and I'd still call every ten days to two weeks, but the answering machine wasn't on. And she wouldn't pick up the phone. I had suggested having the remote phone handset near her recliner, but nothing changed. On occasion, she'd eat some to appease whoever was there encouraging her, but she stopped eating in late September to early October. She was ready, and in November, she passed. A day after the funeral, I was back home; and within the first week, I saw my mother in a dream, passing her on the stairs in our old house, dressed in purple, her favorite color, smiling and happy and finally at peace. Lord knows I tried to get her to stand up for herself and for what she wanted and not do what others wanted to avoid a confrontation, but in some ways, she may have liked the chaos and conflict. Losing my mother was sad, but because of how she had deteriorated over the last decade or so, it was a blessing to know that she was now at peace and no longer tormented by the pains of this world. Of course, some, if not all, use humor to deflect our pain, and someone had "joked" it was out of jealousy. My father's ex-wife had died a few months earlier, and she didn't want her anywhere near him.

As for the rest of my siblings, with most, it is distant and unlikely to change, at least not, in my opinion, until they have some kind of an awakening. We are just vastly different people on different paths. Some are Kool-Aid-drinking blind sheep cult followers; another reminds me too much of the worst traits of our mother by inflicting the same chaos and conflict on their kids. Thankfully, their children's eyes would be opened, seeing the truth, learning from the experiences of their aunt and uncles, and breaking the chain of "abuse." They had suddenly stopped communicating with me without so much as a middle finger in the air in 2012. It was just silence, and I wanted to know why. And when I read the comments my niece was making on a Facebook post, I knew; and it would be the catalyst in me writing an impassioned letter, the first of four, where I felt like there was a hand on my shoulder helping me write it. It was likely my father's hand on my shoulder. Without going into specific detail, it would allow me to confirm my beliefs in how I would live my life, my approach to people and things, and my expectations in the relationship between us. I broke it all down into eight items that were what they had said, and then I'd add my thoughts and feelings on them: (1) Ultimately, the lesson to be learned could only be for themselves, not taught by another, and as experience is the best teacher, they would have to go through it. (2) I wasn't trying to change their decision but challenging them to be better by using their arguments against them to start the process of opening their eyes. (3) The sun, the moon, and the truth are three things that cannot be long hidden. They would start to see things and make their own decisions, which I am grateful they did. A cycle is broken, and I was hoping it would last through eternity. I mean, evil still fights for oxygen from time to time, but they have the antibodies and tools to prevent it from disrupting their lives. (4) They didn't know everything that happened, but they never sought others' perspective or side before making their decision. (5) They wanted to avoid an unpleasant conversation and give people the benefit of the doubt. They didn't want to get involved or be put in the middle but had already had because they chose not to communicate their decision to me, which I would not have tried to change. (6) They appeared to accept the accusations about me stealing money or some other bullshit. Still, they never sought my side of the story to determine for themselves if there were any truth to the accusation or statement. They parroted or regurgitated the outrageous claims against me but didn't want to be in the middle of anything. (7) They were dependent on those making the false accusations and statements, so supporting their decisions was done out of fear and self-preservation. Doing the right thing for the right reasons is the only natural choice we can make. Silence is consent. (8) They admired individuals for the wrong reasons, not for who they were but for what was received or done for them by the individuals in question. No matter what, a lie is a lie; but they were unwilling, unable, or avoiding anything that might contradict the lie. And the truth would have.

In the second reading of the Gospel, I mean in the letter to my siblings, not including Ann, was the third impassioned letter, where I felt a hand on my shoulder writing it. I'm not going to air any dirty laundry of theirs. It's not my place, and I have no desire. Those impactful things for me, the highlights, have already been disclosed. I called them out on contradictions to the values we were all raised with, especially those who learned the hard way. One of the most powerful understandings for me came as I earned the title *Honor* (integrity, responsibility, accountability); *Courage* (doing the right thing in the right way for the right reasons); and *Commitment* (devotion to the Corps and my fellow marines). My older sister wrote everyone a year or so earlier, proclaiming to be a victim and blaming others for what had occurred to her and her family, which were self-inflicted wounds. My letter would be, in part, a response to hers. I wasn't going to let that stand. Still, I waited as I was trying to get copies of the pictures in the family photo albums and maybe some background on who was in the photographs when they were taken and the event. I tried to do this while my mother was alive because she likely knew all of that information. I had arrangements with a Toledo company to digitally scan them, repair any damage, and even enhance the colors, if necessary, for those in color. I had my mother's permission, which I videotaped and sent to everyone. I offered to pay gas money and shipping costs to get them to me or have them delivered to the store directly. Unfortunately, Marie had them, and it was a control thing.

My father and younger sister helped me out financially when I was in need due to car-related issues. On a trip home from North Carolina, I decided to try one of the southern routes from West Virginia to Columbus and then home. When I entered Ohio, my brakes began to squeak. I called my father to tell him that I would be late as I didn't want to risk significant damage to my brakes or rotors. He allowed me to put the repairs on his NTB card, and I gave him a check dated for my next payday for the entire amount. My younger sister would help a year later as I discovered I needed new tires, and she let me use her credit card. And I gave her a check dated for my next payday for the total amount. If you have to borrow money from family or even friends, don't let it become an issue that strains your relationship.

Not everyone can afford to lose what they gave you, so confirm it's a loan or gift. And if it was a gift, repaying them in kind with something is just a show of respect when they came through for you. Not doing so—well, for me and my belief—is death before dishonor. Aside from these two examples, I never relied on my siblings for assistance—financial, emotional, spiritual, or anything else. I'd come to feel that I couldn't trust them not to bring it back up and throw it up in my face, including the false accusations later. My faith was in the truth eventually coming to light, and it did. I would have a conversation with Joe, whose wife talked with Ruth as I was married to Lynn, and the stepson was six months old. I would call him and tell him how things are going, which were good. But everything I'd say to him, he'd tell his wife, and she would end up telling my ex. And she had no reason or right to know. She just wanted to stay connected to someone in the family for whatever reason. I would explain to my brother that I'd no longer talk to him about what was going on in my life if he couldn't convince his wife to stop having anything to do with my ex. I mean, it wasn't as if they bonded or had any real friendship. He said he wouldn't ask or tell her to stop, and I said that he left me no choice to back away and stop letting him know what was going on in my life. We'd be cordial at a family event, but beyond that, not much else. That's changed now, but it took a few years before it would. Not much else to say as I've indicated other issues I may have had with my siblings already. I'm sure if this becomes a published book and they become known, they may want their fifteen minutes of fame, but I'm not interested in going back and forth over anything. And I do still have the letter I sent them all with embedded images of the various things addressed in the letter.

The underlying theme was that we were all most likely closer to the end of our lives than we were at the beginning. If we couldn't put aside petty things, taking an honest look at ourselves in the mirror, then there wouldn't be much of a chance of becoming a close-knit family, helping one another without the need for reciprocation or being critical of another unless the decision specifically impacted us—common sense things, or so I thought. Some of the things I highlighted in bold were "an honest person doesn't have to remember a lie," encouraging professional or intensive psychiatric help for the one who took the worst traits of our mother and amplified them toward their children. I told the individual to "come down off the cross you put yourself on, use the wood to build a bridge, and get over it." Thank you, Christopher Titus, for that. I even embedded a picture of The Emotional Guidance Scale, hoping it would become one of those life-changing moments, but it wouldn't. One thing I would repeat a few times in the letter was "We teach people how to treat us by what we allow, what we stop, and what we reinforce."

Tom, Marie, Mark, Joe, and his wife knew what I was trying to do with the photo albums and why. They never called out of common courtesy before, during, or after they changed things. So when I got the DVD and USB, I broke the DVD in half and returned one half to Joe and the other to his wife, who had her section in the letter and a separate mailing, telling them, "You know what you can do with it." Mark received the same instructions but with a USB drive. I no longer wanted anything to do with them, which included the picture images of the family in front of my father's open casket. I wasn't going to be a part of it but did so only because my mother asked, but after I told them all, "I never wanted to see the pictures. You assholes couldn't come together when he was alive, so now that you're acting like you want to be a family, it disgusts me." The second-to-last time we were all in the same house or place together was in '82 when we got family photos done as an anniversary gift for our parents.

The last time was while I was home on leave, and I told them I was buying pizza because some would never have considered coming over unless they had something to gain or benefit from. And a free meal did the trick. I wanted more of how my extended family was—not perfect by any means, but there was love and respect and a willingness to see one another succeed. To be overwhelmed by that is worth every tear you might shed because isn't that what family should be? Jillian was still angry and bitter over how my mom treated her during her last few years of high school because she chose the foster child over her, and I didn't blame her. I only wanted her to be comfortable in her skin and be able to live with it, should she not attempt to heal from the hurt or see our mother before it was too late. The skills and talent to go to college on a volleyball scholarship were there, but the desire wasn't. She is probably doing the best out of all of us, at least from the financial perspective. I still think she needs to consider a kickback to all of her siblings because she benefited from learning from our mistakes of which there were many. She would visit with our mother every single day after she became aware that she was starving herself. She saw her more in those six weeks than the sum of everyone else, including me, but I wasn't living in Ohio. She could heal from the hurt and wouldn't have to live with regret when it came to our mother.

In every family, there are problems or issues to some degree, even disappointments, but that doesn't mean you have to carry that with you forever. At funerals or celebrations of life, it's an opportunity to reflect on your life, the relationships you have, and the potential for bridging any divide that may be there. Take that honest look in the mirror and see if you are part of the problem or could have done anything to contribute to it. We are all capable of being unfair, stubborn, pigheaded, or opinionated, and I know the saying "You don't speak ill of the dead." Still, you can't view everything with only rose- or blue-colored glasses, not if you are honest. The deceased may not have done anything to you, or maybe that had both a positive and negative impact on your life. Reflect and see what you can or should have learned from the experience, and don't be afraid to share the story with another or even write it out just for yourself in a journal. It could be therapeutic and healing for you. Looking at the brutal truth, I realized why I am not as excited or sentimental about my heritage. I'm not ashamed or embarrassed by it. Still, in those moments that we did try to learn or celebrate the traditions and even stories, they are not positive memories for me, and that stems from being alone in a house full of people and having to find my way out of the darkness. I thank the Creator every day for that smile and friendly voice who helped me regain mine. I don't lose sleep over it, but I'm not going to be sentimental about things to appease someone.

My extended family has issues or problems. Which family doesn't? But none of it will ever change how I feel toward them and how thankful I am for them being a part of my life and adopting

CHAPTER 6

My Extended Family

Family isn't always blood. It's the people in your life who want you in theirs, the ones who accept you for who you are, the ones who would do anything to see you smile and who love you no matter what.
—Unknown

The summer after my freshman year, I was "adopted" by friends who became family—unconditional love by people who take an active interest in your well-being, successes, failures, or hurt. Even if you haven't spoken in a few months since your last time together, when you do, you pick up right where you left off from your previous conversation. Every family has issues, but that doesn't mean it impacts everyone. And you can still have great conversations and laughter, even with those who you may be currently at odds with. It's never a competition, want, or need to feel one is right or justified, and they won't gather others to their cause. It is something my father tried unsuccessfully to encourage my siblings and me to do. Still, like everything else, if you're the only one even willing to travel down that two-way street, then you'll come to realize that you've done all you can or will do and will no longer expend any energy or effort on it. The course of my life changed in such a positive way that it's impossible to think of my extended family not being in my life. The fun, laughter, and feeling of being loved just because was overwhelming, but it was our interactions while together and, oh my god, the healing power of Mrs. C's hugs were what brought it all home for me.

In a typical summer, I'd be playing baseball every day, all day. This summer, I'd be spending virtually every day with my extended family—Mom and Dad C, Jerry, Casey, and Jim—swimming, hanging out, and having lunch and sometimes dinner; and Sara would also be there most of the time. Jim was playing baseball in the younger league, and we had several games over a three- to four-week span that were within an hour or so of each other. So I'd watch him, and he'd watch me. Mr. C had played semipro baseball for the South Amboy, New Jersey, team either before the army or after. He watched me play more in three weeks than my father ever did. In one of the best games I had, he and Jim were watching, and I had a hot bat. And nothing was getting by me in the field, although not much ever did no matter which position I was playing—which was first, second, or third base or right field—as my arm was the strongest. I'm not sure if it was a close game or not; but my last at bat, I hit one to about twenty feet from the fence on the large diamond—which, I want to say, was somewhere in the neighborhood of three hundred feet or more—with a wooden bat. I liked the feel and sound of a pure hit, and the bat I used was mine and had a tapered knob at the end. I cleared the bases and stretched it into an in-the-park home run, sliding headfirst into home. I was on top of the world, even as the cut on my left forearm started to bleed, probably not much more than a deep scratch. When we got back to the house, Mrs. C patched me up, but it was more about how she immediately went to work on cleaning and bandaging me up. I was like, "This is different, someone showing their concern and doing what they could to fix me up."

Jerry wasn't into baseball or other team sports but ran track that spring. He was pretty fast in the 100-, 220-, and 440-yard races. Casey wasn't doing sports that summer. I think she was interested in a guy from Waite High School, but it lasted maybe a week or two longer than she and I did. But I never saw him at the house. One of the craziest yet impressive things about these three is that they knew all of the lines from *Smokey and the Bandit* and could recite the movie with exact timing and inflection; it was crazy. My jaw hit the floor when they showed me with the volume on low or off. I'm sure the routine would come back to them if they tried it today.

As great as that summer was, it was the end that would break my heart as they moved to Liverpool, New York, just outside Syracuse—the nature of the job market at the time. I can't imagine that the multiple moves helped the kids build relationships, let alone having others be part of their extended family like Sara and I were. A few years earlier, my parents, or rather my father, considered moving to Ghana, Ohio, outside Columbus for a new job. I'm not sure how I would have reacted had we moved. It would have just been my parents, me, and my younger brother and sister, not even sure if we'd take the dog or not. I wouldn't have met the extended family, and since I'd be the oldest in the new house, it could have been a significant change. But I suspect that I would have had greater responsibilities or crap thrown my way. My older siblings would have stayed in the old house and continued attending the high school until they graduated, but it would have been volatile, considering the personality clashes. Once I found out about the move to New York, I started trying to hang out there as long as possible, even taking the dog on a walk up there, which began when the sun was out, but I got back about thirty minutes after sundown. Jerry was with me on one trip, and when I got home, my father was pissed about how late it was for me to be walking the dog. But that was just a BS excuse; it wasn't even 10:00 p.m. I attempted to remind him that I mentioned where I was going and that I'd be back by ten, but as soon as I opened my mouth, he slapped me across my face and in front of Jerry.

Jerry headed home, and I went upstairs to my room and closed the door, pissed off and sick and tired of the BS. On the day they moved, Sara and I were there to say goodbye, and then we walked back to our neighborhood. We never said a word on the walk home; we were just both crushed. I headed up to the K-Mart, which had

93

turned a section of their store into an arcade. I spent about two to three hours playing Donkey Kong and Tempest. When I came home, I just went up to my room and lay down for several hours. I liked to sleep, especially when I was stressed or mentally exhausted, probably because I'd have a good dream or was just able to ignore what was ever bothering me. I'd learn later that when my energy was low for whatever reason; the sleep would help rejuvenate me.

I began running cross-country in my sophomore year, but I wasn't as good as several others on the team. And while I enjoyed it, I didn't have a competitive desire. In the fall or early winter, the extended family would return for the funeral of Sara's mom, who had died during surgery to repair a problem with her heart. Sara and her brother were adopted, and their adoptive parents and Mr. and Mrs. C were friends. I went with them to the funeral instead of my mother. We did get a chance to hear how the new school was for them, and we were able to laugh and joke. One of the strangest things that happened was Casey asking Sara and me to kiss each other. I am not sure why, maybe because she wanted to ensure we'd be okay or test our love and friendship with Casey. We were extraordinarily reluctant but eventually did because we promised her that we would. The bond we had created in such a short time was strong, and we all shared in the pain of not being together. But having kept our word to her, I believe made it stronger.

I kept busy that school year, got a part-time job, and played intramural basketball, which was terrific, playing with kids who had already graduated for the fun of it. But in competition, we'd play for several hours once or twice a week, which allowed me to sleep very well. I also coached a basketball team of fifth and sixth graders, which was a great experience that I'd repeat in my junior year. I made the JV baseball team and was one of the fastest, being put into pinch runners when we needed runners to score on a long single. I also tore my right quadricep muscle about halfway through the season, which was pretty painful, and it took me more than six weeks to recover fully. And by then, the season was over. That spring, Sara, her brother, Dad, and I drove up to see the extended family over spring break, and it was great. I was grateful that my parents let me go. Later that summer, we'd make another trip up for two weeks, which was just as fun as ever. One of the best times was when the neighbor across the street, who also happened to be a photographer, not sure if it was just amateur or professional, offered to take family pictures after church or some other event where we had gotten dressed up—some great photos of everyone. He made us laugh. He made some smart-ass comments to Jerry and me before he took a picture, and Jerry began to make an offensive gesture, similar to flipping the middle finger but with his arm. And it was in the picture.

I wouldn't see them again until I was on leave after my first deployment. They lived in Cary, just outside Raleigh. I walked off the plane in my dress blues, and Mom C took my cover (hat) and wouldn't give it back. I can laugh now about it, but then I was like, "Holy shit, I hope no one sees me." And it wasn't like it was a long walk to the car. A screwup years later when I was attending Jim's graduation from the CIA (Culinary Institute of America) in Hyde Park, New York—I forgot my cover at the house. How? I have no idea, but we got some excellent pictures from it. When I told them I was joining the marines, they were concerned about why but still happy for me because it was what I wanted to do. Letters and phone calls would keep us all connected.

Before my second deployment, I came home to Ohio for two weeks with a cast on my left ankle. I spent time with my family and Kristen, splitting my time with each. I thought the relationship with Kristen was, or was becoming, serious, which felt great. It was Duke, the family dog who hadn't seen me in almost two years, that was hysterical. He went crazy running on the family room sofa and love seat like a NASCAR track. It lasted about twenty minutes before he calmed down. I think I scared Kristen when I asked her to consider moving to California when I returned from my next deployment—not marriage and not the smartest thing to ask. But I'd learn a few days after she picked me up from the airport after my deployment that she was in a relationship with someone else. I guess she could have told me at any point in a letter or even before we spent the night together on that first night, but oh well. "I'd rather you hurt me with the truth than comfort me with a lie." I had to leave town, or I'd be out of my damn mind. So Sara's brother and I went down to North Carolina for about two weeks. He would also become a marine, and I figured it was an opportunity to help me focus by working out with him to prepare him. June through August in North Carolina is brutal because of the humidity, but I still ran a few miles every other day along the country roads near the house. I was still in pretty damn good shape. I would meet Ruth on this trip, a friend of Casey's, and I was young and dumb. Ruth would fly out to see me in California for a weekend, and like a moron, I proposed to her. And of course, she said yes because, well, I am still one hell of a catch.

Yes, Captain Obvious, I was rebounding and not in a positive way. In September, I drove for two days straight on my way to Raleigh. I visited for a few days and then onto Richmond, Virginia, reporting for independent duty. Mom C asked me three times in succession if I loved Ruth, and I just danced around it, never directly responding yes or even in the affirmative. But it would be good for my career. I could go to war, focus on the job, and not have to worry about things at home. I did consider breaking things off with her, but then her father died. He was her stepfather who adopted her a decade or so earlier, and I still lacked a certain amount of courage when it came to hurting people.

Jim was the youngest and the funniest; he could go into and out of some interesting characters that would have you laughing until your gut hurt. He got into cooking while working at a golf course's grill, which prompted him to attend the CIA in Hyde Park, New York. Mom and Dad C moved to Homestead, Florida, and Jim came to Raleigh on Thanksgiving break and cooked the turkey, which was terrific. The man can cook, and he enjoys it. And by default, he cooks most of the main dishes for family holidays and get-togethers. He and I traveled to see the folks and Casey on his summer break. I needed to get away from the situation with Lynn, so we took the stepson with us and drove down. I should have driven my car because it had AC, but Lynn needed a car there to use. I think it was over the Fourth of July weekend. Mom and Dad C watched the stepson, who was one, while the rest of us visited Islamorada in the keys, playing volleyball and drinking beer.

Jim would meet Silvia, who he would marry a few years later; and her friends, Michelle and Bridgette, who were sisters, were also there. Michelle had me enticed almost immediately because of her energy; laughter; and fun-loving, carefree approach to most things in life, and she was *my kind of beautiful*. Michelle would recommend a book to me, *Many Lives, Many Masters*, which was the first of many books similar in nature. When Casey got married a year later, I had orders for a year in Okinawa and figured I'd be able to buy a new stereo there, so I packed up one I had and gave it to Michelle. Michelle and I would keep in contact over the next year while I dealt with the BS from the command. She was involved with someone when I came to Florida for two months in the summer of '96. She wasn't at Jim and Silvia's wedding for reasons that weren't important. I will always appreciate all the conversations we had during a turbulent time. I hoped we would have remained friends or kept in touch. And I have reached out, but no response is a response. I do have her picture in the photo collage in my hallway. I'd meet Jill a few years later, but thinking on it now, both Jill's and Michelle's energy and personalities were very similar. And both were my kind of beautiful.

Jim and Silvia and their daughter had moved to Vermont to be closer to her family after Jim had enough of the long late-night hours in the restaurant industry. He loved the job and cooking, but it can also be rough on the family and homelife. Years later, they would relocate back to North Carolina, where the rest of the family was living or soon would be. When I can, I like to do things for the family, and a few years ago, I purchased a smoker for the family as a Christmas present and had it shipped to Jim as he was the family cook. Everyone would benefit from his cooking. Jim's hugs are just as strong as Mom's, though they are mainly "bro" hugs. His daughter is talented in writing and drawing—bright as anything and just as friendly and loving as her parents, who will be celebrating their twenty-fifth anniversary this year.

Casey is a strong and independent woman whose path has had roadblocks and issues that she would always overcome, gaining new strength and courage from each of them. I'm not sure why or what it is about society or men in general, but why they feel threatened by a strong woman is beyond me. She can have an initial rough exterior and may seem to be abrasive, but she isn't. She doesn't play games and sees no point in sugarcoating things that are just a waste of time. Her trust has been taken advantage of by a former employer or two, but she persevered. Her hard work and effort to break the rules so they could be expanded on and improve the efficiency and effectiveness of the office are what drove her and the teams she's managed so they could serve their clients better. She owned her own business with a small number of clients and, last year, graduated from East Carolina University with a bachelor's degree concentration in management and accounting. She's now heading up an accounting firm as the CEO because the partners finally realized her talent, skills, and work ethic. She met her husband at the nuclear power station in Homestead as they both worked there. They married, divorced several years later, and remarried a few years ago, always remaining friendly as they were raising their son; but it was more than that. Yeah, who didn't see the remarriage coming? We all did; it was so obvious. Her son would arrive first as I seem to recall it being a difficult pregnancy. In August, the first wedding was in Southern Florida—no way in hell was I wearing my dress blues, opting for the dress blues delta, the short-sleeved shirt, and dress blues trousers. It would be the last time I'd have my picture taken in uniform—good time, great reception. Years later, an action taken by Casey would cement my respect and admiration for her strength, character, and determination. Think Sandra Bullock's character Leigh Ann Tuohy in *The Blind Side*.

Someone was critical of her decision regarding temporary custody of her son. A bad relationship after her divorce wasn't a suitable environment for her son, so she gave temporary custody to her ex-husband. She drove from Florida to North Carolina and talked with the individual face-to-face. If nothing else, she deserved to be respected for standing up for herself and confronting the individual because sometimes, a phone call isn't as effective as a face-to-face, "come to Jesus" moment. Her perseverance has paid off significantly in her most recent promotion. Her husband retired a few years ago from his career in the nuclear industry. Her son has his degree from

East Carolina University in health and fitness, has worked in physical therapy and personal training, competed in CrossFit training or competitions, and is now taking computer science classes.

Jerry is one of the most resourceful people I know—a hard worker and a jack-of-all-trades. My two older brothers had taken me out for an impromptu bachelor party at a strip club before my first marriage, and I never called Jerry to let him know. And I know that stung. My head wasn't in the game at that time, and I'd figure it out much later that I didn't marry for love but because I was rebelling against my father. I was an adult now and could do what I wanted. Boy, I showed him. When he married, I was his best man a few years later, and I didn't initially think they'd last. But that was envy or even a bit of jealousy. He was my best man when I married Ade in 2005. Jerry and his wife will be celebrating thirty years in 2022. Their kids are doing great. His son works in IT, and their daughter is attending the community college. And I'm not sure if it's for clothing design or another art-type degree. One of the funniest things I remember Jerry doing was getting plastered on a concoction of fruit soaked in Everclear in his first apartment in the late eighties. I didn't eat the fruit and drink to excess as I had on my first deployment, but Jerry and his roommate felt the pain the following day. He helped me move to Charlotte in the fall of '99, and we went to the Coca-Cola 600 NASCAR race in May 2000, which would be a first for me and a last.

I'm not a fan of the sport but respected the hell out of the drivers and teams, especially Dale Earnhardt. I am not likely to go to another race because it took us four hours to get out of the parking lots after the race was over. I'm sure there's better traffic control now as demonstrated by his son and friends recently who went to the same race this year, and it only took them thirty minutes after the race ended to get here, which is a few miles from the track. In February 2013, Jerry would be involved in a single-car accident where he slammed the driver's-side door into a barrier. The impact would break his hip, forearm, and collarbone, all of which would require metal rods or plates. I hit the road for Raleigh as soon as I got the call, packed a bag, and took the dogs over to the soon-to-be ex's as we were still sharing custody of the dogs at that time. His recovery would be difficult, and he'd be out of work for six months or so. Had he not been in as good a shape as he was, I suspect it would have taken much longer—a wake-up call for the family as it was the first major incident to any family member. A few years later, Jim would need emergency surgery to remove several inches of his large intestine due to diverticulitis. Casey would have several injuries that would require surgery, but none had an emergency associated with them to the best of my knowledge.

Sara lived on the same street I did, but we didn't hang out or get to know each other until the extended family. And even then, it was limited. She is a remarkable woman—a high school English teacher of all things—loves what she does, connects with her students, and even adopts them to a certain degree. Like so many teachers who love the job, Sara teaches for the outcome, not the income, and that passion is unmistakable. She married early, giving birth to a daughter; divorced years later; would marry again a few years after that; and have another daughter. What brings a smile to my face and heart is that her oldest daughter swore off having kids. She was as tough, strong, and independent as her mother, and she got the strength of character from both parents. Her father is a marine. A few months after she gave birth, I reminded her of what she had said five years earlier about not having kids and would do it again a few years later when her second would come along. It brought a smile to my heart, thinking how much she changed, and it was such a beautiful thing to witness and a true testament to Sara, who she is, and how she raised her daughters. And the fact that she is now a grandmother three times is just amazing, but I know she is enjoying it. It is refreshing to see and feel the power of love and how transformative it is. Recently, however, I have been irritated with her and Casey as they have kept the secret of Sara's latest few trips down to surprise the family. I was like, "Damn, you should have at least told me so I could have made arrangements to either board my dog or have someone come over and let her out in the middle of the day." It's three hours to Raleigh without traffic, so it's a full day even if I spend four hours there. Sara's younger brother is also a part of the extended family, although it's been years since I've seen or spoken to him.

Mr. C was the consummate provider for his family in every sense. With a quiet, reserved mannerism, he is a man who loves his wife, children, all of us, and baseball. He was successful by any definition of the word; and he rarely, if ever, said no to his wife. I have never heard him raise his voice in anger; and he would talk with you, not at you and certainly not down to you. They've lived in several states over his fifty-plus-year career, retiring several years ago and moving back to North Carolina. Mr. C's sister and brother-in-law were a great couple and funny, salt-of-the-earth people. Their son is just as fun-loving as his parents. I don't recall meeting anyone else on Dad C's side of the family tree, but I may have. Mrs. C's family, however, I've met most, if not all, of her family, except for her dad. Every year, I was invited to attend the Fourth of July family reunion in Pennsylvania, but for some unexplainable reason, I avoided it until 2005. Mr. and Mrs. C will celebrate their fifty-fifth anniversary this year, which is a fantastic accomplishment for any marriage, and I'm sure they have had ups and downs, even a few arguments with as many moves as they made. But no matter how they did it, they did it. Unfortunately, the roles are now reversed due to Mr. C's diagnosis a few years ago with Lewy body dementia. Mrs. C has stepped up and taken on things she never had to before, primarily the financials, with the help of Casey. I'd call them both a few days before or after birthdays and Mother's and Father's Day because they usually have something going on the actual days, and I wanted quality one-on-one time since I couldn't be there in person.

I'd call or drive up depending on my situation on holidays, which primarily meant having someone watch my dog. I never had an issue with bringing Nitki with me while he was alive; he was well-behaved and laid-back like me. Dad C did use him once as he wanted to teach his dog a lesson about space; so when his dog began to get curious and invade his space, Nitki let him know to back away, nipping him on his nose—lesson learned. Nitki felt terrible, but I reassured him it was okay. And as he did warn the other dog, sometimes you have to let the dogs work it out among themselves. It would be at their place for Thanksgiving in 2015 that Nitki would show me that he was struggling with his hind legs, and I'd have to carry him up and

CHAPTER 7

ADRIENNE MARIE

I used to believe, I mean I still do, that if you give something your all—everything you have—it doesn't matter if you win or lose as long you risked everything. Put everything out there. And I've done that. I did it in my life. I did it with the game—but not with you. I never gave you that, and I'm sorry.
—Billy Chapel (Kevin Costner) talking to Jane Aubrey (Kelly Preston) from the movie *For Love of the Game*

Adrienne Marie, she preferred Ade, would realize too late that I did give her every part of me—all of the love I had to give and then some and then more. She had every chance or opportunity to return it in kind. *If only*, two of the biggest words that speak to regret. I met Adrienne in November 2002, which was about two months after she kicked her husband out the door. We would connect on a dating website, chatting via Yahoo! Messenger for about two weeks before meeting for dinner. It was a great way to "test the water" to see if the other was legitimate or batshit crazy before meeting in person or even giving out your address or phone number. We would be together for about two months before we stopped. Without realizing it at the time, we were both scared about the feelings we were having for each other. Her scars from what her soon-to-be ex did throughout their marriage were still fresh, and I was in denial that someone could bring about light in me that others could see. But I couldn't. Taking my advice, she would trade in the vehicle her soon-to-be ex-husband bought her out of his guilt of being caught cheating again. He'd intentionally not make the payment, forcing the creditor to call her, and she'd have to call him. From my own experience, I mentioned that it wasn't worth the aggravation—best to cut those kinds of financial ties.

We would chat with a psychic named Michelle at different times in a Yahoo chat room back when you could actually have some great discussions with others about whatever the subject of the chat room was. On more than one occasion, Michelle indicated to each of us that Adrienne and I were supposed to be together. We had both moved on. I had met someone, and I'd learn later that Adrienne had been on several first dates, all of which she proclaimed they proposed to her on that same date. The psychic, Michelle, contacted me on instant messenger one evening in May or early June and told me I needed to call Adrienne ASAP to warn her. I didn't want to. I didn't want to get involved no matter what it was, but I called and told her what was going on and that I was relaying what Michelle was instructing me to say to her. As I relayed the information, Adrienne looked out her bedroom window, which faced a cemetery. Yes, there was a car running with what appeared to be an individual in the vehicle. I told her to call the police, have them check it out, lock her doors and windows, load her 9 mm Ruger, and keep it ready until the police gave the all clear.

In mid-June, I bought my house, and the woman I had met in May also moved in but as a roommate—nothing more. Adrienne had also taken on a roommate for about a month. When I got back from Raleigh after meeting with Jill's son, I sent out an email to everyone I knew to ask for updated contact information and provided mine, and I explained why I was asking. Adrienne replied first, and then we talked on the phone. And she told me what happened after I called and relayed what Michelle was saying. The police confirmed that the individual in the car was wearing all-black clothing and had a mask and a large hunting knife on him. She had gone out with the individual once, who worked for the same company she did and in the same office building. She said no to his marriage proposal. It was mind-blowing. On Thursday nights, Adrienne invited me to join her team to shoot pool a few blocks from her office in Uptown Charlotte (it's what they call downtown Charlotte because it's up a slope). It would be over the summer that the most challenging part of the "brutally honest assessment" I was going through from Jill's passing, and Adrienne is who I would speak to about it—all of it. The conclusion or realization I came to was that I was afraid or extremely hesitant in opening up and being honest about my feelings, fears, concerns, or worries to anyone, sometimes even to myself. I'd withdraw to my man cave on Mars to try and sort it out or wait for it to pass. Our Thursday nights shooting pool were fun times, and we'd talk for hours about everything under the sun. And we were more alike in virtually every aspect.

Ade would act like her skin would melt off like Dracula in the sun if she wore a dress, although I suspect it was just because of her weight. She was a few inches shorter than I was and weighed a good deal more than I did, but her weight was never an issue for me. I would fall in love with her for being herself, not her waist size. Besides, I figure as long as I can breathe when I eat, I'm good. I'd come to learn that it was a primary reason why she didn't like crowds or her picture taken, which was unfortunate because her smile would light up a room. In October, she invited me to Sullivan's Steakhouse for my birthday, and she was wearing a dress and looked great! At the end of the dinner, she gave me a Viking pool cue with an eagle on the bottom of the shaft. I was blown away by the gesture and told her I wouldn't let up on my billiards game, letting her win more because of the gift. She just laughed, and no doubt because of how I responded, she began plotting for Christmas. The questions she'd ask about what kind of dog I'd love to have, well, she wasn't very subtle no matter how coy she tried to be. A week before Christmas, she called me from the road and slipped up, saying she was on the way to pick her up, and I said, "Her? What about him?" She called on her way back from the rescue shelter and would bring over my present after she stopped by her place. In the background, I could hear the dogs, and she played it off like it was in the car next to her or on the radio. Once she arrived, she rang the doorbell and asked me if I wanted to meet my present. She had a big-ass grin on her face, and I was slightly embarrassed. I was uncomfortable with people doing things like this for me, still am to a certain degree. I stepped out my door and stood there, then all of a sudden, I was pushed in the back and fell face forward. And I swear I heard "Get out there and accept this gift" in a loving but stern voice as I braced myself before hitting the ground. It was my father doing the pushing. I'm sure of it. I got up, went to the car, and picked up my boy. I would name him Nitki. A few tears escaped, and I was speechless but managed to kiss Ade and say thank you. I picked up the girl, who Adrienne would name Sasha, and got kisses from her too.

We headed to the local pet store, where Adrienne bought me the "starter kit" for puppies, including a crate. She went all out. It was overwhelming but was one of the best things anyone has ever done for me. I drove home from work during my lunch hour to let Nitki out when my roommate was working. A few days later, I was on a day trip to corporate offices in New Jersey, which made no sense, and I never understood the purpose of the trip. I finished up, got to the airport, and was speeding excessively to get home quicker to see my boy. A few days after Christmas, I told Adrienne that we should try dating again, and from that point on, we were inseparable—as were Nitki and Sasha. Adrienne also had two other dogs, Ginger and Maggie, but Maggie didn't like to travel in the car. So Ade's mom would stop by her place to let them out in the morning and afternoon when Ade had spent the night at my place.

We started getting serious in the summer of 2004, talking about marriage and concerns we may have. She didn't indicate any, but I had two things that I wanted to ensure we were on the same page with. And I wasn't going to hold back in talking about things that may be uncomfortable, especially with my best friend. The first was the number of animals we'd agree to have after the furkids we had—four dogs and five cats—were to pass on. She agreed with me on no more than four animals, cats or dogs in any combination, because getting someone to take care of them or even boarding them when we were on vacation would be challenging to find. The second was that I wanted and needed her to be willing to tell me if I was unreasonable, unrealistic, or just an ass and provide me with examples of what I was saying or doing that backed up her observation or point of view. She knew what keeping my word meant to me, along with my honor and integrity. I always wanted my best friend to be my best friend, which required us to be honest and upfront about everything without reservation.

She agreed and understood where I was coming from and why. On a drive, we stopped in a log cabin place just off I-77 and went inside. I wanted to retire in a log cabin on several acres in the mountains, away from the world. She also liked that, which sealed it for me. We went up to the mall near her house and popped into a jewelry store to look at rings, to check out the styles and prices. I'd go back a day later and buy the one she liked, but it would take a few weeks for sizing. Once I had the ring, I suggested a trip up to the Blue Ridge Parkway to see the fall colors, which weren't at peak yet, but it was just an excuse. We pulled over on one of the outlooks and just took in the view. I pulled out the ring and put it in her line of sight and asked her to marry me. Her response was of pure emotions—smiling bigger and with a brighter glow around her than I'd ever seen before, and the tears let me know it was true. We set the date on Valentine's Day 2005.

As the plans were coming together, I screwed up and wished I wouldn't have been allowed to. Maybe if Ade had pushed back on the idea, even a little, it could have changed the outcome years later ultimately, though it was all on me, even though I had her support. I would give my two weeks' notice at work before we married and planned on taking time off from the rat race. Adrienne had convinced me that if my employer wanted to keep me, they'd have to pay me what I was worth. Still, the amount she had in mind and what they had in mind was way off. Our management styles were very similar, and I wasn't offended or felt less of a man because she made almost twice what I did. I used my bonus and cashed out my 401(k) and pension to pay off the ring, pay for the wedding, and have enough left over for several months of expenses. I'm sure she still had some scar tissue from her ex in this area, but she never said anything. Since I'd be home, she'd ask me to do things around the house, which I would do but not until she was an hour or so from getting home. My sleep was off as I wouldn't go to sleep until well after midnight and would sleep until noon, feeling drained. By the summer, she told me to get checked out by my doctor. The only bright spot in this was that my thyroid was not functioning correctly, and it took two years before the medication and dosage were at the right level. I also had acid reflux, which caused problems for me during my sleep. Had I kept working, I might never have known about it, but it was the beginning of a few more health issues that would follow.

I was diagnosed with sleep apnea a few years later after she observed that I stopped breathing several times in the night. I missed the scheduled sleep study appointment, but I rescheduled it when she said it was getting worse. I'd discover the multitude of problems that were a direct result of having sleep apnea, type-2 diabetes among them. I had to be hospitalized after the sleep study because I had a rash on my right arm, which had gotten worse in the two days since it first appeared. Some suspected MRSA, but it was undetermined. The funny thing about it was having the most potent antibiotic available being administered and watching the rash disappear as the antibiotic reached it. I know she was worried for those few days I was in the hospital. Adrienne had been in the nursing program for one year before switching to IT. She would indicate that it was what she wanted. However, I'd learn later that the situation wasn't how she described it but rather because of her butting heads with the program's head. She'd be required to submit a letter for readmission, which would be an apology of sorts, but ultimately, it was the best move for her. In hindsight, it was a mistake to quit my job when we married, and I wish I could turn back time. But it's unlikely things would have turned out differently.

In January 2006, I accepted an entry-level position within a brokerage call center with the same company where Ade was working. She encouraged me to take it because we could have lunch together. It was about getting a foot in the door. I was overqualified for it and had more management experience than most of the current managers on the floor, and it became frustrating after about a month. It was because of incompetence, and some of the upper call center's management team had zero experience in the investment industry. Our instructions were to upset customers with low balances to encourage them to move their accounts so the company would comply with a rule or regulation surrounding threshold limits. I wasn't going to do that, and I showed Ade the emails. The department wasn't as described, and they sure as hell weren't living up to the corporate marketing slogan. I interviewed in May for an operations management position, which would be in the same building as Ade, actually interviewing with someone who knew me from my days with First Union. A few days after, my manager brought me into his manager's office, where they asked me to resign because I had missed more days than allowed within their rolling window. Still, I suspect it had more to do with the new position I was about to be offered, and I'd be at a higher management level than him. I resigned and immediately began writing a detailed letter to the top five in executive management, including the CEO, indicating the problems with the direction of the call center and provided emails backing up what I was implying. I asked Ade to read it to ensure it was clear, concise, and on point. She did, and she supported my position to ensure there wasn't anything negative concerning my rehire status. A month after I sent the letters, they called and confirmed my rehire status as "eligible." A few months later, HR canceled the attendance policy and the call center's management team.

In the summer of 2006, Ade's nephew would come to live with us because he didn't graduate from high school, and she knew better than her sister how to raise and motivate him. Yes, you heard my eyes rolling. Over the summer, we built an outdoor storage building from a home kit. He was a hard worker when he had to be. We enrolled him at the local high school for the two classes he needed to earn his diploma in the fall. Ade and I would have to constantly contact his teachers and counselor to ensure he showed up and did the necessary work. That fall, I would return to work in a management position with a new brokerage firm in the area, but their headquarters was in San Diego. For the first month I was in San Diego, I met up with Rick and his wife on the weekends. Rick was still on active duty. Upon my return, I immediately got to work on interviewing and hiring staff, including mentoring an individual who moved from San Diego for the opportunity to be a team leader on my team. He had been in the navy and was very rough around the edges, but I took him under my wing. My manager was the friend of the CFO, and it was obvious that she got the position because of that relationship. She had zero management experience—no securities licenses or experience in operations. Along with her counterparts in San Diego, she would manage the processes and departments by the hour instead of building something long-term. I stressed that we needed to approach things long-term as the short-term wouldn't achieve lasting results.

I got to work getting my team the materials for the securities licenses and creating a standard operating procedures, training, and resource manual, which I had experience doing. For the most part, it was going well, but there were issues with my manager trying to hit on the male employees on my team, confusing the hell out of my team leader, and trying to micromanage me in an attempt to prove herself. I was ambushed by her and her counterpart "friends" on a call. Several minutes into the call, I asked why HR was not on the call, and they indicated that they didn't want to involve them. I stopped the meeting and told them that if they wanted to discuss their issues with me or my management style, an HR representative should be on the call. I talked to the senior manager on-site the next morning, and he agreed with my position. Unfortunately, his discussion with those who ambushed me didn't work, and I would resign a few days later. But what sealed it was that my manager informed me that she was going to hire a personal friend of hers for my team that my team leader and I rejected. I would write a letter to the CEO, CFO, director of HR, and senior manager on-site about the issues and statements backed up with emails. Most importantly, I would show the progress I made with my team leader on his management style. I asked Ade to review what I had written to ensure it was clear, concise, and on point, and she did.

A few months later, several of my old team reached out to let me know what had transpired. My manager had a few months to get her security license and improve her management skills. She didn't and was either fired or quit. They offered my team leader his position back and would return his salary to what it was before my manager had reduced it in an attempt to control him and punish him for not bad-mouthing me. Ade would later attempt to throw both letters to employers back in my face. Still, I wasn't having any of it, calling her out for not saying or trying to talk to me out of it as I was writing them or before I mailed them and reminding her that she said she fully supported what I was doing.

I signed up for a Six Sigma Green Belt Certification course that began the same week I resigned and would begin delivering pizzas until I could land management, business analyst, or a project-management position. Ade's nephew was graduating from the local high school; and she went all out to celebrate his accomplishment, bought him a new stereo and clothes, and threw a party for him. I disagreed with him being allowed to have an occasional beer or smoke pot in the backyard with his friends, but it wouldn't stop Ade from doing things her way. When Hurricane Adrienne had her mindset, the best thing you could do was tie things down and brace yourself for the storm that was to come. He would host a party with his friends at his mother's house over a weekend, and Ade tried to caution him about it. But he didn't listen, and she decided to make a point. She contacted the sheriff's office and told them about a planned party where underage drinking and drug use were likely to occur. He'd be arrested and charged with four counts of contributing to underage drinking and four counts of having drug paraphernalia. I drove him to a lawyer to discuss the case; he paid the retainer.

Ade had also cosigned a loan for him as a means to help him build up his credit. Thankfully, she had listened to me in restoring her credit, and she made good money but used that money to try and influence others as a means of changing them. Most just took advantage of her, but she'd have to learn those lessons the hard way. Her nephew ended up getting 60 hours of drug counseling and 150 hours of community service. He would become a major pain in cleaning his room and going to classes at the community college that Ade convinced his father to pay for. He wasn't showing up, lying, saying he was and was doing pretty well in the classes, but he never showed up or completed any assignments. Ade would start to charge him weekly if his room wasn't kept clean, and instead of doing it himself, he paid her the money after she cleaned it for him. A change to his behavior never occurred, but her efforts were negatively impacting our relationship. She would later accuse me of being too authoritative with him. He was acting out because I reminded him of his father, which I called bullshit on as he played on her heartstrings. Her nephew and I were going to see the counselor at the community college to inquire why he failed, but he said he wasn't going. I told him his aunt knew the truth already about him not showing up for classes or doing any of the work. I told him if he wasn't going the see the counselor, then he had an hour to pack his shit and get out. She was upset with me for that and placed no accountability or responsibility on his shoulders for anything. I was hands-off and letting her do what she felt she needed to.

He lied to her repeatedly about paying on the loan she cosigned for him. She had legal access to his bank accounts and knew he had more than enough money to pay off the entire balance and could have paid it off from his account, but she didn't. As it approached ninety days, she paid off the balance on the account, which was more than $1,500. The lies from him continued later that fall as he stopped by asking for her help in creating a résumé, again playing on her heartstrings, and indicated to her that he was done with the drug counseling and only had a few hours left on his community service. I didn't believe him, so the next day, I called the lawyer's office and spoke to the legal secretary and found out the truth but didn't immediately tell Ade as he was coming by the following week to pick up the résumé she had created for him. I didn't speak to him or engage him but listened to the conversation. She asked for specifics, and he confirmed what he previously told her and that his court date was in the middle of December, where they'd dismiss the charges. After he left, I told her that I loved her and appreciated what she was trying to do for him, but it wasn't working. He was lying to her, playing on her heartstrings. It was my job to protect her from things like this, and I asked her if she wanted to know the truth. She did, so I told her, "His lawyer is pissed because he's only completed 2 hours out of the 50 required for drug counseling and only 6 hours out of the 150 required for community service," and that his court date was a week earlier than what he told her.

She needed to see this for herself, so she took the day off work. And we went to the courthouse and sat within a direct line of sight to him. We left without speaking to him, and she didn't speak on the drive home. She heard it for herself; and yet she still bought him Christmas gifts, nothing like she did for his graduation or birthday, just plain socks and underwear, explaining that he'd know he screwed up when he'd notice the change in gifts. I said, "He, his mind isn't wired that way. He can't comprehend what you're trying to communicate to him," and I was right. He didn't react the way she hoped he would. No doubt it would taste like vinegar coming out of her mouth if she were ever to say I was right, but she knew it even if she never admitted it. Damn, that sounds familiar. I've been here before.

Barkwells is a dog-friendly retreat near Asheville, and in May of 2007, we went up for a weekend with the furkids. In 2009, we'd spend eight days around my birthday there, which we already planned. I was laid off at the beginning of the month, but it didn't faze us. It was a very relaxing vacation. We spent some great time together, just breathing again as we escaped the rat race, even if it was for just a week. A long drive along the Blue Ridge Parkway was peaceful and beautiful, seeing the beginning of the fall colors coming out. We visited the Cherokee reservation and took in the wonders of it. Adrienne was one-sixteenth Native American—Huron, I think. We also planned to visit Biltmore Estate and take in both the garden and house, but she wasn't feeling well but told me to go and take pictures of everything. We would relax each night in the hot tub, enjoy the gas fireplace after, and just really enjoy being together. While on vacation, I began looking for another job, but companies weren't hiring. So I'd return to delivering pizzas to keep myself busy and bring in some income. She wanted me to try Home Depot or Lowes, but I knew that it wasn't for me. And I rejected her suggestion about getting my real estate license as sales just weren't for me. Toward the latter part of the year, I felt like I was slowly losing my best friend, and I tried to talk to her about it. She would become very dismissive about my thoughts, feelings, or concerns, so I began to write on my computer to express it somewhere.

Facebook wasn't responsible for the decline in our relationship. But it didn't help, not because social media is evil—it was because of her reconnecting with two friends (LYLAS—love you like a sister, my ass) from school she never really liked. But I think she liked being more successful than either of them. And it made her feel good, but it wasn't healthy for her or us. She was also frustrated with her weight and appearance, but she could have used the elliptical I bought her. And I used it almost religiously every day. Plus, I was walking the dogs at night and invited her every time to join us. She would discover my journal on my computer, and instead of asking me about it, she had written a page and a half of wondering what the hell it was, which was obvious. But she thought I was documenting plans to divorce her, which had never crossed my mind. It took me about a month to see it, and I asked her, "What the hell?" Had she bothered to ask me or see what I had written and why I was writing it, she'd understand that our relationship was not like it once was.

Her fortieth birthday was in 2011, and I began to hatch a plan to celebrate it forty days ahead of her actual fortieth birthday, with *forty* being the overall theme. I was surprised that we could keep it a secret until she walked in the door after going shopping with her sister. I wanted to let her know that she was loved beyond measure, appreciated for who she was and for everything that she has ever done for those who responded or were in attendance. Her aunt and uncle on her mother's side drove down from New York for it. Her sister in New York flew in, and her other sister and brother drove down from their homes. Her brother cooked up spiedies, which was a hometown favorite of theirs from New York. Her sisters went crazy packing up forty of everything—paper clips, tissue packages, rubber bands, just anything and everything they could get their hands on in amounts of forty. An aunt sent a quilt with *40* all over it, and others sent birthday cards with stories about her or pictures, which I had asked them to do. When she walked in and saw "Happy (40th) Birthday Adrienne Happy 40 days til then," she began to shed some tears, and I pumped my arms like Kirk Gibson did after he hit his walk-off home run. And I got it all on video. She thanked me several times, but the good mood wouldn't last.

About an hour into it, she started showing her ass in front of everyone because she wanted her goddaughter to go and get a dog she wanted to take in. In the weeks before the party, I told her god-daughter to make excuses if she needed to but that the dog wouldn't be taken in by us. I also tried to reason with Ade about it at that time, reminding her of the agreement we had and introducing a new dog to the pack wasn't a good idea. I didn't want anything to ruin the party's surprise. Her goddaughter went and got that damn dog and brought it back. It didn't take long before it approached Nitki, who was near me by design because he didn't like a new dog coming into his house, and when he approached Nitki, he let it know that he wasn't going to invade his personal space. The other dogs were just as apprehensive around it but never bit or attacked it. I would tell Adrienne about an hour after its arrival that the dog wasn't staying, and if she wanted it, she could keep it at her place in Concord. The dog went back to its original owner, and a week later, Ade tried to tell me that the owner released the dog into some field and that it got killed, which wasn't true. The owner had found another home for the dog a week after Ade's party. Needless to say, because she showed her ass, her uncle told her that he wouldn't visit her or North Carolina again. It would be after her actual birthday that she got baby fever. I was on board with that, and we both got tested to ensure everything was good to go. She had a slight problem with a prolapsed uterus, but the issue was mine. I had a low sperm count. So I went under the knife so the fertility specialist could go right to the source and retrieve them directly for in vitro—no luck. Approximately 95 percent of my sperm ducts hadn't fully matured. We weren't going to wait ten years or more for possible medication to reverse it, so we decided on using a sperm donor. And she went through two rounds of in vitro. She had three the company would pay for, but after the second didn't take, she said she didn't want to do the third. She had told me that she had a miscarriage in her first marriage at four months; but when I mentioned this to her mother, Ade had never been pregnant, let alone had a miscarriage.

Ade knew her goddaughter's family for over sixteen years as they lived across the street from her place in Concord, and whenever there was a fight or argument, they'd come over and confide in her. Sometime later that summer, her goddaughter began giving her parents a hard time. And they gave her a week to find her own place, or they'd toss her ass on the street. When this came to light, I confirmed with Ade that we wouldn't help her goddaughter out and just let her parents do what they thought was best for their daughter. She agreed, but I'd learn a few years later that she lied and had put up all the money for rent and utilities for an apartment. It didn't matter if the goddaughter paid her back. Her parents were trying to teach their daughter a lesson, a life lesson, but she was Adrienne. She knew better than the girl's parents about what she needed—déjà vu all over again.

In the first few years of our marriage, Ade would start yearly home improvement projects primarily because she needed to establish good credit again. It helped that there were tax deductions that we could take from improving the house's energy efficiency. No way on earth that what she was spending would ever be recouped when we sold the house; and I tried to caution her about it, suggesting she sell her place, we buy a new one, and then sell this one. But once she got something in her head, there was just no stopping the hurricane. We watched DIY shows, so she thought we could do some of the work ourselves. That thought went out the door after an estimate of more than $90,000 for a new kitchen remodel that would enclose the screen porch as a living space, which she disagreed with because she knew better than the guy with thirty years doing that kind of work. The kicker would come when we needed to get the grout in our main bathroom removed and redone. She bought the supplies but stopped short of doing anything because she realized that the task at hand would be significant. She found someone who did it, and he underestimated what it would cost him. But when he finished, she paid him what he usually would have charged. Many of the painting and other projects we could do were done by me, especially painting. Ade wanted to get straight to it, but I stressed over and over that prep work was necessary before you started painting, which would make cleanup that much easier. I painted all the rooms in the house at different times, but I suggested she take the dogs and spend the weekend at her place while I did all the painting and shampooing of the carpets. It was so much easier than getting frustrated with her half-assed job, which I would then have to fix.

I put up a small shelf in the workout room, which was also her office for when she worked from home, and I drilled into the wall and hit an electrical line. Her drama-king nephew from New York was down, and they both began to tease and ridicule me. I took it the first few minutes and then walked back to the bedroom to wait for the electrician. An hour later, I came out, and they started right back into me. I said that was enough and to stop. When they didn't, I went back to the bedroom. At hour 2, I came out, and they started in on me again. But I spoke up in a reasonably quiet but stern voice, "I've had all I am going to fucking take from the two of you. I gave you the initial fun and, an hour later, asked you to stop, but you can't or won't. So if that's the case, then your nephew can spend the rest of his vacation at your place, and you can stay there with him."

They stopped. The electrician repaired the break in the electrical wiring in the wall, surprised I didn't get a jolt from hitting the line, and I paid him. A week later, she proclaimed to her mother that I would blow my top when I found out what she did and had her on the phone when I got home from work. She told me she was removing a casserole dish from the microwave. It slipped and smashed the glass oven cooktop. I asked if she was okay before looking at the damage, and she was.

And after I saw the damage, I said, "Oh well, shit happens."

She was in shock, but that's who I am. And my response didn't surprise her mother. She had already contacted the place where we initially purchased all the appliances and ordered a new one. It was only slightly more than a repair would have cost.

That summer, she would have the kitchen cabinets resurfaced and a granite countertop installed; and while we were at the granite place picking out the top she wanted, she would show her ass again. And her mother was not happy with her. She didn't want a backstop installed in the back of the sink, which was also a window. She was adamant, even after the expert advised having one to prevent water damage on the backside of the cabinets. I tried to reason with her, but Hurricane Ade was in full force. After the countertops were installed, a young apprentice prepared a three-quarter-inch section for the backstop behind the sink. I knew what he was doing and why but asked him to explain his thoughts on it. He did, and then I asked him to explain that to my wife, which he did. And lo and behold, she agreed to have it done. She refused to talk to me for a fucking week after that, and forget about any touching or kissing. I was tired of the BS of which this was just the latest.

Months earlier, after I had gone to bed, she came in and turned on the light and then crawled into bed. I woke up and asked her, "Aren't you going to turn the light off?" No was her reply. Two hours later, I woke up again, got up, and turned the light off. Another moment came when I folded clothes and put mine away but couldn't squeeze any more of hers into her armoire and told her about it, placing the clothes on her side of the bed. When I came to bed a little bit later, she had just moved the clothes to my side of the bed. The next day, I went through her underwear drawer to count how many pairs she had—seventy-fucking-four! When she got home, I acknowledged that she earned more than enough money to buy whatever her heart desired and usually did. But if she was going to buy new clothes that she'd want in her armoire and not hung up, she needed to do some spring cleaning, perhaps by throwing away some of the seventy-four pairs of underwear she has before buying more. A few days later, she went through and removed items but gave me the silent treatment for several days. She would typically go to bed an hour or so before me, and I would give her a kiss good night. But when she asked one night after one of these incidents, "Are you going to come in and give me a kiss?" I replied no. I was sick and tired of what I felt was abuse.

Sex was nonexistent, not for lack of trying to romance or show her how special she was. She continued her attempts to emasculate me, redirecting her issues onto me as though they were mine. I was no longer attracted to her, but I still tried to be playful and all. But she wasn't interested. Another issue she may have had was that I was back to work again and earning significantly more money and could easily cover all household expenses, including my truck payment. I encouraged her to put more toward her 401(k) as it would benefit her in the long run, especially after I recommended changes to the investments she had. I also said we could buy property in the mountains in a year and plan on building the log cabin a few years after that. It would be in June 2012 where she recommended that we separate, and she'd move back to her place in Concord, which I guess is why she never really wanted to sell it. She was unwilling to accept anything short of what she thought her house was worth instead of listening to the real estate agents with decades of experience. Not doing so meant we couldn't buy a place with all the perks and then put this house on the market, which was still only in my name as hers was only in her name.

I said no to the separation and said we needed to get some counseling, and we had our first session on Friday, June 15. And it was nice to relive what we loved about each other. The counselor said he could help and that if Ade felt like she needed to move back into her place, there shouldn't be an issue. I didn't want that but said if she wanted to after sleeping on it for the night, then I'd accept that. The next day, she asked me to take the queen-size bed upstairs and take it to her place. I didn't want that but did it. I broke it down and loaded it up in my truck as she began to remove the drawers from her armoire. It took me two to three hours to drive over, put the bed together, and come back. She hadn't moved or done any more with her packing. I asked why she wasn't loading up her SUV if this was what she wanted. She never answered, and I said, "I don't want this. You do, but if you think I am going to do all the work of packing up your things and taking them over to your place, then think again."

She asked her LYLAS friends and their boyfriends to help me with the armoire and other things. One of the last things was her cats. She said she'd come by each day and feed them and change their litter boxes.

I said, "No, you take them with you. I don't want the reminder that you aren't here by hearing them cry for you in the middle of the night."

Adrienne was indeed a pain in the ass, a bitch even, but she was also one of the most generous people around, no matter if she had ulterior motives or not. I'm not sure if she ever took the quiz to find out her love language, but I suspect it was affirmation. And it wouldn't matter how much I would tell or attempt to show her how much I loved and appreciated her, complimenting her or doing little things to express my appreciation or love for her. Even my nickname for her, PITA (pain in the ass), was out of love to which she would respond, "That only makes you the ass."

She was both fire and ice at the same time or within seconds of each other. I found a picture titled "Fire Ice Angel Wings" that allowed me to visually see what I felt and how I would describe her years later. All the cats we had were indoor cats, and for years, we never had a problem with them. The two males began a pissing contest in her office; and when she caught each of them, she banished them, Jack to the backyard and Max to the front—her decision, not mine. For the last year or two of their lives, they would be outdoor cats. I think it was late in 2011 when Jack passed and early in 2012 when Max did, both of which died in her arms as she held them. The next day, I came home early from work to help her bury Jack. She already had a hole started. We planted a crepe myrtle tree over him, and I placed a Saint Francis of Assisi coin with him. I don't think she had the emotional strength to do the same for Max, so he would be taken to the vets to be cremated. But she wouldn't keep his ashes or spread them herself. She had a very tender side, which she hid, and reinforced a hardened, tough outer shell; and she'd toughen up, no matter the situation, if someone were getting too close to that warm and gushy side of her, which may help explain why things would become so extreme in the last years.

The counseling sessions were every other week, and we'd drive together. Almost two weeks after our first session after our "date night" before our next counseling session, she wasn't looking for intimacy but had the need, which would be the last time between us, but we'd continue "date night" two to three times a month until late October. Counseling seemed to be going well until the middle of August. She had bought a brand-new corvette, which made zero sense because she didn't trade in the old one. So she went from having no car payments to now one of about a grand a month. I was happy she was happy, but quietly, I knew it would put our plans for purchasing land in the mountains off for a while. In the last week or two since its purchase, she'd also become a lot more distant, and I wouldn't find out why until New Year's Eve. I tried to talk with her about it after she dropped off the dogs, all except Nitki. He stayed with me full-time, but I'd take him over there when I took his sisters home. Sasha was the purest soul of them all, and when I brought them back to her, I would let them out. And they'd play in the front yard as we got them inside. During one of these drop-off sessions, Sasha refused to go to Adrienne, wanting to jump back in my truck, and she did. Maggie and Ginger did not want to go to her, but I got them all inside by promising treats. It reminded me of what the stepson had done to his mother when I told him he had to go with her.

The following week when she brought them over, I tried to talk to her before she left, and I said I was hurting more inside because it felt like I was losing my best friend. Her response of "Suck it up" did not sit well with me, and at our next counseling session, we drove separately. And I told the counselor what happened, and you could see the steam rising from her ears. He asked her to excuse the two of us, and we talked for about ten minutes after which I left. And she was giving me the coldest stare I'd ever seen from someone. He'd recommend that another counselor see Adrienne, and then the four of us would come together every other week to continue the overall effort of reconciling. But she became worse the following week when she mentioned that she'd be going to a corvette convention at the end of August up in Pennsylvania and then asked me if I cared if the car salesman who sold her the car went with her.

I said, "Hell no! We are supposed to be working toward reconciliation, and I don't see how that's possible if you are spending the weekend with the car salesman. But if you want to act like your single, then I guess we know where our marriage stands."

She went alone, but in our joint sessions, she was becoming more and more bitter. In October, she bought a brand-new Chevy Tahoe from the same car salesman who sold her the corvette, but he was at another dealership this time. Great, now she has two car payments that were close to $2,000 a month. I needed a break by the end of October and recommended having one final joint session before taking the holidays off. We had our session in early November but were canceling the one at the end of the month and would pick things back up in February. But she showed up at the counselors in late November and got pissed because I was late, texting that she was done instead of calling. I asked about what because we canceled the session and would pick it up again in a few months. She just repeated it, so I asked again, "Done with what?" No response.

A third time, I asked. She never said divorce in the text messages, which I would later present in court as evidence that we were still trying to reconcile the marriage. The next day I went out and bought a new cell phone, a new number and under my plan, and canceled my number on our joint cell phone plan. She was pissed. What the fuck? I told her I was more than capable of paying my bills, and she wasn't going to ease her conscience of hurting me by paying my bills. Now, she did pay my house payment for two months in the summer we split so I could pay off the credit card we used for Sam's club. The kids and I were going to Barkwells in early December for a week. Her mom had bought me *The Five Love Languages* by Jerry Chapman and made me promise to read it, which I did, a few chapters each night, and I'd send her a text indicating what I liked about each chapter. My love language is acts of service.

December 31, 2012, was the day I would learn the truth. I was near her place, and this feeling that I needed to stop by was just overwhelmingly loud. She was out of town, and I had to go to the bathroom. I texted and told her, also letting her know I brought in her mail. I was already in by the time she replied not to, but what

I saw would be both crushing and eye-opening. On her office desk was a Christmas card addressed to her and the car salesman at her address from a couple she met at the corvette rally. Then one of her laptops, she had three of them, was on, and I decided to look at her emails. And, boy, were my eyes ever opened. In early September, she began dating the car salesman while we were in marriage counseling and took him to meet the couple in Boone, North Carolina, a week later, spending the night at the Marriot Courtyard in Boone, North Carolina. In early October, they looked at a house together. She was telling the couple from the corvette convention about her pending divorce. In the middle of October, she was paying for his hotel room when he drove down to Florida to pick up his kid. In late October, they spent another night at the Marriot Courtyard in Boone, North Carolina.

December 31, they spent the day and night at the Fairfield Inn & Suites in Wytheville, Virginia. I forwarded them to my email address and then deleted them from the Sent folder and emptied the Trash folder. She would have one of her LYLAS friends come over and check things out at her place when the neighbor's kid down the street stopped by as I was there. She bought the kid a cell phone so he could call her if he needed to. I didn't have any of her passwords, but she never created them on that one. I wanted to drive up to the hotel in Wytheville and confront them both but just went back to my place and had the locks changed that night. She had been cleaning out my house, taking most of her things but also a few of mine. The leather-bound *National Geographic* books on people in the Bible, the footsteps of Jesus, the Founding Fathers, and three on the indigenous peoples of this country were mine; and I took them.

I wasn't sure if she knew that I forwarded the emails to myself; but when she called in late January, asking if I wanted to file a joint return for 2012, I told her that I had already filed my taxes and that my refund was due in about a week. I don't think I said anything sarcastic about her new boyfriend or even let on that I knew, but she knew something was different in me. In early February, I noticed her dating profile on a dating site, which I thought was interesting. I asked her out for Valentine's Day, which would have been our eighth anniversary. We had a good meal and conversation. She received the roses I had ordered with my note, still considering her my better half and hoping we could work through our problems. She invited me over to her place after dinner, and lo and behold, there wasn't a single thing from the car salesman wishing her a Happy Valentine's Day. She could have hidden it, but why? Sometime in April or May, a big thunderstorm had come through the entire area, and I had the dogs. I intentionally turned off the home answering machine and set my cell phone to silent. The next day as I was walking the dogs, she drove around the neighborhood looking for me as she probably stopped by the house first. She was concerned and worried that something had happened, so I pulled out my cell phone and said I hadn't gotten any phone calls and that I'd check the home phone when I'd get there. A few minutes later, she left, but I knew that she still loved me. She was too afraid of admitting it, probably out of some kind of fear that I'd be an asshole to her if she indicated she wanted to try again, but that was not in my DNA.

In May or June, as the requirement of being separated for a whole year was coming up, she asked me if I'd pay half for the divorce; and I said, "No, I don't want the divorce, so if you want it, you'll have to pay for it."

She then attempted to play me, being all nice and sweet as she asked me if I would consider giving her $25,000 when I sold my house because of all the home improvements she had paid for, which was over $90,000. I did try to stop her from doing as much as she did, arguing that we were never going to recuperate what was being put into the house and saying we'd be better off selling both places and buying or building. I initially said I had no plans to sell anytime soon, and then I remarked, "I guess it would have been better had you sold your house so we could buy or build the one we wanted and then sell my place before you decided that it would be best if we separated." I hung up.

My reply to the divorce filing requested alimony, not because I needed or wanted it but as an attempt to stop the divorce and attempt more counseling without the car salesman in the picture. My lawyer called out her act of illicit sexual behavior during the marriage and before what I was claiming to be our actual date of separation of late November as we were actively engaged in attempting to reconcile and resume the marital relationship. My lawyer screwed up by waiting until the last day to file it. I was on a business trip to Denver, Colorado, for the week, and she was pissed when she read the response. And I named the car salesman in my reply. I had the phone records showing that he began calling her a week after she bought the corvette, late in the evenings, usually after 10:00 p.m. just before going to bed, which is a con man's tactic so that she'd feel good right before going to bed. I've seen other marines do the same things, and unfortunately, he also served in the Corps. He was considered a shit bird by those he served with—fired from a job in Florida because he got caught stealing from the company and forced to leave the state and go live with his mommy in North Carolina because his ex-wife was planning to use that against him for more child support or whatever else. The major downside was that I never thought about getting an agreement in place for the dogs. She brought Nitki back to me when I returned from the business trip but not the girls. She wouldn't let me see them again unless I changed my response about her illicit sexual behavior and cheating. I wasn't going to because I wanted to go after that son of a bitch under North Carolina's alienation of affection law, and no doubt she knew that.

The court was in mid-September, and I had screenshots of the text messages showing that she never asked for a divorce, that we were still in counseling and trying to reconcile. The judge would rule at the end of the month something to the effect that only one of the parties had to have the intent to separate permanently or some other BS. So the divorce was final, but the alimony request was still an outstanding issue. But I told my lawyer to withdraw my request, and he knew why I was asking for it. And it had zero to do with me wanting or needing any support from her. I had to tell that son of a bitch three times to do it over two days, reminding him each time that I never wanted alimony. Once the divorce was final, any assets of hers that remained in my house were mine. Now I had already loaded up my truck twice during the summer, packing up her things and taking them over to her. After the first trip, I suggested she come over and go through the items and sort them into what she wanted, what she would donate, and what to toss; but she never did. Several furniture items, including a cedar chest that her parents bought her when she graduated high school, were still in my possession. I packed all of that up and delivered it to her mother's garage as she was on a two-week trip to New York, and I had asked her if I could put the items there. She allowed me to; and the trailer filled with the combination nightstand and dresser I had made for her, the cedar chest, tools, and other items she gave me as gifts during the marriage. I delivered the compost bin, and a friend helped me get it into the garage. I texted Ade, including her mother and siblings, that the remainder of her things were in her mother's garage. Her sister would call me soon after, begging me to give her the cedar chest at least back to her because it was a graduation present from their parents. I told her to speak to her mother, who confirmed that I had asked permission to put the things in her garage. It would take Adrienne more than nine months to get her stuff out of her mother's garage—but not all of it. The following summer, her mother had tripped on one of the items and hurt her hip, and she asked me to take the things to the dump if Ade wasn't going to keep them.

What was so sad about all this is that she married the car salesman in late December of 2013 because she needed the marriage tax break, which she admitted to her mother and siblings. She had never changed her tax deductions to Single. Less than a month later, I'd start having her visit me in my dreams, crying and upset because she had seen emails and text messages from her new husband to several other women. In one, he said he only married her because it's what his mother wanted. It sounds like a marriage made in heaven, right? That pattern of her connecting to me in our sleep would happen every four to six weeks. She'd always be upset and, most of the time, cry about the same shit. I suspect she was attempting to tap into my energy to tolerate the BS she was going through. It would take me some time before I'd be able to stop the intrusions or "stealing" of my energies, and it would require advice from psychics that I began communicating with in July 2012. It would take me some time to figure out which ones were full of BS from others who were pretty helpful.

Eventually, I stopped asking questions and began strengthening up my "defenses" against Ade's intrusion into my sleep, where we would talk, but she wouldn't do what she knew she needed to, to change the direction her life was heading.

In August 2014, I'd get a text message from Adrienne about Sasha going under surgery to determine what the mass was that she had and had asked me to bring Nitki up so they could try and use his blood since it would be better to have his than use another dog's. They shaved his neck but could not tap a vein; and while I wanted to bring him to see his sister, who he hadn't seen in over a year, Sasha needed to remain calm before her surgery. I went back to see her and got a few kisses from her, and she was thinner and shallow-looking, not like the fluffy polar bear cub she resembled. I tried to do some work but left after she came out of surgery and was in recovery. Adrienne would try to engage me in conversation to avoid thinking about Sasha, and she did spend some time with Nitki when he came back to the lobby. It would be an aggressive form of cancer, and they felt like they got all of it. But in late October, Adrienne would send me a text message, letting me know they put Sasha down as cancer had returned. I was pissed at first because I should have been there with her, and later, I'd hear that her piece-of-shit spouse tried to convince her not to tell me. I called the vet's office and asked if I could come up and see Sasha with Nitki, and they kept her in the exam room for us. I wanted Nitki to have the opportunity to say goodbye to his sister. We spent an hour with her, and I asked for a blanket to put her on the floor so Nitki could say goodbye. I cried and apologized for not being there for her and her sisters as I kneeled over her. I collected her fur and would have a cuddle clone made of her with some of her fur stuffed inside.

I let Adrienne know that I was grateful and appreciative that she let me know about Sasha, but that didn't last long as I learned that she didn't plan to keep Sasha's ashes but let the vet's office discard them. Not sure if it was the cost or not, but I asked the office staff if they could call her and let her know that I would pay for the special cremation of just Sasha so she could keep the ashes. But as soon as they mentioned it was me who was asking and offering to pay for it, she got all bent out of shape. They would try another call an hour later to see if she wanted to keep the ashes or allow me to have them, and she was a consummate bitch. I coordinated with the office staff that I would be allowed to spread her ashes on-site, which Nitki and I did two days later, placing three white roses with baby's breath and a ribbon, along with a St. Francis of Assisi coin, as we spread her ashes. I took a picture of the spot so I could easily remember where we spread them. Had I been thinking clearly, I should have just taken Sasha's ashes with me or poured them into another bag and taken them home.

A few of the vet's office staff ladies were pretty pissed off with Adrienne for acting the way she did and not allowing me to pay for the special cremation and keep her ashes. They knew Sasha and loved her, along with her brother and other sisters, and would let me know about it. In the spring or summer, I had a feeling that I'd be seeing Adrienne up at the vet's office; and sure enough, when Nitki and I finished up our appointment and were paying the bill and walking out, Adrienne was sitting by the entrance with a cat carrier. Nitki would go toward her, and she lifted her hand to try and pet him.

I lightly flicked his leash and said, "Let's go, buddy."

She withdrew her hand and never got to pet him, but I'm sure he recognized her or would have had he been given a few minutes with her. I know that it hurt her; and yes, in hindsight, it was wrong. But I was still very pissed and angry about what she did with Sasha. The hurt was still pretty raw about what she did to me, and she was still refusing to do what she needed to, to change her environment and forcing me to continue to block her from trying to tap into my energy at night. Losing Sasha was the worst individual pain I had felt to date—yes, even more than my father. But I attribute it to the distance I felt with my family, even when we were in the same room. Sasha was more than a dog. She was my child, and not being a part of her life for the two years prior was difficult to bear but necessary. Her belly bumps were part of her character, and she used them for various reasons—"Pay attention to me." "Snap out it." "I'm cute!" She has made her presence known from time to time, the first being about six months after she passed. Nitki played with a bone in the living room, tossing it up in the air and catching it, which only Sasha did. I asked Nitki why he was acting like his sister. She gave me a spiritual belly bump, which brought on a few tears.

> When the student is ready, the teacher will
> appear. (Buddha)

As you get older and become an adult, the script flips. In school, you are taught a lesson and given a test to determine if the lesson was learned. But life lessons are the opposite. Most times, you are tested to learn the lesson. It's essential to learn the lesson, or else you are doomed to repeat it. Everyone can be a teacher. Everyone is, or should be, a student, and everyone can be a messenger, even if it is only by the example they provide. It doesn't require us to wear multiple hats. We seem to have lost touch with the ability or desire to seek wisdom and guidance from those with greater experiences. We should agree that having even a tiny amount of knowledge or information that might help prevent a mistake or pain of a potential hurt is preferred over not knowing anything.

> You can preach a better sermon with your
> life than with your lips. (Unknown)

Once you know, then it's up to you to live it and pass it on. We all have life lessons to learn while we are here, and we may not even know what they are until we are through the storm. But we all have them, whether we are a teacher, a student, or the messenger. We all can learn and grow on this spiritual journey as human beings.

CHAPTER 8

TEACHERS, STUDENTS, MESSENGERS, AND LIFE LESSONS

A man whispered, "Creator speak to me," and a meadowlark sang. But the man did not hear. So the man yelled, "Universe, speak to me," and the thunder rolled across the sky. But the man did not listen. The man looked around and said, "Let me see you." And a star shined brightly. But the man did not see. And the man shouted, "Show me a miracle." And a life was born. But the man did not notice. So the man cried out in despair, "Touch me, and let me know you are here," whereupon the Great Mystery touched the man. But the man brushed the butterfly away and walked on. Don't miss out on a blessing because it isn't packaged the way you expect.

—Unknown

A fellow was stuck on his rooftop in a flood. He was praying to God for help. Soon a man in a rowboat came by, and the fellow shouted to the man on the roof, "Jump in, I can save you." The stranded fellow shouted back, "No, it's OK, I'm praying to God, and he is going to save me." So, the rowboat went on. Then a motorboat came by. The fellow in the motorboat shouted, "Jump in, I can save you." To this, the stranded man said, "No thanks, I'm praying to God, and he is going to save me. I have faith." So, the motorboat went on. Then a helicopter came by, and the pilot shouted down, "Grab this rope, and I will lift you to safety." To this, the stranded man again replied, "No thanks, I'm praying to God, and he is going to save me. I have faith." So, the helicopter reluctantly flew away. Soon the water rose above the rooftop, and the man drowned. He went to Heaven. He finally got his chance to discuss this whole situation with God, at which point he exclaimed, "I had faith in you, but you didn't save me; you let me drown. I don't understand why!" To this, God replied, "I sent you a rowboat and a motorboat and a helicopter. What more did you expect?"
—The Drowning Man

Life teaches all a lot of lessons, but Love reveals your true purpose. Don't be disheartened; there's something good in every bad and something positive in every negative.
—Tushar Raj Luthra

I 'd be willing to bet that those teachers who love the profession teach for the outcome, not the income, and the great ones inspire, empowering the student by helping them learn how to think and not what to think. I've known several teachers personally—meaning they were classmates, family, friends, including Jill—and those I've had the pleasure of being in their classes (Mr. Stevens, who made learning Ohio history in the seventh-grade fun and rememberable). Mrs. Sandwisch, whose accounting classes I loved, was excellent. Those I've learned from, no matter how long it may have taken to learn the lesson, I thank you. No one can predict when one's labor will bear the fruit they seek, but our subconscious can play a significant part in delivering the solution. Epiphany, inspiration, realization, or awakening, whatever you want to call it—have you ever had a moment of clarity that left you stunned and speechless as you searched for the words or response?

I had precisely that happen to me in late April 2013. I found out Adrienne had been cheating in the afternoon of New Year's Eve 2012, and no doubt she knew there was no coming back from it because she showed no signs of interest in the truth about herself. She would act more like a man in this regard by going to her cave on Mars, denying what she was struggling with inside—a process to discover and find the courage to talk to me or anyone else about whatever it may have been or could be about. She may have known the issue or issues, but if she did, she'd keep that so close to her chest that no one would ever know. The rationalizations or justifications that we can convince ourselves of to avoid that reflection in the mirror can be pretty powerful. I was still cordial even after noticing her profile on a dating website after our dinner on what would have been our eighth anniversary. We talked at her place, and no other Valentine's Day gift was present other than the flowers I sent. We were still sharing custody of the girls at this time. She'd have them during the week, five days, and I'd take them for the next nine, each weekend and the following week. I should have gotten the arrangement into an agreement, but I was still hoping we could reconcile. In March and April, her dating profile was still on the site. When she had brought the girls to my place in mid to late April and noticed the changes I was making around the house, she asked about the wooden bathroom cabinet that either she or someone else had made for her years ago. I said it was upstairs in the storage space; and she was more than welcome, encouraged even, to pick up more of her things. But she didn't. I also asked about the dating profile, and she became quiet. I told her I still loved her and wanted to make it work, but she also knew that she would have to come to terms with herself and what, if anything, was hiding beneath the surface. Even if she were too afraid to share or even bring up, she would have to confide in me as I had with her for any real chance at reconciliation.

> Sometimes the mask we hide is beautiful; however, as long as we are hiding, we will never live an authentic life. Our lives may appear perfect and beautiful on the outside; however within, we will be fighting our biggest battle that, over time, will haunt us more than just facing the reality of who we are. Only from there can we fulfill our purpose and experience all the wonder life is meant to hold. (The Inspired Approach)

Of course, it could have just been me who was in denial about who she was as "sometimes it's not the people who change; it's the mask that falls off" (Higher Perspective). She would leave, not answering or saying a word, and I was dumbfounded and asking WTF to myself.

Early on during an individual counseling session, I had remarked about not making changes around the house until we had reconciled. She would either move back in or sell both houses and buy or build a new one, but the counselor suggested that I make whatever changes I wanted. I took down the picture in the dining room and the four porcelain plates hanging around it. I ordered several vinyl decals with inspiring quotes or sayings when I got home from Raleigh at Thanksgiving. "Live Every Moment. Laugh Every Day. Love Beyond Words" was one that I cut into sections and placed around a picture of a quote by Mother Teresa called "Life Is."

Life is an opportunity; benefit from it. Life is beauty; admire it. Life is a dream; realize it. Life is a challenge; meet it. Life is a duty; complete it. Life is a game; play it. Life is a promise; fulfill it. Life is sorrow; overcome it. Life is a song; sing it. Life is a struggle; accept it. Life is a tragedy; confront it. Life is an adventure; dare it. Life is luck; make it. Life is too precious; do not destroy it. Life is life; fight for it.

The framed picture is missing "Life is bliss; taste it," which is part of the actual quote, but you get the point. I had put Spackle in the nail holes from the plates I had taken down and sanded but didn't paint over it. In late April 2013, I talked with Adrienne's mother on the phone about what had transpired. I asked out loud, "Why was I alone in this? Where was God or my guardian angels? Why me? What the hell am I supposed to learn from all of this? What was the purpose for this pain?" And as I asked the question, I turned from the living room toward the dining room. The image struck me hard, and I couldn't speak. I explained to her mother that I had just got my answer, took a picture of it with my cell phone, and sent it to her.

I'd post the picture on Facebook, asking, "What do you see...?" Ade and I were "friends" on Facebook, and she wondered why there was a face on the wall. And I replied I noticed it just as I finished asking a question out loud. You have to be looking at the wall from the right spot and angle with the kitchen light on. She had made a snide comment about painting over it or something crazy like that, and I replied, "No, I find it enlightening because it answered my question." Looking the same way at things can leave you stuck, so what is required is a change of angle or point of view to see it from a different perspective. It may bring clarity to observe something that catches your eye like it never did before, and that is something we should all be thankful and appreciative of seeing. I would delete her comments when the image popped up in my memories a year later. It would be that moment that I would come to terms with and begin the process of standing tall, dusting myself off, and taking the necessary steps to recover. A booster shot arrived in the early summer; a neighbor and her daughter delivered the Girl Scout Cookies I had ordered. I invited them in, and the mom remarked that she was feeling so much love in this house that it was a bit overwhelming. I wasn't sure how to respond except to say thank you and indicate that it was just Nitki and me. Adrienne may have felt the same way when she had come into the house before the WTF moment, but I wasn't going to spend my time thinking about it any longer. We all receive messages from the universe, and they come in various forms. So asking or praying for something and not having an open mind or heart to receive the answer seems like a waste of time.

As for me, I feel it is better to walk alone in the right direction than following the herd walking in the wrong direction. How close people get to me or how much I let them into my life depends significantly on the individual's character, actions, and impact on my life. I do not put my faith, loyalty, or belief in people first. My faith, commitment, and trust lie within certain ideals, values, and universal truths that are beyond reproach. An individual who exhibits these values and standards, in word and action, is someone I can respect, even if I may not necessarily agree with them. What is right for you may not be suitable for me. Music has always been a driving force, a saving grace for me, especially in dealing with grief and the overall process. I would find a path that I didn't know had a name. On this path, I discovered and was able to further connect with the memes that I had come across that spoke to the ideals, values, and universal truths that are beyond reproach and withstand the test of time. For me, movies were an escape of sorts—two hours in front of a big screen, a big bucket of popcorn, and a drink. I found further definition and inspiration about the kind of person I wanted to be and how I wanted to live in those movies with great stories, character development, and universal messages. They would help renew my faith in the better angels of our nature. I'd purchase them when available on DVD.

In 2014, I would meet a few women, and something was nudging me to help them by offering them a place to stay as they sorted out the issues in their life. None of them were friends with benefits or a quid pro quo kind of arrangement. The first turned out to have a problem with heroin, and she had lost custody of her daughter. Her parents were still in the picture but wouldn't do any more to help her out until she got clean, which she would eventually do, and then she moved a few months later back in with her parents. She contacted me six months after I asked her to move out, thanking me for giving her a safe place to stay and recover from the addiction. She began to see her daughter again soon after.

The next was a bit more volatile, and she only remained about a month—no drug or alcohol problem but major mental and attitude issues. Her uncle had passed months earlier, and she would confide in me that the messages she was receiving from him were to accept the offer when it was made, which happened to be a safe place to stay and get her life back on track instead of living out of a motel. We actually slept in the same bed but had no physical intimacy, but I would place my hand on her hip to let her know she was safe. And she would sometimes cuddle. Her friend came to help her move to South Carolina, and she would go on to get her cosmetology license and begin to build up her life. I would receive a text message from her late into the summer saying thank you and apologizing for being a raving bitch. I wished her well and am glad I was able to help.

The third and last one moved in late summer because her boyfriend had beaten her up and needed a place to stay to get away from him. She would move out a few months later for what she said was a job opportunity in Reno, Nevada; but it turned out that her ex, the one who beat her, had moved to Oklahoma and had convinced her to move there. About six weeks after she left, she'd return to the area after he had beaten her again, and she ended up in the hospital for several days. We'd reconnect several months later; and she told me the truth, thanked me, and apologized for lying to me. But she had finally learned her lesson when it came to her ex. Last I heard, which was a few years ago, she was doing great in her job at a coffee shop and in a stable relationship. All three had remarked similarly about my helping them understand finances and budgeting and appreciated my honesty. They learned that it's better to be honest in all things, no matter how difficult it may be, because you don't have to remember the lie.

> If you tell the truth, it becomes part of your
> past. If you lie, it becomes part of your future.
> (Rick Pitino)

> Hurt me with the truth *but never* comfort
> me with a lie. (Unknown)

In September of 2014, I wasn't feeling well at work and decided to leave work and go to the hospital, and no way did I want an ambulance showing up while I was at work to take me to the hospital. Walking from the office to my truck was tiring, and I only got a hundred yards before I had to sit down with chest pains and shortness of breath. I made it home and changed into more comfortable clothes and headed to the hospital. The monitoring wasn't indicating a heart attack. A blood test seemed to; so they would take me via ambulance to the hospital in Concord as they had space, bed availability, and equipment to do more tests. I would be diagnosed with blood clots, and the MRI or ultrasound scan showed it going from my left ankle to my groin. I called Myrna to let her know and asked her to watch Nitki for a few days since I couldn't reach the roommate I had. She said she'd be happy to and went to my house and picked him up. I'd be in the hospital for five days, and Adrienne would contact me after hearing that I was in the hospital, offering to watch Nitki. But I said I had someone watching him. She wouldn't know or find out that it was her mother who was watching him. It's unlikely that it would have been any different even if I hadn't heard from a mutual friend who was at Adrienne's "new" residence, and he conveyed that her husband had picked up a new husky by the throat, yelling and hitting the dog to get in a crate. I was shocked when I heard this because I would have never thought Adrienne would have ever allowed something like that to happen to any animal she owned or even had under her care. If I had heard about him doing that to Sasha, Maggie, or Ginger, I'd be in his and her face even though I hadn't seen them in a year. And I knew that if Nitki were with her and her husband so much as stepped on his paw, I'd end up in jail for what I would do to him. Adrienne did go over to her mother's house to visit; and her mother had put Nitki up in her bedroom, knowing that if Ade found out, she'd go ballistic. She and her mother had a somewhat strained relationship at times. Nitki was good, not moving around on the wooden floors, and he was sleeping on her bed. Ade never knew.

In January 2015, I'd end up in the hospital again for blood clots for four days. The doctor wanted me to come off the blood thinners for a few weeks to run an additional test to confirm it wasn't hereditary. During one of my surgeries while on active duty, I suspect the damage was done by a large blood-pressure cuff on my left thigh attached for more than ninety minutes, sixty minutes longer than advised, causing the damage. The combination of that and my ankle injuries were contributing factors, but I'm sure my poor eating habits also played a significant role. Adrienne's mom and oldest sister would visit me in the hospital, and I would discover that Adrienne blocked me on her mom's Facebook account. It was probably because she'd complain about things I still had of "hers," which was only the king-size bed, but if she had no intention of getting back together, why didn't she want that moved instead of the queen from the upstairs bedroom?

I received Sasha's cuddle clone after I got out of the hospital; and in the spring of 2015, Nitki began playing in the living room, tossing up his bone and catching it, which is how Sasha would play with large treats. When I received a belly bump as I watched Nitki, I knew Sasha was present, and this was her letting me and Nitki know she was okay—a beautiful feeling from the messenger herself and a few tears of happiness. Sasha was the purest of souls; and no doubt she accepted her fate as a means of getting Adrienne to change her ways, which she had been told over and over again by me when she connected with me in my dreams, crying and complaining. The answer would always be the same: "If you can't change the situation, then you should remove yourself from it. I've done all I can or will do—no more stealing my energies to deal with your life as it is now. It's only you who can change this. Stand up, set the expectation, and use your voice." Years earlier, I had read a few articles on how toxic and negative energies, including emotions, helped feed cancer, so when I felt Sasha's presence, this also came to mind about her sacrifice. She was the youngest of all the animals. No doubt the girls weren't being walked, and the yard they had was only a quarter acre, if that, while my backyard was a half acre. And she, her sisters, her brother, and I would go for walks each night we could.

In September 2015, Adrienne had an intestinal blockage and would have a tumor and about a foot of large intestine removed but not her colon. It was cancer—stage 3. She'd begin chemo and other treatments in November. A feeling had come over me that a point-blank message needed to be delivered. If she didn't change her environment, the worst was likely to happen. The second impassioned letter I wrote was to Adrienne. But it would come from Michelle, the psychic. If I had signed my name, she'd never read it. She wouldn't listen to anything from me or anyone else if they criticized her or indicated in any way, shape, or form that she was wrong or even could be. A hand was on my shoulder as I wrote it, but this one didn't seem to be my angels or a loved one I knew. I wrote the letter over several days, and in looking back, I believe it was her father that was there with me as I wrote it. And what it did for me was close the karmic loop for me. Rather than explain it, here it is:

Valentine's Day, a day to celebrate love, but for each of thee, it's a day like every other, a direct reminder that there is not an ounce or trace of real love that exists within the relationship, let alone the marriage—never was and will be.

It's not a marriage; it's a façade, created so that each can cover up and avoid problems, issues, and deficiencies within. Oh sure, he loves her money and what she does with it (buys gifts, clothes, gadgets, private tutor, pay his mother's mortgage, and being more of a father figure to his kid than he'll ever be). And for her, she loves believing that she can buy some kind of control or obedience in him, manipulating him, emasculating him, deflecting her issues onto him as his own so he never becomes wise to what she is doing or unwilling to speak up if he did. Had he cared for her even slightly, it might have worked, but he never has. He's a player, a con man who continues to play her for everything he can. Hopefully more evidence of this isn't required, but the universe has its way. She married because she needed the tax deduction, and he's been wanting a sugar mama who he could easily manipulate into believing his bullshit and paying for everything while he played around. He saw her coming a mile away and started to play her after she bought the corvette, telling her exactly what she wanted to hear, stroking her ego—a move right out of the players and con man handbook. Rasputin is envious at the snow job he continues doing on her.

Great track record on him. Since meeting, he's been a car salesman five times for four different companies, a cemetery salesman (she coached him on what to say to get his job back at the last car dealership), out of work because of a boo-boo on his foot, became a real estate agent (she wrote his presentation), worked for three different real estate companies but couldn't sell a house even with fake reviews from her or her pressuring her family, friends, or coworkers to buy from him. Gecko (actual name withheld) Ventures LLC was nothing more than a "Ponzi name recognition" scheme now administratively dissolved just the like Another Time Inc. (actual name withheld), and now he's back to being a truck driver. Less than a month into the marriage, she finds his communications to one of his many girlfriends and confronts him, but the communications continue to this day. A few months later, he says a friend of a friend has a Siberian husky who needs a home. Well, it's not an Eddie Bauer Ford Explorer, but the premise is the same. He wasn't making it at the second car dealership; so she bought a new SUV because she, the twisted female Cliff Clavin, knew exactly what to do and how to motivate or, rather, manipulate. She always knows the answer to everything and for everyone and quick to tell others what is right for them, how they should live, and how to grieve, all while ignoring the same, similar, or any advice given to her. He is someone she can control, letting her hide from herself and avoid being accountable or responsible for the things she's said and done; deflecting her issues onto him; getting him to become dependent on her; making him easier to control, manipulate, and

emasculate; ensuring she is the dominant part-
ner, which is what she wanted. Unfortunately, it's
not what she needed.

He's not her soul mate. He is not a part
of her life because of his cancer experience but
because evil can serve a purpose in the divine
plan. No mystery why she hasn't introduced him
to her family in New York, except the drama
king. She avoids having that mirror in front
of her because she knows as they do that she
screwed up *big time*! No one she knows—family, friend, or acquaintance—likes him. *No one!*
His "friends" and family can't stand him. And the
excuses she makes for him. Before they met, he
was let go (fired) for stealing from his employer
and assaulted his ex-wife—police report filed but
no charges because he agreed to move to North
Carolina. But she blames his ex and accuses her
of lying. Yes, the only thing he sold her was a
line of bullshit millions of miles long and oceans
deep. Instead of rescuing dogs in order to avoid
issues and being reminded daily of a loveless marriage to the con man, she should seek counseling.
Animal hoarders start out like this.

The unavoidable truth is that her ego, arrogance, self-righteous attitude, negative energy,
and stubbornness are preventing her heart from
being heard, messages the universe is sending
from being received and acknowledged, or the
lessons from being learned, which keeps her
from finding the strength and courage she needs
to take that necessary first step in her heart's
direction. Her tattoo—meant to be a representation of what she believes or who she is or trying
to portray herself to be—isn't. Her words and
actions are not in harmony with each other. She

is unhappy and miserable but unwilling to do what she knows she must in order to move in the right direction. She has shown classic narcissistic behaviors, lashing out at everyone who questions or challenges her false logic, rationalization, or justification excuses. Such an intelligent woman, she is, but by the time she figures out she's being played, the damage is done. And instead of putting her disappointment on the shoulders of the individuals responsible, she condemns those trying to protect her. Relatives have manipulated, lied, and stolen from her. She knew better than her goddaughter's parents on what was right, and her goddaughter played her. Other friends use her because they refuse to help themselves, except to her gullibility. And for those who tried to warn or caution her, she is unmerciful, crucifying, punishing, belittling, and degrading to them. Love isn't a contest. But they could never be right, and she could never be wrong—about anything.

Saying that acknowledgment and apologies are required to those she has done this to is understating the obvious. Penance would be nice; but all of it requires humility, being gracious, finding strength, courage, and being genuine. Unfortunate if these aren't realized because acknowledging, apologizing, and making amends is for her—no one else. They will allow her to be free; and even if forgiveness isn't received, peace can still be found in knowing that the effort was made, presuming of course that it's a pure and honest one. It's about being proud of who one sees in the mirror and being able to live with that image—nothing more. Once the first step is made, the others become easier and easier. It does however come down to free will—a choice, one she is afraid to make. He—along with her other enablers, drama king included—will continue to try and keep her distracted in order to prevent any movement forward, which will only work if she allows it.

A universal truth is, "The lesson will continue until it is learned." The lesson and its delivery become harder and harder the longer it takes to be learned, which is why she finds herself where she is now—health and all. A very humbling thought is, the little polar bear, such a beautiful spirit on four legs, knew her path and accepted it as it was supposed to help her mommy change course to be a catalyst for change. Most would be humbled at the remote possibility of such a sacrifice, but she was quickly replaced so it wouldn't have to be thought about. Imagine if that little polar bear had continued to be treated like the child she was or used to be instead of a dog, fostering her pure and loving spirit, taking her for walks, spending time with her, playing with her, doing special things for her the entire time instead of just at the end—if only. It would have done wonders for both, and cancer would never have been an issue then or now. No one can buy their way into heaven. Denial isn't just a river in Egypt; it's her security blanket and needs to be let go before regret is all that remains.

She has a heart bigger than the great outdoors; but her ego, arrogance, self-righteous attitude, and negative energy are her toxic environment, attracting enablers and denying her heart. It's time she found the strength and courage to take steps toward healing her heart. The mind and body will follow. Einstein's definition of insanity, "doing the same thing over and over again and expecting different results," or words to that effect are applicable. So if the required changes aren't made, then neither will her paradigm. The good news is that she will survive this cancer, but cancer has been known to come back. And if the environment that allowed it isn't changed, then it may come back quicker, harder, and to the extent that nothing can be done. There is no "perfect or good time"—no point or "situation" in her treatment or after will be "the right time."

He is a player; a con man continuing to feed off her for as long as he can; an adulterer who has no intention of giving up riding her gravy train as long as he can keep her from having the strength, courage, or desire from doing anything about it; an adulterer with STDs in his future. He's already found other women along his route who believe his BS.

The time is now—nothing is worse than regret!

I had traveled up to a small town called Harmony, which was about an hour away, to try and get the postage stamp showing it came from there. When she received it, she called and questioned me about it and why I sent it. I played stupid but wasn't going to listen to her BS and hung up. It would be the last time we would ever talk. Adrienne would survive cancer, initially becoming cancer-free in December 2016, but in February 2017, it was back. And just as indicated in the letter, it was back with a vengeance. During all this, she continued working, and I think that helped keep her mind busy. Her treatments began again, and I can't recall how long her hospital stay was. But it wasn't working.

Adrienne passed in the early morning hours of April 21, 2017; her mother was by her side. She had begun planning her celebration of life and had everything written from hymns to sing to readings because that is who she was. Adrienne was very thorough and "professional" in approaching most things, which was an admirable quality. Adrienne was able to heal her relationship with her mother as she relied heavily on her to help her get to appointments and take care of her. Even though she probably never apologized for the things she had said or done, she did in her way. She would tell her mom on several occasions during this that "she was glad that she was her mom." It was about the only blessing that came from her illness and passing. Her husband was always on his phone or the road, which was also a blessing for her. Her mother would tell me later that before she had gone into the hospital the last time, she was done with her husband and wanted to end things, but she needed to get through the treatments. In mid-April, her mother was with her in the hospital, holding her hand when she called out my name as she woke up; and when their eyes met, Adrienne said, "Yeah, Mom, I know."

I would have come to the hospital or her house at any time if asked. Adrienne and I would never have got back together; that wasn't in the cards or grand scheme of the divine plan. Okay, you never say never, but it would have been improbable. And for me, it's because of what happened with Sasha, which sealed it for me. It was likely because she would have to admit that she was wrong, which she never did. Her mother would describe her as a younger version of her grandmother. While I do wish the love felt would have been killed off long ago, the path helped ensure there wasn't a karmic circle left opened by regret or anything left undone or unsaid, at least for me.

> We cannot force someone to hear a message they are not ready to receive, but we must never underestimate the power of planting a seed. (Unknown)

I'd find out about her passing early that morning when a mutual friend would send me a Facebook post via text that one of Adrienne's LYLAS "friends" had posted about her passing. It hit me hard—more challenging than I expected it would. I'd leave work and come home, working remotely, and I immediately sent a text to her mother and siblings with my condolences and prayers for them during this difficult time. Unfortunately, my day would be consumed by it and also with the woman I was seeing who was sending me information about hockey games or things we could do. And I told her that I couldn't think about things like that right now, needing a day to come to terms with her passing. We planned that next week to see Neil Diamond in concert for his fiftieth anniversary tour. It was a great show, and I enjoyed it all. But when we got back to my place, I said I wanted to step back from our relationship and potentially move in together that summer. It was too much work. I tried to help her lighten her load with the baggage she had, but it wasn't helping her. And the financial component was too much when she floated a check to buy a puppy a week after she had put her older dog down due to cancer. I helped her help her son by putting up money for bail and a lawyer for an incident seven years earlier when he was in his senior year in high school. It went on a high-interest-rate credit card, one that had a zero balance, and I should have closed it as soon as I paid it off. Four years later, he had only paid me back half of what he owed and would stop paying on it. In the future, if I have the money and don't need it in the foreseeable future, then no problem, but if it's a loan, we will sign an agreement.

The next day was better, but I went across the street in the evening and let my neighbors know as they knew Adrienne when we were together. I was getting emotional; and when I got back to my house, I stood in front of the kitchen sink and screamed at her and cursed her stubbornness, saying if she had only been able to be brutally honest with herself, this likely wouldn't have happened. I also said that if she wanted to apologize, then she could do so by letting me win enough money in the lottery that it would allow me to help as many people as possible. Early Sunday morning, about 2:30 a.m., she was in my bedroom, screaming at me for twenty to thirty minutes, proclaiming that it wasn't her fault, that she had tried to fix things, etc. I was still asleep but heard her plain as day, and I told her, "Bullshit, you ran away. Leave me alone." She did for about thirty minutes and returned, again proclaiming her position, and I was still asleep and told her again, "You ran away. Leave me alone." She came back thirty minutes later and started in, and I woke up and shouted out loud, "You didn't do anything to fix things! You ran away instead and tried to deflect your issues onto me as though they were mine. Now get the fuck out of here and leave me alone!"

If only she had asked for *a little forgiveness* from me or apologized to me before she passed, it would have been appreciated, but that wasn't who she was. It would however come in time. It would be a few months later that I'd get another visit in my dreams from her, which was calmer, and she appeared to be making progress in coming to terms with the truth but still resisting a bit. There were two more incidents a few months apart, the last one being in January or February 2018. She had come to terms with herself and was no longer upset, angry, or trying to deflect or justify the things she did or said; and while I never heard an apology, I felt it or about as close to one that I'd ever get, albeit in her way. I took it and let her know that I hoped she was indeed at peace. I still hear from her on occasion, usually in my dreams, when there is something that I can help her mother with or even her nephew, the one she reported to the sheriff. In June 2018, he was in jail, and his father was boarding his dogs at the local kennel where his sister worked. But it cost him. When her mother and I spoke and she mentioned this, I offered to foster the dogs until his former girlfriend was in a position to take them, which would only be three to four weeks. Ade was here as I was writing about her to ensure that I was accurate in my description and quotes of what transpired between us. It was a challenging chapter to get through, and I would end up speaking to her mother later that night for almost two hours because of what it took out of me. We've never spoken for that long, an hour at the most, at least on the phone.

In late April of this year, 2021, she would revisit me and encourage me to do something with her mother for Mother's Day. The Michelangelo Sistine Chapel exhibit would be in town for a few weeks, and I thought she'd enjoy that. And I wanted to see it. I hate having to have an app on my phone, but it was the only way to buy tickets. And I initially bought them for that Saturday before Mother's Day, which I thought was best in case any of her children wanted to do anything on Mother's Day with her. I'd cancel them to buy

VIP tickets, but unfortunately or fortunately, they were for May 1. And afterward, we'd go to a late lunch or early dinner. The pictures were on large canvas or cloth prints to show the detail, but what I found extremely helpful were the placards next to each one of them that explained the elements within each print. While we were eating, we talked about Ade and what we both went through with her. Two people suffered similar abuse from the one they loved, finding strength in our shared experiences. This time was different for me. As I talked, I was still hurt and angry about what she did and said, and her mother made a comment she had made many times before in that "she just wasn't able to." She was more like her grandmother than anyone else—tough exterior with a warm and soft gushy side that she would protect and not allow others to see or touch. I knew I had cracked open that tough exterior and reached that emotional soft gushy side of her when we had the surprise party for her before her fortieth birthday. As I heard those words again about her not being completely honest about her feelings, fears, or issues, peace came over me. I was no longer hurting or angry about the events. Even though going through the process of describing them was painful, I was no longer mad about it. We would both agree that had she only been able to, she could still be here, doing all of the same things she had done for people but without the fire-and-ice treatment. The real heartbreak of it, while her mother still has some pain from her ordeal, is there is nothing but love there, and she is also grateful for the time she had with her.

Adrienne Marie was a trip. When her death was published online, I would be the first to leave a comment "To [names withheld], her mom, both sisters, and brother, my heartfelt and deepest sympathies to you and your families. Adrienne was many things to many people. Her loving spirit was fire and ice, and its impact will be felt for the remainder of our days. May the Lord bless and comfort each of you and your family during this time of grief. Our love and prayers are with you always. My name and Nitki."

I attended the memorial service that Monday and sat about halfway up on the right side. One of her LYLAS friends was in the same pew, but I only offered up an acknowledgment nod. I wanted to laugh out loud and call bullshit on some of the things the minister was saying about her marriage, and my god, her mother-in-law cannot sing. A cat being strangled would have sounded better. I would leave just as it finished up and didn't wait for the family to meet people by the doors—couldn't because of the raw emotion for the family and anger toward her piece-of-shit husband. And I couldn't leave Nitki alone if I ended up in jail. I would unfollow her sister, who posted almost every day about her passing, and it was just too much to continue to see. I would change that around a few weeks later and noticed they had her ashes buried next to her father on what would have been her forty-sixth birthday. Probably good that I didn't know because it would have been tempting to drive up with Nitki, which he would have had a difficult time with his arthritis, and I know her relatives and family would have greeted us and happily engaged with us. Adrienne does know that I gave her all that I had and then some and did everything I could to keep her from her fate, but it wasn't on me to do any more except protect myself and my energies. If a change were possible, then it would be up to her to find and use her voice, standing up for not only what she wanted but what she needed—a brutal truth that may have been too difficult a task for her to come to terms with.

Losing Adrienne, well, to be honest, she was lost to me long before her passing. I have no regrets; I did all that I could and then some to save the marriage. I'm not claiming any high ground, nor will I take away from the good qualities she had. People do come into our lives for a reason, season, or a lifetime, and it's unlikely we will honestly know until we pass on if then. Still, all of it impacts your spiritual journey as a human being to fulfill that purpose, which helps bring us closer to the Creator.

Nitki was my anchor, a quiet alpha, my best friend. He was living proof of unconditional love. Lovable and protective of his home and all in it and easygoing, he was a four-legged version of me. His blue eyes were the main reason I wanted a Siberian husky, but I suspect that he had some malamute in him as well because he was bigger than your typical husky. He had caught a few squirrels, which I was upset about but never punished him for because that is part of the

Siberian husky drive. The breed has a high prey drive, which means they can be aggressive when it comes to smaller animals or prey, and to hear him bark when he and his sisters had one cornered in a tree in the backyard, you could feel the bass in his bark. And while he would bring the dead squirrel up to the back porch, it wasn't certain if he had killed it or if it was Sasha. He was better behaved than most children I've met; and while most will tell you that you can't let a husky off-leash, I could when it was just him and me but only did so when I was working in the front yard, not while we walked. He'd lay in the grass and soak up the sun while I did yard work. He was affectionate and gave kisses often and was always happy to see you.

It was just him and me, and I spoiled him as much as I could. Even when Ade and I were together, he'd jump on the arm of the couch and sit on the arm, staring out the window, waiting for me to come home. He'd perk up as soon as he heard my truck, and there was nothing better than greeting him at the front door, his tail wagging. I would joke with Ade from time to time that I wish she showed some enthusiasm like the dogs or like I did when she came home. Her reply would typically center around getting the same amount of treats they did while attempting humor, which would fall flat and leave me feeling empty inside. We were always together on walks around the local park, our neighborhood, and the National Whitewater Center. On our birthdays, which were just a few days apart, I'd get a large porterhouse steak with all the trimmings and usually a large lobster-tail that I'd cook separately. He would get some steak but only wanted the bone, and he was okay with lobster but only took a bite or two.

It would be difficult the last two years of his life as on a trip to Raleigh for Thanksgiving in 2015, he would struggle going up and down the stairs, so I had to carry him up and down. We would go to the vet as soon as we got back to Charlotte, and he had arthritis in his back legs and hips. We'd use medication, acupuncture, and massage therapy over the next few years. He could function, but I would let him out in front to do his business instead of the backyard because we'd have to navigate the stairs from the porch. We would go to the local park for walks because it was a flat walking area, not the small hills around the neighborhood. And he loved kids, and they loved him, always willing to let others pet him. I knew that the day would come when Nitki would no longer be by my side, but it was a decision that I didn't want to make. It was April 2018, and I had been negotiating with God to call him home and not force me to make the decision. The treatments weren't working anymore, and I would get a visit from Ade, who was trying to indicate that I should have him put down on the first anniversary of her passing. I immediately rejected that and said that I'd be pretty pissed off with God, and I'd give him CPR for a full day to ensure he didn't pass on that specific date.

Monday, April 23, 2018, Nitki was at the vet's office getting a bath, acupuncture, and massage, and the vet tech who was doing the massages called to let me know that the treatments weren't working anymore. He had cut himself when he tried to stand up and fell over and hit a small nail on the wall, and it required a few stitches. I did not want to hear it; I didn't want to decide but knew it was time. I called Myrna and let her know. I also called the stepson, who drove up with his boyfriend. I also called a friend that Adrienne and I knew. He was ready to go home when I arrived, but we wouldn't be going home together. I had cut some of his fur and put it in a sandwich bag for his cuddle clone as I had done with Sasha. I waited until everyone showed up, and they prepared the IV. I held him; he laid his head on my lap and tilted it up so we could look into each other's eyes. The entire time I was telling him I loved him, thanking him for loving me unconditionally and being by my side as I navigated the worst storms in my life and being my best friend. It's been three-plus years since that day, and I still cry like it was a few hours ago as I recall this. I carried him to the back room and laid him on the surgical table. Myrna would also say goodbye, and she stroked his head. He loved his grandma, and she loved him. And every chance we'd get, we'd visit her. The next morning, he was picked up from the vet's office by the local business that did cremations. I could not function for the next week and would work from home. I didn't want to break down in the office. On Wednesday morning, I went to the pet crematory to finalize things and say my final goodbye. I was surprised when they called me in the afternoon and said his ashes were ready to be picked up. I asked them to put some of his ashes in one of the small heart-shaped urns for Myrna, which she could either have placed with Adrienne or hers when she passed. I ordered his cuddle clone during that week and sent his fur to them. Nitki was my favorite hello and my hardest goodbye. To say that it was and has been the hardest thing I have ever had to go through is an understatement.

I let my family and friends know of Nitki's passing when it happened, posted it on Facebook, and asked people not to call to check on me because I could not speak about it. I also let them know that I would take at least a year before I considered getting another and asked them not to try and rush it by surprising me. I began thinking about two Siberian husky puppies after I fostered the two dogs of Adrienne's nephew. I was thinking of a male and female but not related—one red who I would name Phoenix and uncertain what I would call the other who would be all or mostly white. Only this time, I would breed them just once or twice before getting them fixed. The mythology of the *phoenix* resurrecting itself from the flames, rising, emerging stronger, is a powerful sign or symbol for anyone who might also be dealing with grief or pain, needing to shed that which no longer serves them. I love the symbolism and power of it.

A month later, I went to Sacramento for a week for work, which was a wasted trip for me. I should have tried to visit Lake Tahoe while on the trip because I had heard it was a spiritual energy location, but I was paying for everything out of pocket, which pissed me off. I talked to another about it. He and his wife lived there for fifteen years before moving to Arizona. I have heard that Sedona is also like Lake Tahoe as it relates to spiritual and healing energies. I know there was no way I could afford to live there unless I won a boatload in the lottery, but the thought and close proximity to Sacramento helped me heal.

Still, I needed the distraction as the stepson and his boyfriend were getting on my nerves, eating everything, and the stepson wasn't working. I was still pretty pissed off with him because a few months earlier, the condition of him staying with me was to ensure he was home in the late mornings and early afternoons during the week to help Nitki get up if he needed to. I checked the security camera around 11:00 a.m. one day to see if he was home yet, and he wasn't. But Nitki was in the middle of the living room where I had left him. I called several times—no answer. I texted him—no reply. When I noticed his paw marks on the carpet, showing him moving in circles as he tried to get up, I immediately left work to come home. I was fucking hot and livid, especially when I finally heard from the stepson after 3:00 p.m. A month later, I'd evict the stepson on his birthday because of the bullshit, and the little asshole would convince his boyfriend to press a simple assault charge against me because I wouldn't allow them to remove items that did not belong to either of them. I'd get Nitki's cuddle clone a few days later, and I swear I saw him when I looked at it while it was sitting on the recliner.

In the fall, Adrienne was whispering in my dreams; and when a picture of a red female Siberian husky appeared in my Facebook feed, I applied to foster her. It took a while, and I wouldn't get any background information on her. She was a handful, a challenge, still is sometimes, but she also has many of the characteristics of Nitki and his sisters. About five weeks later, the rescue had called and claimed that someone wanted to adopt her unless I wanted to adopt her. I thought about it for a few days and then decided to. Several months later, I noticed a Siberian husky needed transportation from the local animal shelter to a rescue in Raleigh. Since I had nothing major planned, I offered to do it, driving the entire way. The dog was at the shelter located on Highway 49 in Concord and would be on my way. The girl at animal control remembered me from her days as a vet tech at the veterinarian offices where Adrienne and I took the dogs and cats. It also gave me some time to stop by and see Mom and Dad C before coming back to Charlotte.

> There are signs everywhere. What did you say? You look lost; there are signs everywhere to help you find your way. (From the movie *Fools Rush In*)

I do not hate Adrienne or anything close to it. If you think that because of what I've written about her, which has been pretty painful, you'd be wrong. I hate the things she said and did, especially those that tore my heart and left deep scar tissue, but what is no longer present is anger at those things or even anything that was associated with them. I'm not likely to talk more about it because it no longer impacts me, except to ensure that I am who I say I am, and my actions continue to support my words along these lines. She is loved and fondly remembered, but I don't and likely won't have any pictures of her hanging up in my house. I have all of them on my computer, but I've also moved them to a distinct folder containing all of the legal proceedings, etc. It shouldn't surprise anyone that I don't have pictures of my ex-wives hanging up in my house because what I went through with each wasn't a pleasant experience. Even in the last day or two while Ade was alive, had she reached out to me and attempted to apologize, maybe I'd feel different about having a picture of her in the photo collage or elsewhere in the house. The best way for me to describe how I feel now when it comes to Ade and what we went through, I'm glad I didn't know how it would end. I could have missed the pain, but I'd have had to miss the dance. For the actual lines, listen to "The Dance" by Garth Brooks.

I was able to see the movie *I Still Believe* before the pandemic closed everything down, and it would provide me with a powerful message about recovering from the pain and grief. At the end of the movie, a stranger approaches the actor portraying singer Jeremy Camp, who indicates that she felt like she knew his wife, who was in the next bed in the hospital, dying of cancer. She heard him praying over his wife. The stranger expressed that the experience of those events rescued and changed her life, and she would explain how. When she turned around and began to walk away, he noticed the stars on the back of her jacket, and it reminded him of the conversation he had with his wife on the subject of stars. He would ask what her name was, and she replied, "Adrienne"—yes, a coincidence. But it didn't take away from the power behind the message for me, which was that real and lasting love would return to my life, without any trials and tribulations, at least none to the extent they had been—lessons learned. My time in the sun was about to begin—on the horizon or just beyond it. Who knows genuinely how the messaging from the universe works? But I believe. Sure, we can delude ourselves. But sometimes the message isn't meant for you, or you aren't ready to hear it. Our guardian angels know when you will be prepared and continually try to move you in that direction. It can take some time, and there is no rushing the process. But you can also help them out by doing the work once you realize it.

These are the seven teachings. *Love*—love, like a river, will cut a new path whenever it meets an obstacle. *Respect*—in the end, we are all separate: our stories, no matter how similar, come to a fork and diverge. We are drawn to one another because of our similarities, but it is our differences we must learn to respect. *Courage*—when your bow is broken and your last arrow is spent, then shoot, shoot with your whole heart. *Honesty*—honesty is the first chapter in the book of wisdom. *Wisdom*—nothing will work unless you do. *Humility*—humility is the foundation of all virtues. *Truth*—if you cannot find the truth right where you are, where else do you expect to find it? These universal truths are at the foundation of my beliefs and who I am and will continue to try to be; and I've gotten reminders, guidance in my dreams from loved ones who have passed on, and déjà vu, all of which has helped me through those dark times. As a US marine, I found a set of principles and ideals that helped further a spiritual growth that began in my early teens and has seen me through some dark times. The paths previously walked prepare you for your next. My previous relationships and marriages did that for what I would endure in the last one; so while the outcome was regrettable, wishing it had been different, I don't regret the experience or lessons learned. I am wiser and stronger as a result, with a greater sense of humility, respect, and hope.

I am not sure if it's this way everywhere; but it seems we, as human beings, have lost the skills or even desire to listen and learn from those with experiences greater than our own, which might help us avoid the same or similar mistakes. People come into our lives for a reason, season, or lifetime. It shouldn't be a surprise to know that we all have a purpose, even if we don't understand what that is or may be yet; but each of us can be a teacher, a student, a messenger that we can learn from. We all can live our best lives, but it can be a struggle for most because they may not yet know their purpose for being. It may be the intention, so it forces you to change into the loving child of the Creator. Teachers, we are and can be. Students, we are and can be. Messengers, we are and can be. And by our example, good or bad, we can help others learn and grow without much of an effort. Whether it's movies, music, books, church, or something else, find out which speaks to you to become stronger, endure the storm, and be more focused on living your best life.

For me, music would be powerful, instrumental messages that would allow me to find some level of comfort in understanding what was, expressing painful feelings and heartache that I hadn't been able to come to terms with yet. "Here I Go Again" by Whitesnake is the classic anthem for those going through similar things, I suppose. Still, all kinds of music would help me find and build up courage and strength to rise and strengthen my foundation, primarily in finding the right words that expressed my feelings. Some songs conveyed the complicated emotions that most would like to avoid having, but the only way you will get through something is to go through it. "Vicious Circles" by Aaron Lewis was one key song because it described what Ade and I were doing: going in vicious circles until we were dizzy with disdain. It was an emotional *roller-coaster* ride, from the ups and downs, which became more downs than anything else; but it helped me find the strength, courage, and resolve to rise from the ride that I didn't want anymore, not because we didn't respect each other but because we just kept butting heads until we stopped trying. If you listen to the song and read the lyrics, it is how I truly felt—and I didn't leave any word unspoken.

Another, "What Hurts the Most," also by Aaron Lewis, spoke directly to my emotional state at the time. I would first hear those songs sometime after receiving the visual answer to my question while talking to Adrienne's mother in late April 2013. I was mourning the loss and wanted to *"kill this love"* within myself to ensure no karmic circles were left open that kept me trying. It was the beginning of me rising from the hurt and heartache and looking forward again. Unfortunately, I'd realize over time that there was nothing I could ever say or do that would or could have changed anything. Her first husband got fired before their scheduled wedding date because he got caught calling sex lines from a work phone. Her father would die before the rescheduled date. He cheated on her several times, and I think there was a problem with alcohol. We talked about everything, more so when it was becoming serious. I'm not sure she expressed any concerns, but I wanted to make sure the other understood any problems or lingering scar tissue. Had she been honest with me, even remotely, as I was with her in our relationship about any fears, concerns, or scars, things might have turned out differently. If she had conveyed any scars or tender wounds from her ex-husband, I would never have quit my job when we got married. She had several attempts to tell me, but sharing fears and feelings wasn't something she did, always putting on that strong front no matter what. She could never be seen as vulnerable or not the Rock of Gibraltar. She was in denial about so many things about who she was and not how she portrayed herself, especially in front of others. It was such a waste because she genuinely could have done more for many people in this world, including herself.

It was music, movies, and social media memes that spoke to me. Reaffirming universal messages, truth, and perspective would help me, especially Nitki, from acting on my anger and pain as the thought of him being without me if I were in jail or worse was unbearable to consider. But it would be a comedy, specifically Christopher Titus and two of his specials, that would save my life, renewing my strength and resolve to rise like the *phoenix* from the ashes.

CHAPTER 9

CHRISTOPHER TITUS SAVED MY LIFE

*The ability to find humor in the ups and
downs of life can give us a new perspective and
a new way of viewing our circumstances.*
—Heidi Catherine

In mid-December 2012, I went to an individual counseling session because of what had transpired the month earlier. I thought I'd also bring the counselor up to speed about what I learned from reading *The Five Love Languages* while on vacation. He was surprised that I read it because he had presumed that because I was a marine, I approached life with a drill instructor—, Clint Eastwood-type mentality, which I've never done or would do. We had talked about that several times before, but he never changed his approach. I went back in early January because I had found out the truth about the affair, and I immediately asked him, "So how long have you known about Adrienne cheating on me since September?"

He appeared shocked and indicated he wasn't aware, and then I remarked that perhaps he should check with her counselor and see if she knew. I then started discussing the book *Love and Respect*. He again acted surprised that I was reading it. Before he got another word out, I said, "The presumptions you appeared to make about me being some gung ho, in-your-face, macho man who commands the world hasn't helped. I'm not perfect, but I always listen to what others say, especially criticism. I ask for examples to ensure I understand what they say and why, even if I disagree with the observation. But since perception is reality, I may use their feedback to change my approach, words, or actions that might give them that impression. I am the most thoughtful, caring, and understanding son of a bitch out there, and your false assumptions about me led to the wrong approach, failing to realize the problems or issues that needed to be confronted were not mine but Adrienne's. I am done with counseling." Before I left, he apologized again several times for his false assumptions, which was a confirmation that I was right. But who knows, maybe he would become a better marriage counselor as a result.

I purchased the Christian music collection *Keep the Faith* after seeing an advertisement on TV sometime after my discharge. It had seven CDs, and each CD had a specific message or content—"Finding Time to Love," "Emotional Healing and Loving Again," "Nurturing Your Soul," "Finding Strength in Hope," "Album of Values," "Celebrate Life," and "Power of Prayer." I would listen to a CD repeatedly, specifically for the message within the lyrics and the power of the voice. Doing so allowed me to mourn or come to terms with the pain, hurt, and anger before letting it go, learn what I could from it, and take that next step forward. It allowed me to realize that I had the power, strength, and courage within me to rise above the pain and hurt, learn from it, and move forward. Don't get me wrong; but if I can relate to it, even if I've never lived it, it is appreciated no matter the language or genre. Music has the power to heal as much as empower or just let loose. In the personals ad that I had when I met Jill, I would describe myself as having a rock and roll heart with a country soul and that I was old enough to know better but still too damn young to care, which still applies to some degree. Three songs would become instrumental for me in 2013 that allowed me to recognize and put words to my pain and express and acknowledge them if only to myself, and it would add fuel to my fire in rising up and out of the darkness.

"Broken" by Scott Stapp allowed me to acknowledge not necessarily losing myself but the pieces of my heart and, to some extent, my ability to understand or comprehend the reasons or purpose for the pain. The spiritual aspect of Evanescence's music was so powerful for me, especially at this time, and I'd be lucky to see Amy Lee in concert at a small venue in late 2016. Halestorm's music was powerful, filled with emotions, as most music is, that had you shaking a fist in the air or reflecting on life itself, and their live show here in Charlotte was the best concert I had seen since Creed years earlier. "Hold on to the Memories" and "The Light" by Disturbed are excellent, as are the albums *Immortalized* and *Evolution*. Bob Seger is my all-time favorite artist. Growing up listening to his music, I have been lucky enough to see several of his concerts in person. Another song by Scott Stapp "Dying to Live" would encourage and empower me to build up my strength and resolve to live my life, not just exist in it. It required me to remove any mask or filter, reflect and observe the process, and turn the page because all that had happened was only a tiny part of my life story. I would learn and grow, dying to let go and see with brand-new eyes.

"Overcome" by Creed would allow me to put words to hurt, pain, and anger toward Ade for what she was doing, not the divorce but what she was doing by trying to deflect her issues onto me and me breaking free from her bullshit. She tried to play the victim, and I wasn't having it as I exposed the brutal truth of things—damn the consequences. I was entitled to overcome and let her know in no uncertain terms, which is about when I could completely block her from connecting with me in my dreams or at any other time. Part of me was still fighting for her, but she was impossible. And I had to take a stand. In early October 2013, I sent her a text, her family included, letting her know that all her remaining items were in her mother's garage and that nothing else of hers was in my house or my possession. I also sent the link to the YouTube video for "Overcome." She would attempt to turn it around and say she was entitled to overcome, but that was just her attempt to deflect. Her family knew better, not that I was trying to get them involved or take my side as they knew her all too well, and they learned to never say anything to her about the way she was. For if they did, they would suffer the wrath of Hurricane Adrienne. I was giving myself the *green light*, the permission to move on, becoming *unchained* by what connected me to her. My affirmation was that I was worth more than what she had shown or treated me.

Never again would I be treated this way by anyone, and I would never treat anyone in the same or similar manner, not if I were in love with them. I suppose that to some extent or another, I will keep *my hands around my heart*, guarding it against potential abuses or mistreatment, but I also can't be the one who abuses or mistreats another. Those with scar tissue are not as likely to cause the same or even similar pain to another, but things happen, which is why I will need to ensure I keep myself in check and listen. It's a two-way street where trust, honesty, communication, nurturing, and a commitment to each other reside. Pain heals; even scar tissue fades. I was shocked to see on our bank statements that she still had a joint savings account opened with her first ex-husband, and it had about $26 in it. I closed our joint savings account. She was pissed when I closed the savings and took the $25-plus change balance. She said she wanted it back. I said, "No, that was for the gas and the time spent packing up your things and delivering them to you." I also remarked that I wouldn't let it remain open like the one she had with her first ex-husband. What the hell was the point of that? I'll never know, but I was so done.

Since I first saw *Politically Incorrect*, Bill Maher has always been one of my favorite comedians, and I watch his show *Real Time* each week. Adrienne and I enjoyed watching it together, and we went to see his comedy show when he came to Charlotte in June 2006. And we saw *Religulous* in 2008. Virtually everything from politics to religion, we agreed and expanded our views or better defined them as we discussed them. Comedians of all shapes and sizes have been hilarious to watch. George Carlin was so ahead of the times! Robin Williams was belly-hurting funny, and there doesn't appear to be any comedy show or appearance on TV that he wasn't hilarious. Even his movies were hilarious. Even the serious ones had absolute power in the messaging, especially his performance in *Good Will Hunting* while both his and Matt Damon's character were sitting on a bench in front of a pond. It hit home about how you may have the book knowledge, but without the experience, you don't know. When Robin Williams's character talked about his wife and loss, it would set a foundation for me that I will not change who I am, what I believe, and who I would continue to be when it comes to being completely honest with anyone and everyone, especially a significant other I was in love with or if it was moving in that direction. Not only did they deserve that but I also owed it to myself so that I wouldn't have to reflect on if I had told them something important or not.

Christopher Titus's *Norman Rockwell Is Bleeding* was the first comedy show that I would repeatedly watch over and over because of the humor and how he dealt with some hurtful things. His openness and ability to lay it all out there, nothing to hide, was just pure freedom to me—no secrets, no skeletons in the closet, etc. It started with a take on 63 percent of American families being considered dysfunctional and that they made up the majority. And he would go on to talk about his parents and his childhood, being raised by his father, his mother having severe mental health issues. The stories were so funny. Truth can be stranger than fiction but to come to terms with your past so it no longer negatively impacts your future is priceless. Finding a way to learn, grow, and even laugh about it, or watching another doing it, is such a powerful weapon for anyone to have in their arsenal as you find strength and courage in it. Knowing when to step to the side when the shit is about to hit the fan is invaluable. Learning from experience is the best way to avoid future things, presuming that you have learned the entire lesson. Some of the "lessons learned" undoubtedly served him well, even though some of the items were painful on virtually every level, but you can overcome them. His stories ranged from how he stopped drinking at seventeen years old after falling into a bonfire to his father's relationship with his mother—the physical abuse he was on the receiving end of. For the record, I have never hit or struck any woman in anger or any other way. I'd walk away first, especially considering how I was pushed like I was by Ruth back in '91. Now, during better times with Ade and, full disclosure, one time while we were having sex, she wanted to be spanked, which, because of what I went through as a kid, wasn't a turn on for me—but, hey, whatever she wanted. If that turned her on, then so be it. The first two attempts were not hard enough, and she let me know. So the third time, I wound up and damn near broke my hand and wrist. My handprint was on her ass for over a week. I could relate to the mental and emotional abuse, even though his comedy never really went there. Still, anyone who has been in a perceived or actual abusive relationship can likely recognize and relate to it.

Empowerment is what I would take away from that special. Don't blame your present on your past, whatever may be preventing you from moving forward and living your best life. Take a step in the direction you want to go. Figure it out. Don't dwell on the past; you don't live there anymore. Learn from it. Grow from it. Force yourself to look at your reflection, and be brutally honest. No matter how deep the scars you have from the pain and hurt you've experienced in your life are, you can overcome them. If scars remain on your heart, soul, or in your mind, you can overcome them. If anything has negatively impacted your mental, physical, spiritual, or emotional health, you can overcome them. You can move forward beyond the pain and hurt and live your life instead of existing. Forward is forward; it doesn't matter how quickly you get there. Get there and do it in a way so that you never have to return. And one of the best lines I've ever heard, comedy or otherwise, that reinforces this was him telling someone to come down off the cross they were putting themselves on, use the wood to build a bridge, and get over it. I love that line and used it in my letter to my siblings, directed at just one of them trying to be the martyr, victim, or whatever else they were trying to deflect.

Love Is Evol was his third comedy special and the one that would give me hope for the future again and give resolve to my drive and determination to rise above what I was going through—and all while finding a way to laugh through the pain. He spoke about his marriage falling apart, the craziness of it all, questioning God as to why, and then the new love in his life, all joking his way through it. I could easily relate to what he was joking about and found strength in seeing how he responded to it, so I knew I could do the same. Ade tried, for the last two years or so of our marriage, to convince me that I had significant issues when the reality of it was, they were hers. Still, she'd deflect anytime anyone would try to talk to her about it or find a way to distract herself from thinking or even considering the possibility that she had any issues. And when it came to us, sex was used as a weapon, withholding any real intimacy or love, and I tried everything, except kissing her ass and being someone I wasn't. The sad part is that her family received much of her attitude, especially her mother, who took the worst because she was closer physically than her siblings. Her older sister took a good deal from Ade as she was going through a distance in her marriage but wouldn't give up on it, even as Ade pressed her hard to divorce him. To the best of my knowledge, her brother escaped most of the attitude.

When his comedy specials became available on DVD, I purchased the set from his website and paid extra to get them signed. A few years later, I'd buy the box set of all of his shows. I would lend the two DVDs to a much-younger friend who was also in a roller-coaster type relationship, and he found them helpful as he struggled to end his relationship with someone trying to blame him for everything. I'm sure that not everyone will appreciate the stories and humor from it, but for me, it was therapy and helped me through anytime I needed to smile or laugh. Why me? What the hell did I do in a previous life to warrant this kind of pain and hurt? But I was done with the one-person pity party I was throwing for myself. The answer was *nothing*; I hadn't done anything to warrant this kind of treatment. That wasn't why it was happening. I've come to realize that I was the only one strong enough to withstand the storm; it's because I was solid and consistent in who I was and am and in my love for her. It's likely that Adrienne also knew this but would never openly admit it to anyone. She knew that I would eventually reach that place deep inside her that she wanted to keep hidden, even if she didn't know what that was. Two of the worst words about regret are *if only*.

It would be more of his other specials, especially a funny bit on *Voice in My Head* about Tako, the attack dog incident, that would help me laugh after losing Nitki. Had it not been for the comedy and, I say expressly, Christopher Titus in his specials that got me to laugh through the pain, hurt, and anger I felt had it not been for his comedy seeing me through the storm, my life would have turned up differently. His *Armageddon Updates* podcast is funny, and I try to catch more than the brief five-minute trailers of them. Looking forward to his next special, I will definitely catch his show the next time he's in town. As it is now, life is good, and each day is better and better. I know the universe has great things in store for me. Rather than trying to get there as quickly as possible, I remain focused on doing the small things every day to build a life I don't need a vacation from and prepare myself for it no matter what may be on the horizon or beyond. It's not a secret that real and lasting success will require several things depending on your definition of success. But in all things, life requires balance—the ability to learn and grow from experiences even if they aren't yours, ensuring your words and actions are living in harmony with each other.

I, like everyone else, have opinions, which I believe are informed ones and basic concepts about several issues facing our country as a whole. I'm not trying to start any holy war; but my approach is to look at things honestly, realistically, the only filter being myself, answering the questions about what if it were me going through it, etc. A vital aspect in discussing or making decisions is not to allow emotions about any specific issue to cloud your view and reduce your ability to listen to understand instead of just replying or dictating your actions. Passion is great as long as you can reasonably and rationally think and consider another's point of view, even if you disagree with it. If we challenged ourselves to question the information others may give us, we could reason more and react less. We could solve so many problems before they become problems. Most of the problems we face are "man-made," so "mankind" can solve them—yes, this includes women. In reaching the sum of 4, there are multiple ways to get there by addition and multiplication, such as $2+2=4$, $1+3=4$, $0+4=4$, $4\times1=4$, and $2\times2=4$. All it takes is an open mind and heart to hear. We need to stop listening with the intent to reply and begin to listen to understand.

In the Declaration of Independence, it reads, "We hold these truths to be self-evident, that all men are created equal, that they are endowed by their Creator with certain unalienable Rights, that among these are Life, Liberty and the pursuit of Happiness." Great, powerful words to announce in the declaration, but these words' practical application has taken too long to implement fully for all citizens of this country—no matter their race, ethnicity, religion, or sex or sexual orientation. Systemic racism exists in this country because politicians hide behind a holy book or some superiority complex. The most corrupt and morally bankrupt among us in power only want to keep expanding that power; they are servants to the almighty dollar, not the people they represent. So many issues have plagued this country. Slavery, women's suffrage, and the treatment of the indigenous peoples of this country are just a few examples of the national embarrassment that demanded change; and progress still needs to be made as it's a direct violation of this country's founding ideals, values, and principals. We may have made progress, but there is still too much needed to end systemic racism in this country, including racism toward the indigenous peoples. How the hell would this country feel, especially the veterans who have honorably served, if an oil pipeline went through Arlington Cemetery. You're damn right. Virtually every American would be up in arms. Why then is it okay for the indigenous people to be treated in such an abusive and disrespectful manner and have the lands they live on be the new dumping grounds for the greed of corporations that do not think they matter? The US government has broken every treaty ever made with the indigenous peoples in this country; it's no wonder why they are pissed and suspicious of anything coming from the federal and state governments. *And* get rid of Columbus Day since he never stepped foot in what would become the USA and replace it with "Indigenous Peoples Day!" And let's start to walk the red road!

I don't have to be Black or a person of color to be outraged by the systematic racism that still exists in the country. I am White, which is a color. Still, I am appalled by those who want to "whitewash" history because they don't want to acknowledge or be reminded of the past and sometimes current abuses of others because they had no control over it or because of the reflection they see in the mirror brings to light their prejudices. How would I feel if the racism in question were directed at White men by those who aren't? Yes, I would do everything I could to make sure I wasn't doing things I shouldn't be. I would ensure I followed every order by authority humanly possible to prevent abuse, mistreatment, or even arrest. Unfortunately, we've seen, especially recently, that doesn't always work. Why is it that an individual or group of citizens who aren't like "us" must fight and struggle for the same rights already understood or in place for another subset of the population? Simple—it's prejudices, fear, stupidity, and ignorance, thinking that giving someone else a right, freedom, or liberty you already enjoy is taking away from yours. Isn't it or shouldn't it be "equality under the law" for all? Only when "We the People" is actively applied to include everyone will we ensure individuals are not judged by the color of their skin but by the content of their character and, specifically, their actions because we all know words can be cheap. But an individual's actions will tell you more about their heart, soul, and character than their words ever could. Yeah, ponder that and let me know why it shouldn't be the standard.

This country's problems are easily solved *if* politicians, political entities, and organizations weren't allowed to lie, mislead, or misrepresent information when they communicate, no matter the medium and especially in advertising. Politicians tend to use emotional issues to pump up their base, counting on the electorate being too lazy to fact-check them, do their research, listen, or even read for themselves. Some would prefer to be led like lambs to the slaughter. If I am selling a product, it is against the law to lie, mislead, or misrepresent virtually any aspects of the product's benefits, promises, or any so-called guarantees. Politicians should be held to the same higher standard by law with severe financial penalties for violating it. A committee or group of scholars could determine the level of infraction with more significant penalties if the conduct continues, including automatic expulsion from elected office and prevention of holding future office for some time or permanently if warranted. Simple enough concept, isn't it? And yet it's still amazing that most approval polls for Congress as a whole are in the teens. Still, representatives who don't do anything except live to get rich off the taxpayers continue to get reelected cycle after cycle. If we want better leaders, then "We the People" must set the higher expectation and demand that they fulfill it if they're going to be a representative of, by, and for the people. This simple change could solve many of the problems facing this country. Gerrymandering wouldn't be an issue, but we know the politicians will still try to use it so they don't have to worry about being accountable or responsible to their Kool-Aid-drinking blind sheep cult followers, I mean electorate.

Like many other citizens of the world who love their country, I love the United States of America. However, we still have a good deal to live up to the promises in the ideals, principles, and values expressed in the founding documents. Sometimes tough love, which is still love, is required or even demanded, which will allow the individual to realize the detrimental impact they are having on themselves and those who love them—and yes, this country needs a dosage of tough love. Each generation makes some progress, and while some think we are close, close only counts in horseshoes and hand grenades. Financial slavery has replaced physical indentured servitude, which can be associated with individual accountability and responsibility. Still, the other side of that coin is deceptive practices by corporations or institutions that make money by screwing the consumer.

The pandemic has been brutal for every country and its population. The last four years here in the US, especially the last one with the pandemic, have been excruciating for most on so many levels. We forget how young our country is. Unfortunately, arrogance, hidden by pride or some superiority complex, blinds us to the fact that other great nations have different ways to achieve similar or better results for their citizens. We could learn so much if we only asked questions and listened with the intent to understand. Suppose we understood other countries' programs, their methods, and their approaches that show positive results. The purpose isn't to mirror them but to build or adapt them to our system. Identify potential risks and mitigate them by listening to and acknowledging arguments on all sides. Build in applicable measures and steps to address those reasonable concerns. Naturally, there will be attempts by some who will dismiss, intentionally deflect, and misrepresent information that breaks the status quo because it impacts their ability to profit from it. But if politicians and political entities are required by law not to lie, mislead, or misrepresent, then problem solved.

It just doesn't seem like we will come together until we are out of our rebel teenage years as a country and into our twenties. We need to break free from the "quick fix" desire or being distracted by the cost and realize that a strong foundation is necessary for any structure, institution, or program to successfully withstand the challenges it may face. As technology or we as human beings improve, things can't be reviewed, added, or taken down to ensure the foundations remain firm against the storms of life and allow everyone the opportunity to live their best life while still requiring them to do the work. So tailoring them to our systems over the long-term could also help strengthen, reinvent, or repurpose those systems and institutions to achieve the same or similar results for the citizens of the United States. Focus on the issues, programs, and benefits.

Determine a long-term road map into phases. Build in key performance indicators and realistic benchmarks. Improve efficiency and effectiveness whenever possible without increasing risk beyond an acceptable limit. Implement not as dictated by the financial cost but more so for the human capital to be realized, which could have outstanding results on the return of the investment.

If fifteen to twenty people from all walks of life were in a room without the noise from left or right, I believe we could solve 85–90 percent or more of the problems or issues facing this country. Have experts and those with differing views present their facts, data, and resources used in their analyses, perhaps even expanding it to another group after the first one completes their work or even a third group to round it out to ensure greater clarification. It's an investment in this country and its citizens to become as great as we think we are by actually being that bright, shining city on a hill—a beacon for what is best in humankind. So simple, right? But the root of all evil is money. Of course, if politicians, their campaigns, or political advertisements weren't allowed to lie, mislead, or misrepresent themselves or their opponents, most of our problems would get solved, as long as the ego is left behind. "Don't come to me with a problem unless you have a potential solution in mind." My first sergeant at I&I Staff Richmond, Virginia, told me this when I first approached him with what I saw as a problem of the two administrative reservists not being adequately trained to do their actual jobs while on their weekend duties. I came to him with the potential solution and began to implement it. He would use my example as the standard to follow for the remaining staff to train their reserve counterparts to be ready, should the unit ever be activated.

Now, for those who want to cry about your free will, freedoms, or liberties being negatively affected when they aren't, educate yourselves before you speak or regurgitate talking points. It shows your ignorance when you cannot communicate beyond what you've already heard from unreliable sources. Smokers had a choice to start or stop, but that was impacted by having their free will "taken" from them as the tobacco industry manipulated the nicotine delivery system and the necessary changes forced them to stop in the midnineties. Corporations and businesses need to be more focused on being good corporate citizens and working for the benefit of their stakeholders and not just their shareholders and "feeding the beast" to drive up profits ahead of everything else. There is a moral obligation. There has to be to focus on the stakeholders of the business, employees, and the communities served and or operated in instead of only being focused on stockholders and executive compensation. Suppose you place more value on your stakeholders than your shareholders. Money, even if it's not in the billions by the minute, will still be made. Imagine how those involved in the January 6 insurrection feel now, especially after they've been charged and now face the potential of a more challenging future resulting from the lies from so-called leaders and right-wing media. The excuses, reasoning, or justification? Because they weren't strong enough to pull away. It's not my fault; it was "Foxitis." Imagine the lives saved and destruction avoided if honesty, integrity, and maintaining the highest ethical standards in journalism were the norm instead of the exception. Journalism has suffered dramatically since the days of Edward R. Murrow, Walter Cronkite, and those who approached journalism with the honor and integrity it required because it is necessary to keep the powers that be in check.

Some individuals act like freedom of speech only applies to them as they talk, especially when they can't withstand the heat from the scrutiny of or challenge to their words, so they shout over the top of others in order to avoid or deflect from the challenge, which only shows ignorance. The final speech in the movie *The American President* starts with Michael Douglas's character addressing questions to the press corps—free speech, but it's not just yours that's applicable. Can you acknowledge another person's right to say something that makes your blood boil and would spend a lifetime opposing at the top of your voice? What about kneeling during the national anthem, which has become a rallying cry on one side to feign outrage? Unless you've served under that flag, you have no right to be offended. I do not like it, but it is still respectful. But those who are doing it for legitimate reasons are doing so because of an injustice. For those who had done so because they weren't playing or as an attempt to drive up their jersey sales, well, you can see through their actions before they knelt, if they took any, to help out the communities for which they now are so vocal about protecting. Turn the tables, like Matthew McConaughey's character did in their closing argument in the movie *A Time to Kill*, and let's see if you genuinely feel the same way about people of color or different sex or sexual orientation kneeling for the anthem.

> In the First Amendment, the Founding Fathers gave the free press the protection it must have to fulfill its essential role in our democracy. The press was to serve the governed, not the governors. The Government's power to censor the press was abolished so that the press would remain forever free to censure the Government. The press was protected so that it could bare the secrets of government and inform the people. Only a free and unrestrained press can effectively expose deception in government. (Supreme Court Justice Hugo Black regarding New York Times Co. v United States)

There are limits on free speech as there should be—communicating threats or violence, shouting fire in a crowded movie theater, common sense stuff complicated by politicians who take the easy way out to reward the stupid or to help lawyers who are looking for a payday. Unfortunately, with a twenty-four-hour news cycle, news departments now being for-profit, and especially opinion hosts portraying themselves or the information they speak on as actual news instead of the fabricated BS it is, it is the electorate and subsequently the country as a whole that is used and manipulated. The design of the human mind is to see patterns in the world. Propaganda networks and websites will use apophenia, which tends to perceive meaningful connections between unrelated things, and some so-called media outlets use this to manipulate the viewer or user so they can keep the money beast fed and growing. Sheep are always led; none will ever lead. To the best of my knowledge, daytime and evening hosts of CNN, Rachel Maddow, and NBC newscaster Lester Holt *have never had to walk back a story* because they intentionally got a story wrong or were deliberately misleading, not even for the sake of ratings. And, John Avalon, we need your "Reality Check" to be standard for the next iteration of an adult version of *Schoolhouse Rocks*. I don't mean to infer that the reporters and anchors from CBS, ABC, PBS, or any reputable actual news programs aren't worthy of such praise. I can't say because I don't watch them as much.

What if a reporter and/or media outlet were being sued, like those propaganda networks being sued by Dominion Voting Systems Inc. or Smartmatic Corp.? In that case, you should be questioning their trustworthiness. I'll add Shep Smith and Chris Wallace in there, who have never knowingly presented false or misleading information to their viewers. I'll have to defer to Meghan McCain about any other current or former Fox News reporters or anchors with whom she would feel comfortable saying that they have honor and integrity in the same arena as her father's. Perhaps Liz Cheney and Adam Kinzinger will succeed in resurrecting the GOP from the evil that now plagues it because we know that Moscow Mitch and Leningrad Lindsey won't.

On the Democratic side of the aisle, I have always loved Joe Biden. Some things cannot be explained thoroughly in a thirty-second sound bite, not well enough to be fully understood by the masses. Perfect, he isn't, but I know of no one who has questioned his integrity. It's beyond reproach, and even on his worst day, he is a damn sight better than "Sweet Potato Hitler" on his best, if there ever was one. Did you not hear the recordings between him and Bob Woodward? How can anyone believe anything that comes out of his mouth? Because he validates their fears, anger, and prejudices of those he tries to command, but he doesn't give a damn about any of them, only what he can grift from them, again, using emotions to keep people from thinking reasonably or rationally. And his actions shows it to be accurate, even if you don't like it. God bless his niece for speaking out and shining a light on the obvious. Let's be crystal clear about this fact:

Patriotism is not obedience to government. Patriotism is obedience to the principles

for which government is supposed to stand.
(Howard Zinn)

I'll admit. I wasn't initially happy with Kamala Harris as a VP choice but loved the way she conducted herself in the Senate, questioning and challenging the BS coming from the other side of someone's mouth. I was holding a grudge because she attacked Joe in the first debate, but since Joe didn't take it personally, how in the hell could I? Katie Porter is my favorite politician at this time. She is methodical, using her whiteboard or other props to grill those before her in committee. She knows the lies, methods of distraction, misrepresentation, misleading, and regurgitating of talking points and destroys them—nothing better than seeing her put someone in their place. Even AOC has a similar questioning style without the props, but to be honest, I'm not a fan of the progressive positions at this time. Still, I am open to them; and I would recommend that she and others in the squad bring up the data, facts, and science in committee hearings to show the American public the validity of their proposals. We have fifty states and multiple US territories, each with different economics, taxation, and services. You mean you can't take the best of each of them, fine-tune them, and try to implement them on a federal level? Hell, you could even look at other countries and see how they manage or don't and leverage what you learn to better all citizens of this country. Trickle-down economics doesn't work. It's not rain falling on you; it's piss from those at the top.

In the 2018 movie *Robin Hood* with Taron Egerton, a line indicates that the church created hell because fear is the greatest weapon. It's just a movie, but what if the second coming of Jesus was nothing more than something created by those who knew human nature and about how destructive and immoral we can be if there isn't fear to keep people in line by creating a story or prophecy of Jesus's return. I always thought love was enough; and yes, as unfortunate as it is or may be, I believe evil can be used for a divine purpose. There is no need to look any further than the 2016 election of "Sweet Potato Hitler" and all the corrupt information coming to light now that real leaders are in charge again. I thank the Creator for the GOP losing the House in 2018 and the Senate and presidency in 2020, but they are still acting like obstructionists, hoping that it wins them back the House and Senate in 2022. Silly rabbit, you need clear and distinct policies that help the poor and middle class, not just those that keep millionaires, billionaires, and corporations funding your campaigns.

While I am sure there are other shows or movies of similar nature, watch *Start Trek: The Next Generation*, episode 13, "Devil's Due" to hear a story line of how people began to change because they knew they couldn't continue on their current path. Why in the hell do evangelicals seem to want the Israelis and Palestinians to start World War III? So that they can see Jesus's return? Isn't it enough, or shouldn't it be, to live a life that improves your chances of being in his presence when you pass into the hereafter? Akiane Kramarik, who painted *Prince of Peace* at the age of eight, or any of the other children or adults who have all had near-death experiences, brought back pieces of information that tell something that could be the truth to all of this.

> There are more things in Heaven and Earth,
> Horatio, than are dreamt of in your philosophy.
> (William Shakespeare, *Hamlet*, 1623)

And this is just my two cents, but for the leaders of the Palestinian authority and its people, stop allowing Hamas or any other entity or country to use you in their desire to destroy Israel. They do not have your best interests in mind and are just the "devil's advocates." If they did, they would focus their energies on education and training in the jobs and industries to provide for the people. Why continue on a path that ends with nuclear bombs being launched that turns the middle east into a parking lot, when security and prosperity for your people is within reach? So I say to Hamas and any other governments or organizations whose charter or philosophy calls for the destruction of Israel to drop such bullshit and change their approach. Maybe there can be some real and lasting peace. To the Israeli government, not its people, it's your turn, so be prepared for some brutal truth and tough love. Stop building settlements in Palestinian territory in the hopes of driving all Palestinian's out so you can then proclaim they no longer live there. It shouldn't be a land grab. Yes, you deserve to live in peace, and I agree—"never again." But the Palestinians deserve to live in peace, and you are creating more of the very thing you are saying you are fighting—terrorists intent on killing your citizens. If South Carolina or any nearby city tried to do to me what you are doing to the Palestinians, using eminent domain or some other kind of bullshit excuse without considering the human toll or offering up some fair and just compensation, I would be pissed off. If peace is your goal, then stop forcing a population to bow down to your demands under some bullshit moral authority or superiority complex. It's wrong at every level of observation, and the cycle will only continue to repeat itself. Some will always stand up and give their life in opposition to injustice.

I agree that in some situations, peace can only be found on the other side of war. The very definition of insanity is doing the same thing over and over again and expecting different results. Grant Palestinians the same rights and freedoms under the law that Israeli citizens already enjoy and have those living in Israeli settlements leave and let the houses and buildings remain and be given to Palestinians who need a home—a good start. And show your commitment and willingness to a two-state solution and lasting peace. So how about you help us out here? I mean, it does seem to be mostly the American taxpayer funding your war machine. Let's attempt another approach, and yes, all of the things mentioned should start to happen or begin to happen simultaneously or within a reasonable amount of time. If not, then section off a twenty-five to fifty square mile area so that Hamas, Iran's military or militia, meet the Israeli defense forces for a winner-takes-all fight without involving innocent civilians. Maybe then you'll get it out of your system. If your religion requires you to hate anything, check on that image you see in the mirror and determine how lost you are. It's still your choice, and what is right for you may not be suitable for me. And what I believe is right may not be what you believe to be is correct, but that's what free will is all about. Both concepts can be accurate, depending on the nature of the issue, because having the freedom to choose the religion or spiritual path you will follow, or not follow or believe in, is the primary reason why people from all over came to our shores. I'd recommend watching the movie *Silence* (2014) before any attempt to force people into your way of thinking.

I'm for life, but I'll defend a woman's right to choose until my dying breath. I'm not a fan of abortion as a means of birth control, and as a man, I'll never be pregnant and wouldn't want to be. I've had kidney stones, and they were painful enough for me. I'll likely never have children, but I'd be willing to get cut open again if my significant other wanted to try. I agree that the scientific definition of *life* begins at conception. But life isn't sustainable outside the womb until around week 24, even though there may be some exceptions. All life has a purpose, but it comes down to a personal decision between the woman and her god. Hopefully, the child's father is also involved in the decision; but ultimately, it's the woman who will bear the most, if not all, of the burden if they choose to end the pregnancy. If it's a sin, it is above the pay grade of man, so let the Creator alone sit in judgment. For those screaming about life and how precious it is, I ask, what are you doing for those children who are already here? Are you fostering, adopting, being a big brother or big sister to them? Let's focus first on taking care of those children who are already here. Then we can put in some better safeguards for accountability and responsibility on the right shoulders of the individuals having sex without using preventative measures.

The alternative, fine, life begins at conception, but every woman should be charged with murder if she miscarries, right? If it's all about God's will, why would he allow a woman to get pregnant only to take it from her? It seems cruel. You can't pick and choose only your interpretation of specific passages in whatever holy book you read. Terri Schiavo was scientifically alive, but she wasn't living and had no reasonable chance of being able to. So if existing is what you equate to as life, then double-check your reflection. As for me, if I am ever in a similar vegetative state and the physicians and all medical professionals are mostly in agreement, then pull the plug on me and let me go home.

All saints have a past, and all sinners have a future. (Anton Chekhov)

My choice would be to laugh with the sinners, not cry with the saints. If homosexuality is a sin, it is above the pay grade of man and let the Creator alone sit in judgment. I'm not attracted to men, but don't judge those who are or may be. It's something that I wouldn't choose, but attraction isn't so much about the physical as it is the light and energy of the two souls involved. There is no other way to explain how the depth and love between two souls grows stronger and more intense long after physical features have changed. The thing about love is that you can't start it like a car, and you can't stop it with a bullet. Every relationship requires a certain amount of nurturing. When you like a flower, you pluck it, put it in a vase, and keep it on display until it dries up. When you love a flower, you water it, feed it, ensure it gets enough sunlight, maybe even pruning it to help it grow stronger, ensuring it stays alive longer than it would otherwise. I'm not sure how two men or two women being married impacts or takes away from your heterosexual marriage. Perhaps then you're insecure about who you are or that your marriage and relationship aren't as strong you portray them to be. It's not a competition, and it's not a pie where someone else is given something that takes away from your piece of it.

Climate change is real! There are cycles, but this is about extremes that include stronger hurricanes, more drought in areas that need rain, more flooding in areas that can't handle more water, and oppressive heat that you can't escape. It impacts farming, trees, plant life, livestock and buckling roads, and other damage to physical infrastructure. Humanity is responsible for the extremes now being experienced as we continue to burn fossil fuels and allow industries to continue polluting the air and water. Those that turn a blind eye for the sake of politics will have to answer to the Creator for the things they've done and didn't do, especially when they were in a position to do so. All life on this planet requires both clean air and clean water to live, so what is it about this equation that escapes climate deniers. We know why the politicians do nothing and won't as long as fossil fuel companies continue spending big money on them to do their bidding. Still, even those oil and gas companies are now investing in renewable energies because they know the continued approach isn't sustainable. Still, they must take care of the stockholders, forget about the stakeholders. The shortsightedness is disgusting.

> Only when the last tree has died, and the last river has been poisoned, and the last fish has been caught will we realize that we cannot eat money. (Chief Seattle)

Saving money on your energy consumption or having renewable energies like solar and wind power would seem to be a no-brainer. It is renewable; and aside from the initial cost, you will recoup your money over a shorter time frame, especially when federal and state governments offer incentives or tax credits to have them installed. The larger tax refund from the tax credits for energy-saving products means they almost pay for themselves. I've also done my work by turning off ceiling fans in all rooms, except when needed, and changing all light bulbs to LEDs. Sure, a little more expensive, but they should last twenty-plus years and even more for those I don't use as much during the day or evening. When Ade and I were together, she would call me a "light Nazi" because I'd turn off lights in rooms that weren't being used or wouldn't be in a short time. Our electric bill on the equal payment plan was more than $160 a month. I have cut that in half, which means it's money in my pocket and not going to the electric company, and I keep the AC on seventy-two. When the water heater went out, I got the tankless water heater. Yes, it was more expensive, but it immediately began saving me more than $20 per month. And I have all the hot water I want. When I am in a position to have solar installed, I'll replace the gas-tankless water heater with an electric one, saving me from paying out money to another utility company. I realize that there is a cost associated with these kinds of improvements, but the benefits outweigh it. And it will increase my asking price for my house as a result.

I've already changed most of my lawn-care equipment to battery-powered ones and will get rid of the riding gas lawn mower for an electric one next year. And I'll be looking for an all-electric or hybrid SUV, specifically a Toyota 4Runner, because I love them. Still, if another company makes a comparable model, I'll consider switching; so, Toyota, you better get to work on it. And, engineers, there are these things called solar panels, specifically photovoltaic cells, that are clear or transparent that could be on the roof of a vehicle with some windows without impacting the view or perhaps even embedded in the body. It won't charge the car in an hour, but it could give you extra miles on your drive, couldn't it? If you want the government out of your "life" in as many ways as possible, then you need to consider making simple changes, especially if the incentives and tax credits allow you to afford it. It's an investment, and you won't have to worry about a cyberattack on a utility or gas company. It's simple, caring for the earth isn't some "weird, hippie" thing. It's more of a badass survival thing. If we don't have a healthy planet, we won't have a healthy anything. So how about it? Let us stop giving taxpayer subsidies to large fossil fuel companies and provide those subsidies to the American farmer and family farms, especially those that grow organic products. Give them all access to technology that will allow them to monitor their crops and know which areas need water, nutrients, and whatever else to improve the growing season. Poverty exists not because we can't feed the poor but because we can't satisfy the rich.

> A well-regulated Militia, being necessary to the security of a free State, the right of the people to keep and bear Arms shall not be infringed. (Second Amendment to the Constitution of the United States)

The NRA and politicians use this issue facing our country to raise funds, aka grift its members, pumping them up and the rest of their base into a fever at the unlikely attempt by the federal government to come after all guns. While the NRA used to be a gun-rights advocacy group founded to advance rifle marksmanship, teaching firearm safety and competency, it no longer functions or serves in that capacity but instead as a political action committee. Members of the organization appear to be living high on the hog because of the gullibility of its donors. Just how many guns did the Obama administration confiscate? Not a single one but the fear used because the GOP counts on an electorate to follow blindly, who won't challenge or question the BS. It reminds me of the TV preachers in the seventies, eighties, and nineties who would cry and beg for your money to buy a third private plane because God didn't want them to fly coach. I own a handgun and have my concealed carry permit, but I don't carry it everywhere I go, which will change if the circumstances warrant it. The background check for the concealed carry permit was more extensive than the buying permit, which it should be, but I had no worries about it. The training was informative and invaluable, as was the practical application and qualifying, which happens to be the last time I fired it. I am allowed to protect myself, my loved ones, and my property from harm but had no idea that if I were to hit someone else by accident, who wasn't threatening to me, my loved ones, or my property, I could be criminally charged or sued by them or their families if they died.

We should be making voting easier and guns harder to get instead of the opposite being true, especially now that Republican state legislatures are going full speed ahead on voter-suppression efforts. If their policies made sense or were popular, they wouldn't have to attempt such extremes, but they are the party of fear and intimidation. To start a balanced conversation, let's begin with common sense and reasonable points. First, only the US Military and state National Guard units should have fully automatic weapons in their official capacity. No individual should be allowed to own or have any fully automatic weapon or semiautomatic weapon that can mimic fully automatic ones via a modification or other component like the bump stock. Individuals who currently possess them could turn them in as part of a buyback program by the state or federal government. The restriction would be that the only place they should legally shoot them is on a state or federally approved rifle-gun range. All ammunition must be purchased and expended at the same gun range—no keeping any to store at home, etc. All weapons should be required to be locked or stored in an approved safe only accessible by the owner or spouse.

Second, *all* gun sales, private or public, or giving a weapon as a gift must include a successful background check—no matter how long it takes—paid for by the individual purchasing or who will be owning the weapon and then filed and certified by the local law enforcement agency before taking actual possession. All adults living in the home or who might have access to the weapon must complete a background check. Anyone charged or convicted of a felony, charged in domestic violence, or other related matter would preclude them from owning a gun. Anyone suffering from mental health issues or taking medication that impacts the mind wouldn't be allowed to have access to any weapon under any condition. The owner must certify that the weapon is secured and can only be accessed by those allowed to access it.

Third, *all* gun owners should be required to have classroom training, instruction on the laws, and best practices by trained professionals and pass a test showing they are aware of and acknowledge the laws and conduct expected of a gun owner. We require it and a practical application test for individuals desiring to operate a motor vehicle. No harm has ever come from having too much knowledge or training on an issue. Like a driver's license, the gun refresher training should be at one, three, and five years and then the same length of time their driver's license is in the state where they live unless they are a legitimate hunter licensed by the state where they live. Another option to get this taken seriously is to allow insurance companies to increase a homeowners' insurance premium if they own firearms and do not have a safe to store them in and haven't completed the required refresher training and discounts or no additional charge to the premium if they have done all that.

Fourth, no open carry laws unless there are strict training requirements and testing to ensure the individuals understand the laws and what they are guilty of if they hit or kill someone who isn't threatening them, their loved ones, or personal property.

Fifth, unlimited ammunition may be purchased and used while on a gun or rifle range, but how many an individual may purchase for actual home defense per month must be controlled. Allergy medicine is regulated, so an individual purchasing ammunition must show their driver's license and sign an acknowledgment that they are only authorized to have one hundred rounds in their possession for home defense at any given time.

Sixth, all states must enact "red flag" laws so that family and friends of a gun owner could petition the courts for the owner to surrender their firearms. Return the firearms once the courts and medical professionals reasonably conclude that the individual is no longer a threat to themselves or anyone else. If my mental or emotional state could lead to me harming myself, another human being, or a pet, I would want my family and friends to do this for my safety and for another human being or animal that I could harm as a result.

Seventh, hunters do not need a fully automatic weapon or semi-automatic ones that could mimic fully automatic ones. As long as the state has licensing requirements for hunters that include training, the only limitation would be to purchase ammunition for their hunting rifles a month before hunting season begins through the last day. They must certify that they do not have more than one hundred rounds of ammunition at any given time. An AR-15, or other assault weapons, isn't the weapon for home defense as the length of the weapon is too long; and aiming it correctly at an intruder, who could easily move out of the line of sight, wouldn't work unless it's all about being Rambo with a .50-caliber machine gun. If you doubt this, take a two-foot section of a two-by-four piece of wood, which would likely require you to hold it with two hands. See how fast you can aim it, and then compare it with a shoe. Even a shotgun would be better than an assault weapon. These are common-sense solutions and a balance to the equation of allowing competent individuals to own and possess firearms and keep them out of the hands of those who shouldn't. If you believe the Second Amendment is the only thing preventing tyranny in America, then you don't believe in the rest of the Constitution.

A close second issue is the freedom of religion. It is just an emotional distraction about the failure of the GOP to have reasonable policies that help the poor and middle class instead of millionaires, billionaires, and corporations. You're not supposed to talk religion, sex, or politics with family or friends because of the deeply personal nature of each. Still, another reason why it's become so partisan is it's weaponized for expediency. Some can have reasonable and rational discussions on this or any other subject because they perceive the points of view. You aren't wrong if I am right, and you aren't right if I am wrong. The GOP can't counter the arguments on the validity of their policy or position; so they lie, deflect, or distract by moving the goalposts and keeping the individual constantly on the defensive.

Marijuana needs to be legal in all fifty states, regulated, and taxed, similar to alcohol. The number of stress- and anxiety-related illnesses reduced, if not outright eliminated, far outweigh any concerns about addiction or being used as a gateway drug to harder illegal drugs. Each adult can grow a plant or two for personal use or consumption, but the selling and/or distribution outside a regulated dispensary would still be illegal.

Taxes are such a joke in this country because politicians kiss the backsides of donors who want special perks and tax breaks to keep funding political campaigns. If there is any doubt that money is the root of all evil, just look at the corruption of politicians worldwide who are only concerned with the next election instead of doing their jobs to better the electorate for whom they are supposed to serve. The disgusting answer as to why goes right to the heart in what is the worst in human nature; the only truth for those who peddle the worst in us is that "power tends to corrupt, and absolute power corrupts absolutely" (Lord Acton)—the 2017 tax cuts where almost all the benefits went to millionaires, billionaires, and corporations while placing more debt on the shoulders of the poor and middle class, which the GOP will try to screw over whenever they can. I'll repeat it: trickle-down economics doesn't work. It's not rain falling on you; it's piss from those at the top. The tax code needs to be simplified; and yes, everyone needs to pay their fair share no matter how they earn their money—be it a job, investments, or anything else.

Remove all tax breaks for companies who have moved more than 30–40 percent of jobs or their headquarters overseas. Give tax breaks for companies who keep a majority of their manufacturing here in the United States. You get to deduct mortgage interest on your primary home, not your fifth vacation home, private planes, and boats. Corporations pay taxes on their employees by matching what the employee pays to federal and state income tax. Most, because of loopholes, do not pay any on revenue or profit they earn. When the unemployment rate is above 7 percent, each corporation must pay an additional 1–2 percent on all income. If the unemployment rate is above 9 percent, it should be 3–5 percent. No extra tax would be required when the unemployment rate is less than 5 percent, but they could receive tax credits on revenue or profit. I agree with the current progressive tax rate but feel that there should be three more starting at 40 percent, 43 percent, and 47 percent. Develop a plan to tackle the growing deficit over a four- to ten-year plan, although the quicker the better. If you pay off creditors and don't go back into debt, you don't need to earn or take in as much to maintain your lifestyle, and you may be better off. Tax financial investment trades on every US market at a rate that could bring in more than $5 trillion a year. In 2019, there were over twenty-three trillion trades made in the US alone. If $1 on every transaction were charged and explicitly used on the deficit, the credit-card balance would be zero or, at the very least, manageable. No longer would Peter need to be robbed to pay Paul as they did with the Social Security trust fund, which bought up federal notes and bills to cover the shortfalls of the Iraq War and prescription-drug plan.

A fully funded Social Security trust—imagine that. Instead of an individual currently working today to pay the Social Security for those who are now retired, they would support their own retirement. Social Security shouldn't be taxed, and those wealthy Americans who will elect not to take their Social Security each year can write off the amount they would have received from other sources of income. Churches shouldn't be tax-exempt unless they are spending actual money on helping those in need. They should be taxed at the corporate rate and fined if the church leaders come close to crossing the separation line between church and state, losing their tax-exempt status for a minimum of twenty-five years.

In every discussion, emotions can be, and usually are, the enemy of reason. Most politicians will use it to keep their electorate distracted from what they are doing, rewarding millionaires, billionaires, and corporations who fund their campaigns.

Don't do something permanently stupid just
because you are temporarily upset. (Unknown)

Being informed beyond the regurgitated talking points from any media source is mandatory. All problems can be solved using a balanced approach, but it takes a commitment to listen to understand instead of listening to respond. Life is about balance. Be kind but don't let anyone abuse you. Trust but don't be deceived. Be content but never stop seeking to improve yourself. You can make changes in your life no matter where you are in it. The difficulty may lie in knowing where to start, but the most straightforward answer is to take one step in the direction you want to go. And when you are comfortable or it feels right, take another and then another. Take a look at an Emotional Guidance Scale, and you can see the pathways for both upward and downward spirals. If you don't fully understand each component, then look up each one and see if it matches where you are. The upward scale starts at the bottom with contentment, hopefulness, optimism, positive expectation belief, enthusiasm, and passion and ends with joy, knowledge, empowerment, freedom, love, and appreciation. The downward scale starts at the top with boredom, pessimism, frustration, irritation, impatience, "overwhelmed," disappointment, doubt, worry, blame, discouragement, anger, revenge, hatred, rage, jealousy, insecurity, guilt, unworthiness, fear, grief, depression, despair, and powerlessness.

With today's technologies, we have a greater capacity for seeking help and understanding from trained professionals and all from the comfort of our homes via smartphones, tablets, or computers. With social media, we have more ways to connect but appear to be less connected to one another. Sometimes, the craziness of this thing called life can get to the best of us, and for some who seek understanding or acceptance, some groups and websites can help us get to where we want to be. And some will take us to a place we never wanted to be. It may take trial and error. But the key to it all is to follow your heart, but take your brain with you. Don't let common sense be lost or emotions control your life. Find that balance that allows you to take the first steps toward living your best life. Use technology, the internet, and social media to your advantage so that you can find your balance, meaning, and drive to rid yourself of those things that hold you back or weigh you down so you can begin to live your best life.

CHAPTER 11

Technology, Internet, and Social Media

Sometimes people don't want to hear the truth
because they don't want their illusions destroyed.
—Friedrich Nietzsche

The internet and subsequent technology, especially social media and unique applications, can provide such a variety of valuable services that allow individuals to find something without knowing they were looking for it. You can find videos on YouTube from everyday people who have experienced something beneficial and wanted to share it to others who encountered the same problem. Being self-reliant can be rewarding, especially if you don't have the funds to consult with a professional or take something broken to a repair shop. Consider sharing your experiences and knowledge; you never know who could benefit from your experience or what has worked for you. Now, the opposite is also true in that the same combination of the internet, technology, and social media can lead you down a path that may be hard to break free of—so much misinformation disguised as accurate information and individuals or groups going after the most vulnerable in search of validation or some other twisted philosophy. They refuse to seek real help by playing on the fears, prejudices, and anger to serve some warped purpose. Some people will believe things that could never have been true, which is probably a different form of apophenia, the tendency to perceive meaningful connections between unrelated things. A funny picture I have saved is of a maze with a piece of cheese at one corner and a mouse appearing to have gone directly to it by destroying what was in its way, and the caption read, "*Marines*, if you don't understand this, you never met one." Abraham Lincoln, the sixteenth president of the United States, posted it on social media, so it must be true. That's why he is called "Honest Abe." Sorry, just a little tongue-in-cheek sarcasm.

Social media can be a blessing, or a curse for its positive and negative effects, depending on the user's intention, desire, or purpose in using it. We can learn, grow, and decide who we, as individuals, want to be. It can move us forward individually, as a group, as citizens of a country, or as part of the human race that coexist together with all other forms of life on this planet. It could also move us backward or put the individual in a maze that feels like there is no escape. I immediately began seeing posts and memes when I joined Facebook in 2009. I found them funny, intriguing, and some would allow me to place a more accurate description of my thoughts and feelings on what I felt were universal truths or a more balanced way of approaching things in general. Many quotes in this book are from memes I've seen or postings on Facebook that I have come across. Some attributed to the individuals as indicated, others unknown, and some were just general comments or postings that resonated with me. I saved the image or quote on my computer to recall at a later date. Since the seventh or eighth grade, I have been drawn more to the spiritual path of the indigenous peoples (Native Americans) of North America. I would realize that what I was feeling, where I wanted to go, and how I wanted to live my life was to pursue Walking the Red Road.

For all you "keyboard commandos" out there, being anonymous, two-faced, shit-talking, copy-paste, artificial narcissists hiding from the world just to get your daily "fix" from Likes, Loves, and other misused forms of self-admiration so you can stay in denial about yourself or life in general. Hate groups operate this way by going after people to attract them to their BS beliefs or cause, seeking out or preying on those who need a sense of belonging to feel as though they are a part of something that allows them to forget the misery of reality, giving them purpose or drive to continue existing. Look at the stories from those who have escaped these cults; their paths that led them down these dark paths are eerily similar. Today's world has more ways to connect people and places, but we seem less connected as a species than ever before. Perhaps we'd be better off if Snake Plissken were to enter the world code and end all technological activity on the planet, but then technology isn't the problem. It's how some are choosing to use and abuse it. If you want to feed the homeless, then feed the homeless, but the moment you post it on social media, it's likely becoming more about feeding your ego than challenging others to do the same.

Social media companies, you have the opportunity to be better corporate citizens instead of feasting off the algorithms currently in use to drive only specific content to the user by ensuring your community standards are the highest possible. We know that the algorithms have but one purpose, which is that it continues to drive the almighty dollar to your bank accounts. Imagine if there was a built-in periodical reset of the algorithms, perhaps even prompting the user to other research or viewpoints from different reliable sources and more attention to actual news in a fair and balanced way than the propaganda networks currently report.

Want to help reduce bad behaviors or bad actors? Do what the financial industry did in the early 2000s—the Patriot Act but not the most extreme parts of it. Require individuals to verify who they are, even if they are part of an entity or organization authorized to post on their behalf. They can use whatever name they want to on their profile, but their legal names, along with a certain level of contact information, on file. Verify them by requiring a credit check for identity, not creditworthiness. Additionally, you can also require them to deposit $10 to an account associated with their profile if they violate community and best practice standards to help offset the pay for the staff to do the research. Here is an idea of how it could work. In the first violation, the individual is suspended for one week and loses the $10 on deposit. They will be required to deposit then $25, which will be lost if they violate community standards in the future. A second offense will get them suspended for thirty days and lose the $25 required to deposit $100 to restore access. The next violation will be suspension for three months, loss of money on deposit, and requiring to deposit $250 to restore access. Corporations, organizations, or entities will follow the same suspension, but the amounts are multiplied by one hundred. Any fourth violation within a rolling twelve-month period results in loss of funds on deposit and a full-year suspension or even a permanent ban. Allow for an appeals process that they will pay for, but it will be returned to them if the outcome is in their favor. Children must have their parents establish the account. The parent must also maintain an account themselves and cannot be blocked or prevented from seeing what their child posts and notified immediately about important issues surrounding mental health, bullying, talk of suicide, perhaps general bad behavior. Add clear and specific labeling to posts about lies and misinformation as it applies to health, safety, and national security issues.

While no one should see political lies or batshit conspiracy theories, these could be labeled. The user must provide reliable sources for the information before others can see it. These could be defined and periodically updated in the community standards. Keep them clear, concise, and leave no ambiguity. Constantly reviewing and updating the community standards should be fairly easy. It is better to come to terms with doing what is right for the right reasons than having the government attempt to force it upon you. A judge recently blocked Florida's social media law, which would prevent a ban on suspending or annotating the posts of political candidates. The GOP is only interested in manipulating the electorate instead of defending their policy positions by providing the data, science, or facts behind their policies, and the lawsuit proves it. Of course, if there were a law that prevented politicians from lying, misleading, or misrepresenting information on the floors in their respective legislative bodies, their campaigns, and their advertising, then problem solved. We the People are the only ones who can hold elected officials accountable and responsible.

A great concept is that governments should be afraid of We the People, not the people being afraid of their governments. This statement doesn't apply to all countries but is more applicable to those who commit crimes against their citizens that prevent them from life, liberty, or the pursuit of happiness. Any similar version should take notice instead of suppressing freedoms that keep themselves in power. Of course, we here in the US have our self-inflicted version of that in the form of the propaganda channels that only care about feeding the beast and not the validity of the argument or policy positions. Three things cannot be long hidden: the sun, the moon, and the truth. You'd think that people and companies would learn this universal truth, but those who buy into it want to remain blind by choice. The companies who mislead and peddle in lies or misrepresentations do so for the almighty dollar or whatever other currency they value most. Don't be a parrot (aka politician). Most talk way too much, regurgitating the same BS to avoid doing anything of substance. If you cannot speak beyond the talking points, then better to educate yourself than continue to speak the part of the fool. Be an eagle who has the willpower to touch the sky, also known as a statesman or woman.

> When the power of love is greater than the love of power, the world will know peace. (Jimi Hendrix)

Individually, if you can grasp this, even if the world doesn't know peace yet, you may discover it personally. Social media companies and the powers that be within them can help fix this before things get out of hand, and the governments of the world can step in to protect its citizens, which only tends to swing the pendulum to the opposite side to bring back some balance. Of course, challenges will be made in the courts because the beast needs its greed satisfied, but when will you learn?

> When the last tree is cut, the last fish is caught, and the last river is polluted; when to breathe the air is sickening, you will realize, too late, that wealth is not in bank accounts and that you can't eat money. (Alanis Obomsawin)

It's time—actually, past time—for you to be good corporate citizens and start focusing on the overall health and well-being of the individual stakeholders and society instead of only being concerned with executive compensation by manipulating your stock prices. What happened with the 2017 tax cuts for millionaires, billionaires, and corporations is evidence enough that absolute power corrupts absolutely. It's about balance; and most, if not all, evidence is clear that anything done in excess or to such an extreme degree is unhealthy physically, emotionally, mentally, and spiritually. Since the individual user of your platforms is paramount to your long-term success, it would seem logical to bring a better balance to your business models before laws force your hand. You might even be able to set the standard for others to follow. The detrimental impact of algorithms that just keep feeding the need and the addiction to the almighty dollar is nothing short of creating blind sheep cults, where nothing can penetrate that bubble created as a result. How many are aware that they are not truly living but existing in a bubble that reinforces their belief structure and lets them puff up their chest against those who would try to reach out to them? Only those who have had a "come to Jesus moment" or something similar will ever be snapped back into any resemblance of balance. Breaking free is likely equivalent to breaking free from the addiction of drugs, alcohol, or escaping the grasp of a cult.

Technology, applications, and social media, their purpose should be sharing of knowledge, both positive and negative, to advance our personal growth and, subsequently, society as a whole. Yes, some will resist this for whatever reasons they care to manufacture, but it's only an excuse if it's allowed to be. Our interactions can move us forward in a positive direction or a destructive one. It can be head-spinning; but sometimes we need to take a step back, reflect, adjust, and move forward again. Your speed doesn't matter. Forward is forward. As we move forward on our path, we have the opportunity for knowledge, clarity, affirmation of the positive, or confirmation of the steps taken. The option allows us to reflect on the last point where it made sense, correct ourselves, and move forward while hoping that the knowledge and experience remain so we avoid similar mistakes. We can rise or self-destruct, which may or may not have an impact on others. Much like ripples in a pond, the spreading of positive or negative energy, love or hate, knowledge or ignorance can have a remarkable or devastating effect on the individual or others within their circle, who may not be prepared or realize they are in need. Some probably won't reflect or even entertain the possibility of gaining knowledge, a message, or an example to be followed or one not to follow. It is the yin and yang, and all of it has its place on this spiritual journey as a human being.

What is your purpose in using the internet and/or social media? Is it downloading Scripture or porn? Sharing your knowledge or experiences that might help another or conspiracy theories? Learn and grow or be a pawn of a brainwashed cult that only serve on the negative side of life, attempting to give the individual a sense of belongingness or fill what's missing in their heart, mind, or soul with something that is just the opposite of what they proclaim it to be. *No, no,* and *no,* this goes far beyond freedom of speech, rights, or liberties; but *yes,* you still have free will, even if you don't feel like you do. Seriously, that kind of approach will eventually lead to defeat. Still, the innocence that suffers until then may not be fully measurable until long after we've returned home and reviewed the life we've just lived to see if we've grown and fulfilled our purpose. "Love one another as I have loved you, so you must love one another." Granted, this is how people would know that those speaking were disciples of Jesus, but shouldn't we strive for this in our lives, no matter our viewpoint on the lifestyle or conduct? You can love someone without liking their behavior, can't you? And the opposing side will attempt to prove this wrong by bringing up things within human nature twisted to see if the Creator's children follow that guidance. Aren't we tested by life and in our observation of others who may be, in a certain way, have done or said things that you would never do? We may have a good idea or belief in behaving, but ultimately, we don't know how to respond unless we have walked that exact path.

Now for me, *reality TV must die*! It isn't real—just manufactured soap opera, BS stories pumping up emotions. Hence, the viewer hates or loves characters, giving them their "fix" and keeping the money coming in. Some can see this for what it is and enjoy the entertainment, distraction, humor, drama, and craziness of it all—more power to them. There are times that everyone may need or want to forget about things in their own lives, even briefly. But there are those who get drawn in and head down that rabbit hole, unable to find a way back, so when do we say enough? Something similar to this happened to me for a summer in my youth, and looking back, I am glad it was only temporary. I watched the two soap operas my mom watched. I wasn't mature enough to handle the adult-level interactions or content, and I didn't know or feel that I could ask my mom or anyone else that might bring me back to reality. However, I am sure that if my father knew, he would have put a stop to it. He was intimidating, scary sometimes, and could have grounded me from TV in general, and I wasn't going to open myself up to the potential negative consequences. I only knew that I'd be eagerly awaiting Monday's episode after Friday's teaser left me feeling emotions about people and lives who were not even close to realistic.

While on deployment in '88, I became engrossed in pro wrestling in Japan, but we only had the Armed Forces Network or "Forced Entertainment Network," as we referred to it. While not a crazy fanatic or drawn into the story lines, I enjoyed watching the "Ultimate Warrior" and hearing what he said to his fans about himself; his mantra to "always believe" was meaningful to me in more than just entertainment as his warrior persona spoke to the spirit and purpose of the warrior that lies within each of us. I only watched one season of *Survivor*, stopping after Rudy Boesch was booted. I was never a 100 percent fan of *American Idol*, but the fifth season is the only one I watched from the beginning. I thought Chris Daughtry should have won; but it's probably better for his music, career, and life that he didn't. I stopped watching all reality TV after that. Not reality TV, but I recently watched *Game of Thrones* on demand, which allowed me to consume multiple episodes a day or week. I didn't watch it while the series ran and would have gone stir-crazy waiting from week to week or season finale to the next season. I enjoyed everything about it, except how it ended. I wanted Daenerys to align to Jon Snow's philosophy. Unfortunately, Gary Allan sings "Life Ain't Always Beautiful" no matter how much we want it to be, even in TV or movies.

The main problem with "reality TV" is that it isn't real and makes children and teenagers believe they are entitled just because they exist, seeing that it's possible for their fifteen minutes or more of fame if only they can take the drama to the next level to get noticed. I really can't say if Dr. Spock was a genius or a mad scientist, but what I do know is that most parents today seem to be more interested in being their child's friend than the parent. And what the hell is it with participation trophies? A posting on Facebook, and I imagine on other social media sites, was the following:

> My promise to my children—as long as I live—I am your parent first, your friend second. I will stalk you, flip out on you, lecture you, drive you insane, be your worst nightmare, and hunt you down like a bloodhound when needed because *I love you*! When you understand that, I will know you are a responsible adult. You will *never* find someone who loves, prays, cares, and worries about you more than I do! If you don't hate me once in your life, I am not doing my job properly.

The chances of having children are virtually nonexistent for me due to a genetic condition, but it's still possible. As for actual children, I'd like to think that I know what I would do and how I would respond and handle things, but until or unless I am ever in that situation, I really can't say with 100 percent certainty. I know that it is challenging for many parents in today's world, even more so if you are a single parent. Children seem to be "asked" to grow up faster and so much earlier than my generation did if we ever really have. I do thank the stars that the internet wasn't around when I was still in school. I've had furkids, only one now, and I've had people remark that "my furkids" were better behaved than some children. So I'll take that as a compliment.

We need to be tested, sometimes multiple times, to know we've learned the lesson and move to the next lesson, assuming there is one. You must always be willing to truly consider evidence that contradicts your beliefs and admit the possibility that you may be wrong. Being intelligent doesn't mean knowing everything. It's the ability to challenge everything you know—one of those stories with a powerful message that may have escaped you before:

> A professor gave a balloon to every student, who had to inflate it, write their name, and throw it in the hallway. The professor then mixed all the balloons. The students were then given five minutes to find their balloon. Despite a hectic search, no one found their balloon. At that point, the professor told the students to take the first balloon that they found and hand it to the person whose name was written on it. Within five minutes, everyone had their balloon. The professor said to the students: "These balloons are like happiness. We will never find it if everyone is looking for their own. But if we care about other people's happiness, we'll find ours too."

We are all teachers, students, messengers on this spiritual journey as human beings. While learning, possibly teaching, life lessons through our experiences or the example, we unknowingly share to others who may not realize it until it's the right time on their path to see or acknowledge it. A big part of this is using technology, the internet, and social media to discover things about ourselves that we may not have been aware of, like personality profiles, career assessments, or even hidden scar tissue blocking you from full motion. Use social media platforms to learn and share your knowledge and your experiences; you never know who may be helped by it. As a student, seek to understand, learn, and grow to be happy, healthy, mentally fit, and at peace spiritually by getting rid of those things that weigh you down. Become that warrior within that will allow you the strength, courage, and conviction to make any changes that you may require. Even writing in a journal can help you see through the fog and mist, clearing the path and opening your eyes to what blocks your vision. Putting information on a picture about the people, places, and events surrounding the image can help you recall or others know more about the people and events in your life. Write in a journal to help you or others if you choose to share with them your path and the learning and growth you've achieved to date. Others may walk the path you're on with you, but no one can walk it for you. So become the ultimate warrior within; you are the only one who can.

CHAPTER 12

THE WARRIOR WITHIN

*Every man's heart one day beats its final beat.
His lungs take their final breath; and if what
that man did in his life makes the blood pulse
through the bodies of others, then his essence, his
spirit, will be immortalized by storytellers, by the
loyalty and memory of those who honor him.*

—The Ultimate Warrior

H is wife, Dana Warrior, in *Biography: Ultimate Warrior* said, "I believe that that spirit of the warrior lives on in every one of us who decides to do better." I couldn't agree more! Warriors are not always the fastest or strongest people, but strength and speed can be developed with training. Warriors are those who choose to stand between their enemy and all that they love and hold sacred. You become what you feed your mind. Not everyone has self-doubt. Maybe they don't allow it to impact their lives detrimentally or negatively. There is nothing wrong with being brutally honest with yourself, your faults, or your failures; learning; growing; and moving beyond them. Don't forget that you are human and will make mistakes. But most importantly, it's not the load that breaks you down; it's the way you carry it. We are told not to eat unhealthy things; but very little is ever mentioned or cautioned about the harmful things we allow to take up space, living rent-free, in our minds, subtly destroying us from the inside out. We can be our own worst enemy in our minds if we allow negative and toxic thoughts and energies to take up space. Forgive yourself for not knowing what you didn't know until you lived through it. Honor your path. Trust your journey. Learn, grow, evolve, become. The past is your lesson. The present is your gift. The future is your motivation.

> One day at a time—this is enough. Do not look back and grieve over the past, for it is gone, and do not be troubled about the future, for it has not yet come. Live in the present, and make it so beautiful it will be worth remembering. Happiness is a journey, just as life is. Enjoy the ride. (Ida Scott Taylor)

> An old Cherokee told his grandson, "My son, there is a battle between two wolves inside us all. One is Evil. It is anger, jealousy, greed, resentment, inferiority, lies, and ego. The other is Good. It is joy, peace, love, hope, humility, kindness, empathy and truth." The boy thought about it, and asked "Grandfather, which wolf wins?" The old man quietly replied, "The one you feed." (Unknown)

The Red Road or the Red Path is the Native spiritual path when we want a direct relationship with the Great Spirit, the Creator, God, etc. Walking the Red Road means living in the moment connected to all around us, respecting our relations and Mother Earth and Father Sky. It means finding a balance between and attending to our four sides: spiritual, physical, mental, and emotional. It means taking care and respecting ourselves and the Creator. It means being thankful for what we have, only taking what we need, and giving back to those around us and the spiritual world—to remember where we have been, to remember and honor our ancestors. It is walking in the right path of life, where we do the right thing even if it's hard at times.

Simply put, the Red Road is a road of respect, humbleness, truthfulness, and spirituality. It believes that a higher power has a path for us, who guides us on our journey and at the appropriate time, showing us the next step. It certainly does not mean having a perfect life. We fall and stumble, no matter which path we choose; but we also have it within us to get up, change course, find better footing, and keep going. We discover ourselves as we walk and learn from mistakes we have made or even from the successes and failures of others. We grow and evolve. But the goal is to live a balanced life 365 days of the year, to balance our commitments to our family, friends, community, work, spirituality, and ourselves—not an easy task but one we should all strive to achieve. Other roads will lead you to the same destination, but this is the one I am on. I choose it because when I look at the Ten Commandments written in the Bible and compare it to the ten commandments of Native Americans, the latter encompasses or expands on the other.

1. Treat the Earth and all that dwells therein with respect.
2. Remain close to the Great Spirit.
3. Show great respect to your fellow beings.
4. Work together for the benefit of all humankind.
5. Give assistance and kindness wherever needed.
6. Do what you know to be right.
7. Look after the well-being of the mind and body.
8. Dedicate a share of your efforts to the greater good.
9. Be truthful and honest at all times.
10. Take full responsibility for your actions.

Storms are or can be disruptive to life, but sometimes their purpose is to clear your path. When a storm is coming, all other birds seek shelter. The eagle alone avoids the storm by flying above it. So in the storms of life, may your heart soar like an eagle and rise above it. To be truly free, especially from breaking free from your prison, we need to be courageous to face the truth and be resilient about whatever the issue is or may be, breaking free from it. We do that by gaining spiritual, physical, mental, and emotional strength. Sometimes it may feel like we are alone, but we aren't. With technology, the internet, and social media, we have a greater chance to succeed than ever before in today's world without much of the stigma that sometimes happens when you realize you aren't perfect and need a certain amount of help to overcome that which may be holding you back. We all need help from time to time; and it could be as easy as someone listening, really listening, so we don't feel like we are alone, which may or may not be your spouse, loved one, or friend. There are also more advanced issues where you may need a trained and experienced professional to help you navigate the path. A quote from the movie *Lincoln* speaks to what is possible when you look at the whole picture instead of just that one thing being the subject of your focus.

> A compass, I learned when I was surveying, it'll point you true north from where you are standing, but it's got no advice about the swamps and deserts and chasms you'll encounter along the way. If, in pursuit of your destination, you plunge ahead, heedless of obstacles, and achieve nothing more than to sink in a swamp, what's the use of knowing true north? (Daniel Day-Lewis as Abraham Lincoln to Tommy Lee Jones's character, Thaddeus Stevens)

You don't have to fight anyone physically. Get educated. Honor the old ways; and add strength, resolve, and courage to them, creating a new way and walking the path to overcome fear with deep compassion, conviction, and resolve.

> Don't wait for things to get better; life will always be complicated. Learn to be happy right

now; otherwise, you'll run out of time. Do not pray for an easy life, pray for the strength to endure a difficult one. (Unknown)

No one will hit you harder than life itself. It doesn't matter how hard you hit back. It's about how much you can take, and keep fighting, how much you can suffer and keep moving forward. That's how you win. (Sylvester Stallone)

No one can undo the past, no matter how much we may want to; but you can face the future with courage, conviction, and determination even as fear may attempt to stand in your way. Be willing to walk alone; many who started with you won't finish with you. Attract what you expect. Reflect on what you desire. Become what you respect. Mirror what you admire. Don't follow the masses as sometimes the *m* is silent.

Most of us probably know what we want, but I suspect fewer understand what they need, especially in helping to realize things that may be preventing them from living their best life. Social media platforms can be a blessing or a curse, depending on what you want from it, learning and growing or feeling good about yourself by finding people who will validate prejudices and hatred. In the gym, the weight doesn't get easier to lift; you get stronger. In life, events don't get easier to handle; you become better equipped to manage them. I am not sure if this is true everywhere; but it seems we, as human beings, have lost the skills or even desire to listen and learn from those with experiences greater than our own, which might help us avoid the same or similar mistakes. Those in need of breaking free from things holding them back may require some brutal honesty, courage, and empowerment to emerge from their cocoon and rise from the ashes to fulfill the Creator's purpose for them. No one knows it all, and we can all use help at some point in our lives. If you don't like where you are at, move; you are not a tree. Take an online self-assessment test to learn and grow and discover your personality profile or what career considerations might make you happier. Mental health help is available from the comfort of your own home with no stigma about driving to an office. Sometimes our minds can be our own worst enemy; and we all need someone to talk to without fear, judgment, or being labeled a *freak*. It can put us on a better path.

> Mostly, it is the loss which teaches us about
> the worth of things. (Arthur Schopenhauer)

I've spoken about the most impactful losses in my life; but Rick, a friend from high school and fellow marine, his passing in April 2014 shocked and rocked me to my core. I was in awe of his accomplishments as a triathlete and as a marine. His zeal, zest, and love of life were minor compared to the love of his life, his wife Lisa. It was refreshing, hilarious, and eye-opening to hear about the things he did when they first started dating in high school. She was two years younger than him. On her eighteenth birthday, they got married. A few months later, she graduated high school. It was funny to hear how Rick would drive past her house, hoping to see her as he drove by before they began dating. Their adventures in Hawaii, California, and North Carolina were filled with enthusiasm, experience, adventure for life, love for each other, and making their life happen instead of waiting on it to find them. He was a military police officer, and she was a county sheriff's officer.

More than anything, it renewed my belief that such things were possible. It is refreshing to hear stories about other couples' marriages, their ups and downs, which only strengthened their love, friendship, and commitment to each other. Loss can remind us of our mortality, which can be scary, but don't hide from it. If you have things about your personality, character, or principles that make your relationships with others difficult, determine if you can change them to change the dynamics of the relationship. If you can't, that's fine. Don't live with regret. It does take two in the relationship to change things, so if you're the only one, just do what you can for yourself. Life, no matter how long it's lived, isn't long enough, and it's worse if regret has any place in it. Find your purpose, passion, strength, courage, humility, integrity, path to health, happiness, love, prosperity, and live your life. The lessons I've learned from the past relationship have hurt, but they also brought me the strength and courage necessary to weather the last storm. I understand who I am, and a part of that is a healer, a fixer. Make things right. Part of being a libra, I'm sure, needs to bring the ship back into balance when it tilts too far in any direction. I needed to help others to help me through the storm, but that aspect of my nature is taking a much-needed vacation. I know that great things are on the horizon or just beyond it for me, and I'm not going to force it to get here quicker than it's supposed to. For those struggling with losses, mourn in your way for as long as you need but not forever, or at least don't let it prevent you from living. Once you no longer have to remind yourself to breathe, take another step. I ask, hope, and pray that you find a way to find a life worth living again. Nothing will replace the loss, but I've found that sharing things can give another strength, hope, and courage to face the day and peace to sleep through the night, and maybe it can help you. Support groups are out there.

I asked a wise man, "Tell me, sir, in which field could I make a great career?" He said with a smile, "Be a good human being. There is a lot of opportunity in this area and very little competition." (Unknown)

A father used to say to his children when they were young: "When you all reach the age of twelve, I will tell you the secret of life." One day when the oldest turned twelve, he anxiously asked his father what was the secret of life. The father replied that he would tell him but that he should not reveal it to his brothers.

"The secret of life is this: the cow does not give milk."
"What are you saying?" Asked the boy incredulously.

"As you hear it, son, the cow does not give milk. You have to milk it. You have to get up at four in the morning, go to the field, walk through the corral full of manure, tie the tail, hobble the cow's legs, sit on the stool, place the bucket, and do the work yourself.

"That is the secret of life; the cow does not give milk. You milk her, or you don't get milk. There is this generation that thinks that cows *give* milk, that there are automatic and free things. Their mentality is that 'if I wish, I ask, I obtain.'

"They have been accustomed to getting whatever they want the easy way. But no, life is not a matter of wishing, asking, and obtaining. The things that one receives are the effort of what one does. Happiness is the result of effort. Lack of effort creates frustration.

"So please share with your children from a young age the secret of life so they don't grow up with the mentality that the government, their parents, or their cute little faces will give them everything they need in life. Remember— cows don't give milk; you have to work for it."
(Unknown, Cows Don't Give Milk)

I knew what I wanted most: building and living a life without needing a vacation from it. In theory, that sounds like a destination; but in reality, it's a journey, just not as hard of one as it has been. The Red Road would be my guide, and in April 2017, I found and purchased a book, *365 Days of Walking the Red Road: The Native American Path to Leading a Spiritual Life Every Day*. It would be a pilgrimage into my soul, capturing the priceless ancient knowledge Native American elders have passed on from generation to generation for centuries and showing you how to move positively down your road without fear or doubt. The path each of us walks is different; and again, while others may walk with you, no one can walk it for you. But if you don't make an honest effort to improve your life, how will it change? The world will test you and your resolve to continue moving forward, which doesn't mean you can't take a step back and reevaluate your position. Ensure that the action you are taking is where you want to go.

The book arrived about a week before Adrienne passed. Later that year, and with the spiritual visits still ongoing even though they were getting softer, I made a commitment to myself to post each day's teachings on Facebook beginning January 1, 2018. It was hard during the week after Nitki passed, but I am glad I made that commitment early on. I wasn't attempting to preach or convert anyone. The items I post or share on Facebook aren't necessarily things I am going through or in need of but hoping it may help others I am connected with or maybe someone they may know; and sharing things like this can bring comfort, courage, and strength to those in need. You never know if the message is for you or someone else, what it is or may be, and why; but I found it helpful during times of struggle, as suggested by the psychic I went to on a few trips home while in the Corps. I would use visualization by writing out my question or prayer on a piece of paper and then going outside and lighting it on fire, watching the smoke rise to the heavens. Depending on the question, the answer would typically become more apparent to me within a few days as I would take a step forward, adjusting as necessary when I needed to. Truth, honesty, respect, courage, humility, love, and wisdom are universal truths. I have received messages, reminders, guidance in my dreams from loved ones who have passed on and through déjà vu. All of it has helped me through the struggles. Talking to a psychic when I have felt lost or desperate helped, but it has to be done in moderation as it's too easy to get sucked in by those who are less than honest or reputable.

When we doubt, we all want that reassurance, but you have to ensure you think beyond what your heart tells you because it may just be what you want and not what you need. The paths previously walked prepare you for your next, or it should. So when you send out positive energy into the universe, it has a tendency to come back to you threefold. I was definitely in tune with getting my spiritual, mental, and emotional well-being into place, and I should have also started hard on the physical. For some reason, I wasn't mentally ready to proceed full throttle—uncertain as to why this was. It cleared up in late 2020 after the election results were announced or confirmed, and a great relief came over me, knowing that adults were once again going to be in charge and that we were back to some resemblance of normalcy. January 1, 2021, I began to focus on my health religiously.

> If you want to soar in life, you must first
> learn to FLY (first love yourself). (Mark Sterling)

The true warrior fights not because he hates the one in front of him but because he loves those behind him. Some may criticize or try to ridicule you; but it would be nothing more than them fearing what they don't know, understand, or can't comprehend. All they want to do is keep you at their level or below so they can feel good about themselves. But use it to your advantage as a test to strengthen your resolve and harden your mettle until your light and energy are so strong that an individual who might like to see you fail will no longer be a part of your life or be able to get under your skin. Sharing your story isn't and never will be the problem. When people expect others to believe the way they do because their faith is the only faith, well, that's where we have issues. When did we stop listening to elders or those younger than ourselves who may have experiences greater than our own who we could learn from? Even children who haven't lost that innocence of wonder can teach and remind us what it's all supposed to be about. What can be learned can help another sidestep something similar in their own life, still allowing them to know what they needed to but without as much pain or hurt as they might have needed to experience from it. Life is a gift from the Creator; what you do with that life is your gift back, no matter when you start.

> Don't let getting lonely make you reconnect
> with toxic people. You shouldn't drink the poison
> just because you're thirsty. (Unknown)

If you think you know it all, you know nothing. (Robert Kiyosaki)

I knew I had the tools (technology, internet, and social media) to help me understand, and even the psychic helped just through casual conversations. Many people I've spoken to about the events in my life have said, "You need to write a book." And when the psychic said it, I thought, *Damn, I guess I need to write a book.* I inquired with a friend from high school whose daughter had a few books self-published already, and she began writing just because she enjoyed it when she was a teenager. I would take the ideas and concepts that I already outlined and start, but it would be the fourth impassioned letter I'd write to someone that became the road map to this writing. Most of what I needed to do was to lose that which wasn't serving me or my ability to live my best life, which wasn't much at this point. I started to focus on accomplishing at least one thing each day from my "to-do list," which I kept in my head—wrong place for it because I can procrastinate with the best of them. I wrote them down, crossing off those I completed, adding new ones, and reminding myself about things that needed to be done periodically, from flea and tick medication for the dog to changing air filters every three months. I found the Reminders app on my phone and began using it religiously. Simple things, but it's worked. I am closer now to that life that I won't need a vacation from, and I know there is still more work to do. It just isn't as overwhelming as it once was or seemed to be. And even though I should have begun at the start of the pandemic when I was unemployed, my focus was keeping busy and trying to get back to work. I would work outside and walk the dog, exercising a bit on the workout equipment I had but nothing consistent or as aggressive as it is now. More synchronous and serendipitous moments have increased significantly this year, so I know that great things are on the horizon or just beyond it for me. While I used to be impatient in almost everything, it's no longer an issue like it once used to be. A meme I noticed was if you suddenly hear a high-pitched ringing in your ears, it's considered by many to be a "spiritual download"—an individual receiving information from higher realms, which I thought was interesting, even though we may need to reboot to install correctly, which means sleeping.

> Some people find fault like there's a reward for it. (Zig Ziglar)

> You are not the darkness you endured. You are the light that refused to surrender. (John Mark Green)

> Heal so that you can hear what is being said without the filter of your wounds. (Dr. Thema)

Some of the most extraordinary and influential words I would ever hear was in the movie *Act of Valor* by Tecumseh:

> So live your life that the fear of death can never enter your heart. Trouble no one about their religion. Respect others in their view, and demand that they respect yours. Love your life. Perfect your life. Beautify all things in your life. Seek to make your life long and its purpose in the service of your people. Prepare a noble death song for the day when you go over the great divide. Always give a word or a sign of salute when meeting or passing a friend, even a stranger when in a lonely place. Show respect to all people and grovel to none.
>
> When you arise in the morning, give thanks for the food and the joy of living. If you see no reason for giving thanks, the fault lies only in yourself. Abuse no one and nothing, for abuse turns the wise ones to fools and robs the spirit of its vision. When it comes your time to die, be not like those whose hearts are filled with the fear of death so that when their time comes, they weep

and pray for a little more time to live their lives over again in a different way. Sing your death song and die like a hero going home. (Chief Tecumseh 1768–1813)

Healers are spiritual warriors who have found the courage to defeat the darkness of their souls. Awakening and rising from the depths of their deepest fears, like a Phoenix rising from the ashes. Reborn with a wisdom and strength that creates a light that shines bright enough to help, courage, and inspire others out of their darkness. (Melanie Koulouris)

Some may strive to be what others want them to be or some variation, but the reality is that it's no sin to fail at being someone you're not. I've never really cared about my image, status, or how society saw me. I only cared about the reflection in the mirror and whether or not I could sleep peacefully at night. I am by no means perfect, never claimed to be but will jokingly say that I am better than most. It's funny and more for the smile it typically generates, not the reassurance or confirmation from anyone that it is true. In truth, I only need to be better today than I was yesterday. Even though I may fall short on occasion, it's a journey, not a destination. Becoming who you are meant to be doesn't mean having a singular focus on your life. It means coming to terms with things from your past, moving beyond them, learning and growing the gifts and talents you have been born with or learned along your way. For me, it would begin with simple steps and creating an action plan of sorts to get them done. I don't believe I ever had a preconceived idea about who I was supposed to be, especially by anyone's definition except mine, but I know I am succeeding. With a warrior's spirit, I will continue to light the candle and *spread a little light* where I can, sending positive energy into the universe.

CHAPTER 13

SPREAD A LITTLE LIGHT

When you change your energy, you change your life.
—Unknown

For me, this last decade has been a test on several fronts by people I never believed would hurt me or test me or the strength of my resolve. I was enlightened and hopeful about tomorrow because I realized that it was a journey, one I needed to walk if I was ever going to be where I wanted and needed to be. It's unlikely I would be the man I am today if I had not gone through the tribulations in my past—not perfect but better today than I was yesterday or last week for which I am thankful. I'm human. I've made mistakes, as we all have or are likely to do, but am grateful for having learned and growing from them so that I don't or am less likely to repeat them. I reflect on the past, but I don't live there. I have always kept what I wanted in my sights and knew I had the power to achieve them, but the drive and determination haven't been as strong as they are now.

No amount of money ever bought a second of time. (Tony Stark, Robert Downey Jr., to

father Howard Stark, John Slattery, in the movie
Avengers: Endgame)

Great words. And with life, no matter how long it's lived, it isn't long enough for most, although everyone probably knows someone who's tired and just ready to go home. As crazy or painful as life is, I have managed to do a few crazy things now and again to force myself out of my comfort zone, giving myself the *green light* to feel again, to break up the routine, to change the perspective so that maybe, just maybe, I could start enjoying and living life. When I became a manager in 2000, I began working hard to build up the team I managed and write standard operating procedures to approve brokerage account applications and margin requests. "Every job is a self-portrait of the person who did it. Autograph your work with excellence" is on a faux stone I purchased from a company called Successories. Excellence, not perfection, is what I tried to build and live by. My team rallied around this and was instrumental in developing the procedures. The team was solid all around, and a month or two after 9/11, the team began to kid me about my fairly simple set routine because the fifty-five to sixty hours a week that I was working wasn't necessary anymore. It wasn't so much necessary as it became a habit, one that I needed to break.

My routine consisted of going to work and back to my apartment and going to the mall or movie theater, all of which was on one street. In late 2001, I knew I needed to take a real vacation; so I started thinking about what, where, etc. I had convinced myself that if I invited any of the women I knew, they might get the wrong idea of it being more serious than it was, and I wasn't ready for that. I was still running away from what I didn't quite know yet, but I should have asked Jill. Maybe I would have discovered and confided in her what I was unknowingly avoiding. In April of 2002, I took an impromptu vacation to Moscow, Russia, of all places. No, not to find or meet a mail-order bride but because it was so far out of my comfort zone that if this didn't help change the direction of my life, then nothing would. I met a much younger woman, Helen, online in late 2001, and we would talk almost weekly. She was beautiful—just drop-dead gorgeous. I had mentioned that I was planning on taking a much-needed vacation a few times but didn't know where or what. Out of the blue, she invited me to come over for her birthday in mid to late April. I thought about it for a while and pulled the trigger at the end of February. I started getting my passport and visa and reading up on Russia. Had this been six years earlier, I would have asked my father if he wanted to take a trip to Poland; it would have been a chance to bond and perhaps improve our relationship by learning more about my heritage, maybe removing the stigma I felt around it. I know my father would have enjoyed it.

The ten days in Moscow were definitely out of my comfort zone, but it was a great time. Seeing a different culture can make you appreciate your own or even allow you to incorporate something new into your life. I met Helen's girlfriend, Yulia, when they picked me up at the airport; and the next day I met Nina, another girlfriend of hers. I met Helen's mother and brother on a trip to her hometown. So much history and architecture—Red Square, the Kremlin, St. Basil's Cathedral, Lenin's Mausoleum, the Bolshoi Theater, the farmers market, Gorky Park, Kolomenske Park, the Church of the Ascension, and the Trinity Lavra of St. Sergius in Helen's hometown, drinking from the spring, which is said to have healing powers. I even experienced the circus. Not wanting to come empty-handed, I had brought some gifts from North Carolina for her and her family. She didn't ask me to, but it was a surprise and a thank-you for inviting me over. I met her mom and got her a tapestry of all the North Carolina lighthouses, and her brother, who I think I got something from the Carolina Panthers but can't recall. I didn't meet her father, who worked in the construction industry, I think. He was well-respected, and I got him a 1:24 miniature die-cast metal replica of Dale Earnhardt's number 3 black Intimidator car.

Helen, Yulia, and Nina were great, and it was so relaxing to laugh again and enjoy the company of good people, and oh my god, the amount of vodka a male friend of Helen's and I drank at her birthday dinner. I didn't black out or embarrass myself, but I also wasn't feeling any pain. I brought a bottle of it back to the USA.

Helen gave me two matryoshka dolls, which are decreasing-sized wooden dolls placed inside one another that she had painted.

When I got back home, I was so relaxed—not a care in the world. The job was going great. The team did great while I was gone, which is the greatest compliment a manager can get. I still believe in the philosophy of working myself out of a job by making the process as efficient and streamlined as possible, empowering the team with knowledge, resources, and tools to gain the necessary experience to meet any challenge before them, with or without me. I would meet Adrienne in November of that year. Later on, when we replaced the lights in the kitchen, she helped me get out of my comfort zone when it came to working on electrical problems, which was likely due to an incident when I was about six or so at Oak Shade Grove where an electrical wire caught me on the leg. Unless it's something straight-forward, both plumbing and electrical, I call the professionals.

Not working for ten months at the beginning of the pandemic was rough. It went beyond the stress or anxiety of the situation that I felt—the needless loss of so many. For years I have always thought that the best in us would overcome the worst and that evil could serve a divine purpose as an example of what is wrong with human-kind, but some are still in denial because they only seek power. We can never be complacent about evil, especially today because it is still fighting for oxygen. We should have discussions and debates about policies. Still, it will take true statesmen or women, not those who would worship a person instead of remaining steadfast to a set of ideas, values, and principles, which can be easily communicated and shown by their actions. We need to be brutally honest with ourselves, individually and as a country, to fulfill the promise in our founding documents. I was lucky enough to have some savings, and the addi-tional unemployment helped me survive, which is far different from living. I didn't dwell on what I couldn't control and focused my ener-gies on those things I could.

Sometime in early 2020, I began to identify things to work on, which can be crazy because most tend to think we need to do it all to have any real sense of accomplishment, but it's the small things that add up to something big. I would focus on things out in the yard for most of the year, which wouldn't cost me anything but time and sweat. After the election, I switched gears toward the inside of the house and even myself. At the beginning of 2021, I'd write out my "to-do list," not every single thing but initially the higher-priority items, and I would strive to start and work it through completion, take a day or two off, then choose the next thing and repeat. Most of them were easy to complete, such as a reminder to take my medications in the morning and evenings and using my smartphone's Reminders app—household reminders to change the air filters every three months, recycling pickup every two weeks, medications for the dog, and unique items like calling my communications provider to inquire about new promotions that I could use to reduce my bill. Every dollar saved is money in my pocket, and if I could do it without it being too much of an impact on my quality of life, outstanding. I did some comparison shopping on the car and home insurance. The new company would save me $400 per year on car insurance and $500 per year on homeowner's insurance. The company I had been with for more than twenty-seven years didn't even attempt to keep me as a customer or match the offer. I was making the changes I wanted and needed to make for the next part of my journey and having as much of a maintenance-free home as could be had. Most of the items were a one-time event as these were kind of my indoor maintenance-free tasks, and I would just need to be mindful of those things I needed or would need in the immediate future. An example was going through the medicine cabinets for expired products and cleaning out the hallway closet of things I don't need or wouldn't use, donating what I could to Goodwill. It was pretty simple; and I'd do the same in the kitchen cabinets—food that was well past its expiration date, plastic storage containers that I had too many of, etc.

In March of 2021, I reached out to a local landscaping pro after seeing his posting appear on my Facebook feed and asked him to develop a planting design for the natural areas in the front and side of the house and come up with an estimate for doing the work. I wasn't in any rush but wanted a plan and estimate so I could budget, and I'd rather trust a professional who had the knowledge and experience that I knew very little about. I got the plan a month later and hired him for the job, which he would start in late June. I helped prepare the area and did a good portion of the labor I was hoping would save me on the labor costs and help get it done faster. The workout room, a smaller bedroom across from my master bedroom, was also on my list. Per Ade's request fifteen years earlier, I had painted the room "cheerful" yellow because she used it as her office. The change was long overdue, so Navajo white replaced it. And I added a border to the bottom thirty inches with brushed copper linear subway wall tile that was peel-and-stick. I love the look. Additionally, I have been looking at the Bowflex Max Trainer since I began my workouts, and I would need to ensure that I was at least fifteen to twenty pounds below the maximum weight limit. When I initially looked into it, there was a ten-week shipping delay; and in May, it was down to four weeks. And in mid-June, it was just a week, so I ordered it. And it arrived and was assembled by a professional the last week of June, and it is kicking my butt. But I love it.

Next, I needed to get back to a dentist because it had been more than five years since my last appointment. I didn't have dental coverage, and the VA doesn't offer it unless you are fully disabled or retired after you're twenty, which the VA should consider changing. Hell, I'd even pay for it or let them deduct it from my disability pay. I recently bought a discount plan and had an initial appointment and then the intense "digging for gold" appointment—an appointment three weeks later to take care of a small cavity and then another cleaning in the fall, which is just polishing and buffing. But I have learned my lesson big-time. I bought an electric toothbrush that uses an app to help the user brush properly, and I now brush at least twice a day—after breakfast and before bed. And I floss in the evenings. From this experience, I feel obligated to beg and plead with parents to help build and reinforce good habits as early as possible in their children. When it becomes second nature to them, it will follow them into adulthood.

Another item that I wish to ask is to please read to your kids each night, even just a few minutes, so they get a taste for it, and encourage them to read so they become thirsty for knowledge. I wrote earlier about parents being their children's parents first and their friends second—same concept. The expectations you establish early on and reward for meeting them or consequences if they don't will make for good adults who don't expect everything to be given to them as some do. You know your kids better than anyone, and while I am not advocating for spanking, I wouldn't rule it out entirely. But only you can make that decision. I am sure that every child needs to sort through the emotions and life experiences, but that doesn't mean they have to do it by themselves or learn through osmosis. Parents, if you want your children to come to you with hard conversations even though they're scared, then you have to be the kind of person who has hard conversations with them even though you're afraid. I would guess that children who feel comfortable talking with their parents about everything under the sun will be happier because of that love, trust, and connection; so, parents, please speak with your kids about everything, not at them or to them but with them. We seem to have forgotten what it is to learn from individuals with experiences greater than our own, and it starts in the home by the mother and father who brought forth that life. If children know—I mean, to see and feel that they will be heard and listened to—trust is earned to such a degree that even if they choose another path, they will gain confidence in taking their steps and coming back to you for advice or guidance. At least, that is what I believe or hope.

This year, 2021, would be the year that I'd tackle my health and fitness, committing to a workout routine in the mornings and evenings, building them up slowly, and increasing as I could handle more. I created a spreadsheet to track my activities and measurements, taking photos of myself each week to document and see the progress. I started on January 1, 2021, and began using my elliptical and doing some ab work every day, except the weekends. I walked the dog each evening, as long as it wasn't raining or going to, including the weekends. We built up to the three miles around our neighborhood. In February, I added resistance training by doing one set of fifteen reps on my Bowflex on Mondays, Wednesdays, and Fridays, adding a second set in March and the third set in April. Starting in August, I'll add more weight for several months as I want to add strength, not necessarily mass. In June, I added three sets of leg and back resistance training on Tuesdays and Thursdays. In February, I began a diet program, and even though I "cheat" on the weekends, I have lost eighty pounds in six months. And when the extended family saw me recently on the Fourth of July, every one of them said, "Holy shit."

It felt good, and I know I have the other half of the weight I want to lose. But the numbers aren't as important as doing the work and building better habits. There have been a few weeks where I didn't lose but gained weight; but I didn't get discouraged because the other measurements, body fat and BMI, showed decreases. I decided to join a few dating sites at the beginning of the year. Something didn't feel right. I realized that if I had met someone, I could have easily been distracted from my overall goals, so I needed to focus on those items I knew I wanted to accomplish. Thank you to Bill Maher for pointing out our country's obesity problem and Ann's daughter, my niece, who is all about fitness and challenging herself, whose accomplishments she posted on Facebook. It helped keep the issue on my radar.

Some have walked through the fire and will leave sparks of light everywhere they go. Starting when I moved to Charlotte, I did begin to open up, saying hi to strangers on the street, especially if our eyes met. I increased this over the years and have done that more this year, stopping and having conversations with those in the neighborhood on the evening walks. Most of the kids wanted to pet Walker as we approached; and I even had one young boy, Matthew, tell me I was his best friend. And all I did was say hello to him each time we saw him, and I asked how he was doing. I replied, "Thank you," and that I was honored that he considered me his best friend. What you send out into the world comes back to you. I have been moved on the energy side of things when I see a woman whose smile, eyes, or overall energy are radiant or intoxicating. I'd let them know what a great smile and beautiful eyes they had or that the light that surrounded them was bright. While not specifically directed at me, their energy is just because of who they are and telling them hopefully brightened their day. I wasn't flirting and wasn't asking or hoping for any phone number or contact information. I also recall seeing a couple, who looked so beautiful together, so much light and energy from them, so I let them know and went on my way. One of the ladies at the vet's office in Concord, she and her husband are just a beautiful couple, and their kids are adorable as they can be. And all of it renews my belief in the beauty of this world.

> Some believe it is only great power that can hold evil in check. But that is not what I have found. I have found that it is the small things, everyday deeds of ordinary folk that keep the darkness at bay, simple acts of kindness and love. (Gandalf, *The Hobbit*)

You never know what someone else is going through, so one small act from you could mean the world to them. Twenty years ago, I was looking for a new cologne, and the girl at the counter was cute and giving me her thoughts on them. And there seemed to be a spark, so when she asked for my number, I gave her my home number on the back of my business card. A few days later, a guy called me, claiming to be her boyfriend, after finding my card and asked who I was. Not sure if he was snooping, going through her things, or whatever, but I told him she asked me for my number and never said she had a boyfriend. I don't know. She could have just been trying to make him jealous or something else, but it didn't matter. I wouldn't be the reason, cause, or excuse for another's relationship coming to an end. Before giving out my number, I now ask if they are in a relationship to avoid repeating history.

As I write these words, I know the path has led me to this moment, and all of the simple serendipitous moments that I have been seeing have increased significantly since the beginning of 2021. One of them was what to do with the elliptical, and my first thought was about offering it to my friends, Greg and Meredith. If not, then I'd likely donate it to Goodwill or the Salvation Army, but it was something that just fell in line with what I wanted and what they needed. In early June, the refund payment from the IRS hit my account; and a few days later, a check for a refund on the co-pays I had paid for my VA prescriptions was received, which I wasn't expecting. But both have helped me reduce my expenses and add to savings. The latest serendipitous moment came on my return trip from Raleigh on the Fourth of July. Short story long, I stopped at a rest stop about an hour from the house for a bathroom break and to grab a Wild Cherry Pepsi and a snack. I thought it wanted my credit or debit card, but it was cash-only. All I had were $20 bills, so I deposited it and made my selection, hearing it fall. I couldn't budge the door to retrieve it, so I selected it again. And another dropped. I was frustrated until it began to give me my change, which was four $5 bills; and then $3.25, in coins, was dispensed.

I added coins in a third attempt, and after I heard it drop, I was able to get the door open. And there were three Wild Cherry Pepsis, and with the change left, I bought my snack and hit the road. So none of it cost me anything but time. All of it has led me to this point, and there is more to do. But the struggle or climb isn't as great as it once was, but I realize that these moments are about my future and the universe preparing me for what comes next, which I am sensing will be in the fall. I know there will be new clothes that I will need to budget for as I'm hoping to be down another thirty to forty pounds by then. I know I'll be ready once it begins to take off, but I will need to keep myself in check somewhat so I don't go overboard in anything just because of the anticipation of it all and wanting as much as I can get as soon as I can get it because it's been so long. Ever hold sand in your hand? The tighter you squeeze it, the more you lose. So I need to be mindful of it in any new relationship or love interest. I know I will eventually recognize the energy that will captivate me at some point. I'm not worried so much but want to be as far along as I can in my health and fitness goals so that even a pleasant distraction won't stop me from continuing this pursuit. I entered a contest with the company whose diet program I have been using. As strange as it was, I donated to a charity auction to win a C8 2021 Corvette Stingray. I'm not expecting anything, nor will I lose sleep if I'm not a winner in either. But it was nice to be in a position to enter them. One of the last upgrades will be a new kitchen table, chairs, and a bench that will arrive in late September.

The only frustrating thing I experienced recently was jury duty. After thirty-seven years, they found me, and wouldn't you know it, they selected me. Before we began deliberations, they picked me as foreman, which would test my leadership capabilities and ability to drive conversations forward by focusing on facts, not emotions. I was initially told that it would be seven to ten days, which worried me because I'm a contractor. If I'm not working, I don't get paid, and the $50-a-day jury duty pay isn't enough to compensate me for losing more than that per hour. Sure, I could have just logged on, and no one would have known if I was doing any work or not unless they IM'd me or tried to call or text—problem solved. Easy fix, right? Not really as an even bigger problem would be obvious because I would know the truth.

What you send out there comes back to you threefold, so why invite suspicion or questions about your honor and integrity or open up a karmic circle that could come back to bite you? Ultimately, I have to live with myself. I have to like the reflection I see in the mirror, so I let the team and my new manager know and that I'd log in the morning and evenings to check and respond to emails, etc., but that I'd be out for most of the day during regular working hours. It was frustrating in the first few hours of the afternoon, and for a few hours the following day, we began deliberations. We couldn't believe some of the things one juror was saying. He admitted prejudice against the federal government. But everyone who spoke was heard, and it would take three others in the group who were frustrated but initially had raised concerns. I continued to remind and bring everyone's focus to the law and the judge's instructions. The three would approach the juror's argument from another perspective and come at it from a different angle unique to their experience and viewpoint. It worked. We agreed on the verdicts for both defendants and were out of there just after lunch. I thanked each of them for their perspective and ability to approach it from a different angle.

As I complete my maintenance-free projects, I am getting ideas about what to do next on my to-do list and expanding my horizons a little bit more. It isn't about getting outside my comfort zone but having more knowledge and experiences than I currently do. I will look into taking a cooking class, or several, and learning a foreign language, at least enough to be dangerous. Regardless of the country, I am envious of school systems whose early education required or strongly encouraged learning a second language. I attempted to learn Spanish in high school, but my father wouldn't allow me to take the class, telling me that I needed to learn Polish. I knew why he wanted me to, but damn! As I understand it, it's a language that is hard to learn; and most importantly, it wasn't an option at any school in the area. Yes, it could connect me more to my heritage and aunts and uncles who also spoke some and relatives still living in Poland, but not being able to take any language handicapped me.

I'm also thinking of taking a few formal dance lessons as I'm not the most graceful person on any dance floor; and I prefer the excellent seats at concerts, although when I saw Creed in the summer of 2002, the tickets were in the mosh pit. Still, no one was moshing, just hands in the air, screaming and being excited at being so close to the stage, which was a blast, unless that is what moshing is. I'm not sure how high of a priority it is to earn a college degree now as I'm less than fifteen years from retirement. It's something on the back burner. Should there ever be another crisis that impacts the country for any period or I want a challenge, I will enroll in some online courses as it should help keep my mind busy as all the other little projects will have been completed. Reading and rereading some of those books that I learned a lot from is on the list, as is doing cross-stitch. It's my creative outlet. The second one I started, I haven't touched in years, and it's about halfway done. The third is still in the original package, but the Harley Davidson logo was first because it's an eagle. And I love eagles. I'm also going to build a shot glass case for those I have, with room to grow. I always try to pick one up on my travels. An actual release in the last month was me burning the court records from the divorce with Adrienne because I didn't need them after I wrote the chapter on her. It felt terrific to get rid of them and let go. But I saved them all to a CD or DVD—just in case my honor or integrity is questioned surrounding any of it, I can back up what I've indicated.

> We cannot attain the presence of God because we're already totally in the presence of God. What's absent is awareness. (Richard Rohr.)

A proverb cited in several cultures is, you cannot wake up someone who is merely pretending to be asleep; so don't pretend to be asleep just because you don't like the message, messenger, or that bitter pill of truth. No one likes it, especially when confronting the reflection in the mirror and even less when we don't want our faith or beliefs questioned by others, which can reinforce and strengthen them. For some, they see humility as a weakness, but it's the foundation of all virtues, with strength and power that another can't measure. On the path that Mr. Johnny Cash walked, his tribulations eventually forced him to confront things about himself, and what he did with that knowledge spread with open eyes to see the truth about other things, even if it was the truth that only he needed to know. We fear change and being wrong, but it requires a certain amount of humility to bring our courage up to where it needs to be for the challenge. Do you have the guts to challenge your reflection and ask the hard question, face your fears, or swallow that bitter pill of truth you may be avoiding so that you can take a step toward living your best life? We need examples, good and bad, the yin and yang, so that we may challenge or reaffirm our beliefs, faith, or strength of conviction to withstand the storms life throws at us. Without the darkness of night, we would not know or appreciate the beauty of the light of day. Sometimes we do need to reflect on the past but should avoid living there. The phrase "hindsight is twenty-twenty" emphasizes people's clarity about past decisions instead of the uncertainty before making the decision. Our own worst enemy can be our mind.

No one likes to fail, feel inadequate, or fall short of the mark, but if we are not tested, how will you honestly know if your faith or convictions are as strong as you think they are? Yes, seeing isn't believing; believing is seeing. But it's not about proving anything to anyone except yourself if you require that reminder or lesson. Couldn't one perceive Jesus's fasting for forty days in the Judean Desert and Satan's attempt to tempt him toward sin as such a test before he began his ministry? Jesus probably would have known the true power and strength of his belief, faith, or convictions of his father's love, but as for the rest of us mere mortals, would we if we weren't tested or tempted? You probably have a good idea, but for most, you are never going to get through something until you go through it. For those who know every scripture or verse in whichever holy book they hold near and dear, there is a difference between knowing the word and *knowing* it. Suppose you've never done the physical work or applied them through a humbling service and never been tested by temptation, perhaps even losing your way for a time. How will you ever know the full extent of the power of and in your belief, faith, or conviction? I'm not advocating for anyone to seek out the temptation to prove your mettle, but take the opportunity to review the possibility that the reason for the struggle may be a lesson to be learned for your continued growth along the path, preparing you for the next part of your journey. It could also be just a stupid thing you did. Let's face it—sometimes we make the wrong choices to get to the right place. Life teaches; love reveals. We, as a society, shouldn't pursue laws or force our personal beliefs on another just because it may help you avoid temptation. To direct or expect others to believe as you do is wrong on every level. Live and let live while you continue on your path, being an example that another might see when it's their time to see such a reminder. To be clear, what you believe is not the problem. What you think another should believe *is*, and that isn't religious freedom.

> A religious person will do what he is told, no matter what is right, whereas a spiritual person will do what is right, no matter what he is told. (Unknown)

All of this may be the battle between two opposing energies, good and evil, but that doesn't mean you should avoid or run from being challenged out of fear, should you find yourself in that position. Ultimately, if it's our path to walk, there is a purpose, even though we may not fully realize it at the time or shortly after its completion, hindsight being twenty-twenty.

> Rivers do not drink their own water; trees do not eat their own fruit; the sun does not

shine on itself, and flowers do not spread their fragrance for themselves. Living for others is a rule of nature. We are all born to help each other. No matter how difficult it is, life is good when you are happy; but much better when others are happy because of you. (Pope Francis)

My energy has attracted women, broken birds, who needed help in a portion of their lives, occurring primarily in 2014. It was close to the "knight in shining armor" thing I realized back in '92, but this wasn't the same. It was no longer about doing things in an attempt to prove myself in the hopes of a relationship but as a way to feel good about helping someone else out, which wasn't so much money as it was friendship or a safe place to stay without any kind of quid pro quo. Even better was that I wasn't interested in being in a relationship with any of them, and I am just grateful that I didn't fall into any dark holes in helping them. I cosigned a used-car loan for one, which was the biggest mistake ever or could have been. Mechanical issues would prompt returning the car the next day. I canceled the contract; and thankfully, I kept copies of the return acknowledgment, which helped me when they found the car a few months later on the side of the road because it had broken down. They tried but couldn't come after me for it. It was still stupid, bordering on desperate, to help a stranger, which is when I knew I needed to reign things in, and I have. It served its intended purpose, and now I don't mind helping another unload some of their baggage. But I'm not carrying it for them. And whatever baggage I may have, I can handle them myself.

There are two ways of spreading light: to be the candle or the mirror that reflects it. (Edith Wharton)

You can't buy your way into heaven with monetary wealth. It's the good deeds, compassion, generosity, what we do, and how we act in this life that matters. If we are spiritual beings on a human journey, which I believe we are, we will all have to answer for what we said and did that weren't part of the reasons we were to learn. My tribulations to date have allowed me to learn and grow, increasing the positive energy I feel and send out. If I help someone, I prefer to do so without calling attention because it's not about me or my ego but the act of service itself. I do not want the limelight or any spotlight, but I will do all that I can for a significant other as she wishes. I will continue spreading a little light where and when I can, when guided, with simple acts of kindness, generosity, or, if required, tough love, which is still love. All of it has allowed me to become who I am, two of the most powerful words, for what you put after them shapes your reality.

CHAPTER 14

I Am

*The closer you come to knowing that you
alone create the world of your experience,
the more vital it becomes for you to
discover just who is doing the creating.*
—Eric Micha'el Leventhal

I imagine everyone's definition of *success* is different. True success isn't likely to be achieved unless you know and embrace who you are, striving to be the best version of yourself and living a well-lived life by your definition, not anyone else's, and not because others might ask for it but because you deserve it. We have the means to check ourselves by listening to the observations, advice, or opinions of others as they might see something you may not have considered. But make sure you know your circle. Make sure everybody in your boat is rowing and not drilling holes when you're not looking, so you will have to ensure those you treasure also know your value.

Before he died, a father said to his son, "Here is a watch that your grandfather gave me.

It is almost two hundred years old. Before I give it to you, go to the jewelry store downtown. Tell that I want to sell it, and see how much they offer you." The son went to the jewelry store, came back to his father, and said, "They offered $150 because it's so old." The father said, "Go to the pawnshop." The son went to the pawnshop, came back to his father, and said, "The pawnshop offered $10 because it looks so worn." The father asked his son to go to the museum and show them the watch. He went to the museum, came back, and said to his father, "The curator offered $500,000 for this very rare piece to be included in the antique collections." The father said, "I wanted to let you know that the right place values you in the right way. Don't find yourself in the wrong place and get angry if you are not valued. Those that know your value are those who appreciate you; don't stay in a place where nobody sees your value."

Ultimately, it's up to you to do the work, see things through completion, and then decide the next steps to take and in which direction. If you can look in the mirror, be proud of the reflection, and sleep peacefully at night. You are likely on the right path, but you're the only one who knows the truth. So make sure you aren't kidding yourself. It has taken me longer than it should have to come to this place in my life, but sometimes the path is much longer for various reasons that we won't understand until after it's walked. Don't ever mistake my silence for ignorance, my calmness for acceptance, or my kindness for weakness. If you think that I am a pushover because of what I have shared or expressed, you'd be wrong—very wrong. We all have a serious and quiet side, a fun and crazy side, and other sides that likely depend on the situation or people involved. No doubt that for many, there is a side of them you never want to see. For me, I'll likely walk away before I do anything physical because I know myself well enough. If pushed long after warnings are given and threatened or an attempt to hurt me, my home, those I love, including my dogs, is made, I won't stop until one of us is unconscious or worse. Love, not hate, is the driving force and true strength of the warrior within. I don't hate anyone, even though I may hate or dislike the things some may do or say. I don't hate them, but that doesn't mean I have to help them. Take my former stepson as an example. If he were lying on the side of the road from a car crash, hurt, and on fire, I might stop but not to help. In fact, I wouldn't piss on him if that meant it could be interpreted as showing him an ounce of mercy.

> What's broken can be mended. What hurts
> can be healed. And no matter how dark it gets,
> the sun is going to rise again. (Unknown)

I know no one who actively seeks out storms to test themselves, their mettle, or their faith, even though that is precisely what these struggles ultimately do. Not all storms come to disrupt your life; some come to clear your path. Real growth for the best version of you that can be is likely only to happen as a result of pain or struggle, so don't avoid or deny it once it's in front of you. Confront it. Deal with it the best way you can, and look for help and advice from people you respect. People resist change because they focus on what they have to give up instead of what they have to gain. Understand that people talk behind your back for three reasons: (1) when they can't reach your level, (2) when they don't have what you have, and (3) when they try to copy your lifestyle but can't. They will try to bring you down from what they perceive as a higher place than them. Expecting things to change without putting in any effort is like waiting for a ship at the airport. What you deny or ignore, you delay. What you accept and face, you conquer. Reflecting on events in my life that have shaped me—good to bad, wondrous to brutally painful, and most points in between, especially in writing about them—has been therapeutic. It has provided me with a sense of freedom because I won't have to verbally go into the detail required for someone to understand who I am and why.

The circle has healing power. In the circle, we are all equal. When in the circle, no one is in front of you. No one is behind you. No one is above you. No one is below you. The sacred circle is designed to create unity. Change, at the individual level, is the only true power that will change the direction of your life.

> They will come to a fork in the road. One road will lead to Materialism and Destruction for almost all living creatures. The other road will lead to a Spiritual Way upon which the Native People will be standing. This path will lead to the lighting of the eighth fire, a period of eternal peace, harmony and a "New Earth" where the destruction of the past will be healed. (Anishinaabe Prophecy, The Prophecy of the Eighth Fire)

> Whatever your difficulty, whatever your hardship: Dance and make the song you sing your prayer. Sing it courageously, and with each step, strengthen yourself with the knowledge and wisdom of your elders. So that whatever next happen, you can survive and not lose your rhythm. (Red Haircrow)

We all have our path to travel as spiritual beings on this human journey, and it comes down to what is right for you and no other. Too much in this country's, perhaps the world's, forces will attempt to, and often do, destroy the messenger because the message is universal; and they profit off the division or the opposite side of that coin (truth-lie). They will try to use your past and honesty to distract from the message, moving the goalposts, forcing you to defend against each attack, which only takes away from you speaking the truth and sharing it. They do it so others will not hear or listen to the message or quickly dismiss it as it reaches them. Until individuals find out or discover for themselves what is universally true, will they be able to withstand or ignore the attacks against them and see those who attack them for what they truly are. And in doing so, they can rise above and dismiss it.

We as individuals are or can be impatient. What is meant for you will arrive on time. Some will question if there is an actual plan or a higher spiritual being, but it is about what the Creator has planned for us. Dedicating yourself, as some do, doesn't mean that nothing else exists or should. Knowing the word, no matter what book it is read from, if any, is excellent, but living it is far better and shows a more authentic understanding and greater purpose. Some will take this to extremes, but it's not so much about attending religious services every night of the week or reading from the book. But if that provides you strength or whatever it may be that you need, then by all means. We all have our path to walk. And remember, it's not how heavy the load is that breaks you; it's the way you carry it. As you walk upon this earth, treat each step as a prayer. Your thank-you, love, and dedication to the Creator for the life granted to you is where you go from that point on. And the first step toward getting somewhere is to decide that you are not going to stay where you are. Don't tell me the sky's the limit when there are footprints on the moon.

Less than ninety days ago in late April 2021, I began writing this; and on May 3, I stopped briefly to write a fourth impassioned letter.

> Dear (name withheld),
> Your energy, from the smile in your eyes to the beauty, strength and joy in your voice to the universal messaging power of…

I would go through a process of why I felt compelled to write the three-page letter. Once I understood the reason for the message received, I had to decide the purpose or intent of mailing it. I knew it might never reach the recipient, so I wondered if I should light it on fire and send it up to the heavens as a prayer. That letter would serve as a road map to this, which has been therapeutic, a release of sorts. Not that I needed to confess or heal from anything specific, but it did allow me to find the words to how I was feeling about certain things. I am not ashamed or embarrassed by anything in my past or present, and I know my values and beliefs are strong. But I will always listen to constructive observations that might allow me to improve upon them. I asked for guidance from the universe if I should mail it or not. Ade's fiftieth birthday would have been the following week, and I figured it might be a positive-energy booster if it was sent then. And perhaps the recipient would get it. The message I received from the universe about mailing it was undeniable! I didn't send it the following week but that same day via FedEx. The two letters I previously wrote, passionate as they were, were also profound for me. It allowed me to confirm or reaffirm my belief in who I am and who I wanted and would continue to be, and I wanted to ensure that the recipients of those letters knew and understood who I was and would continue to be, not because I was looking for anyone's approval. I know what I wrote wasn't going to wake anyone up who was pretending to be asleep or allow them to have an epiphany, but it did show that my words and actions were in harmony with each other in comparison to theirs. I would realize in those writings that I was on the path I was meant to be on and that I would do all that I could do to remain proud and happy with who I see in the mirror. The third letter to Ade, I already explained.

I sense great things on the horizon or just beyond, and I'm in no rush to get there tomorrow. I will continue to do what I can to ensure that I am in the best position possible to accept any blessings to come and deal with potential roadblocks or events that might alter my course. I may never have come to this point in my life had I not been brutally honest with myself and taken the necessary steps to get rid of those things that no longer serve me or my purpose, which is to live, laugh, and love. And it's not clear if I will attempt to have this published; but I know that when I recognize the energy of "my next ex"—yes, that's a joke—I would rather have this written down than attempt to go through everything again. I'll answer questions; but I don't have the energy, on any level, to revisit these things in sufficient detail. So there are no secrets kept from them. I'm not getting out of life alive, so I will continue my best to continue walking the Red Road; to light a candle and *spread a little light* where I am guided to;

and, most of all, to pack love, light, and beautiful memories inside my heart because I know it's only those things that I will take with me.

> When you follow the crowd, you lose yourself, but when you follow your soul, you will lose the crowd. Eventually, your soul tribe will appear but do not fear the process of solitude. (Unknown)

I realize some may see me as complicated, but I'm not. It just may appear that way. I consider myself to be a simple man—something I love and understand. I am a private person by nature; but with those I love and like, I am an open book about myself, which would be balanced against any need for them to know. I do not want or need to seek any limelight or spotlight, but if a significant other wishes me to be her arm candy, then I'll do my best and all that I can do as she wishes. It's about giving your hearts to each other but not into each other's keeping. I'm not into name brands as a status symbol for others to see or approve. From clothes to cars and virtually everything else I consider purchasing, I prefer quality products and will spend more on them if they are cost-effective for the long-term. A car is just transportation that gets me from point A to point B and back, but I will want those options to make the ride more enjoyable and comfortable, like ventilated seats during the summer here in North Carolina. I will continue to help others when I can or as directed by the universe and won't call attention to it as means of patting myself on the back and would encourage all to do the same when or if they can, especially those who are of means to do so.

I am or may be many things to many people, but it would be impossible to be all things to all people. So I won't make any attempt to be. Above all else, I am honest, trustworthy, and dependable. My integrity is beyond reproach, but I do not claim to be perfect or that I walk on water. I am confident in who I am and how I want to live my life. To do anything less would cheapen the experience. I am purposeful, mindful, and balanced (Libra), albeit with a strange or warped sense of humor at times. I am open-minded, independent, and rational yet still open to spur-of-the-moment, crazy adventures, especially if it's a significant other asking, wanting, or needing. I am considerate, compassionate, and cooperative but will not compromise my values to appease anyone. I am passionate, reasonable, and flexible in virtually every aspect of my life. I won't tolerate liars or BS, even if there isn't an impact on the quality of my life or of those I love. I am respectful, encouraging, and forgiving, especially to those who have earned it or made an honest attempt. I am loving, faithful, and affectionate with those I love and like and especially with a significant other. Yes, I like holding hands, opening doors, and showing love in action. I am reliable, persistent, and hopeful about the future and will speak out against evil and the wrongs humanity does on its behalf.

I am an American, a citizen of the United States of America who is White, male, of Polish ethnicity. I am not a White American, not a male American, not a Polish American. I understand the desire by some to define or describe people by classifying groups in this way, which is fine. It shouldn't be a precursor to them because it blurs the focus on the larger picture.

I am a United States marine, a title earned, never given—no better friend, no worse enemy. But I am not a gung ho type drill instructor reliving "war" stories, nor do I have memorabilia all over my house or on the clothing I wear. But I do have some. I wasn't the best or greatest marine, nor was I a shit bird. I did more than hold my own, earning several awards and recognitions—better in most areas but not perfect in everything. It is a part of me, always will be, as I continue to live my life as best I can because the core values align with my faith in universal truths and living them on my spiritual experience of walking the Red Road. I am a veteran who honorably served his country, its citizens, his brothers, and his sisters, past, present, and future, regardless of skin color, sexual orientation, ethnicity, or religious beliefs. If I am anything, I am all things because it is "We the People," not me, myself, and I.

Honor is what no man can give you and none can take away. Honor is a man's gift to himself. (Rob Roy)

I *am* a son to my mother, father, and Mom and Dad C, blessed as a result. I *am* a brother to my siblings, an uncle to nephews and nieces in both families. I love them all, even if I may not particularly like them or consider them as friends. We don't see eye to eye on political, religious, or spiritual views, but then again, we don't have to. We respect one another even if we don't agree with one another.

I am a child of the Creator and Mother Earth, a member of the human race, not a member of either political party, registered as an Independent. I believe love to be a religion, and its name is spirituality.

I am comfortable in my skin. Whether that is because I am imperfectly perfect or perfectly imperfect will depend on who makes the observation and its purpose. I've never claimed to be perfect in any way, shape, or form, but I am striving to be better today than I was yesterday. And even though I may fall short on occasion, I will rise and start again ultimately to love and be in love with your best friend who brings out the best in you and you in them—a love that isn't just a bond or word but rather a moving sea between the shores of your souls—to laugh and enjoy sharing the simple joys found all around us to be a part of a *youniverse*, not so one is at the center of the others but an integral part of it that nurtures the spiritual, physical, mental, and emotional; and live your best lives together *like no one's watching*. It's not about being perfect but if you are perfect for each other.

> When you like a flower, you just pluck it.
> But when you love a flower, you water it daily.
> One who understands this understands life.
> (Buddha)

Every human inhabitant needs to understand that in this thing called life, no one is getting out of it alive. So when your time comes, will you fear death and beg for more time or sing your death song like a hero going home? I'm in no hurry. I'll be a memory for some people one day, so I will do my best to be a good one. I have to live with myself, loving and liking who I see in the mirror. I'm not perfect and won't be every day, but I will do all that I can to ensure that my words and actions remain in harmony. I will do what I can, where I can, when I can, and especially when called upon to do so. I do this not to buy my way into heaven but so the world knows it will not change me. We should genuinely try to live while we are here, not merely exist. Easier said than done, but we have control over things: who we are and who we want to be. When I pass from this world to the next, I know the only things I am taking with me are those I have packed inside my heart, and I want to pack as much as I can between now and that day.

> My goal in life is to be as good a person as
> my dog already thinks I am. (Unknown)

A dog will love you more than it will ever love itself. What a beautiful world this would or could be if people had hearts like dogs. Nitki was my rock, my anchor, especially during the worst time in my life. Like me, he was a quiet alpha—living proof of unconditional love. He was lovable, protective of his home and his human, easygoing, and my favorite hello and my hardest goodbye. I will always be grateful for his love, affection, kisses, and being a part of my life. I miss him beyond words and more than they could ever say. I know he knows how much he was and is still loved and missed. Ultimately, the people I know and whose lives I've touched will be my legacy, but I will always be grateful for who I am and will do my best to continue to be. I have Walker now, who I love, and I may have other dogs in the future that I will also love. And maybe there will be a strong bond like Nitki and I had. No matter what may be on the horizon or just beyond it, the proudest, most humbling, uplifting, empowering, and encouraging event to date has been to have been loved by Nitki because it never wavered. It never was less than it was the day before. It was never critical. It was never withheld or used as a weapon.

I am and will always be forever grateful, blessed, and humbled to have been Nitki's "hooman."

I am Nitki's Dad.

ABOUT THE AUTHOR

I knew my hooman's path long before he took his first step, which is why I chose him. He grew up in a large family in Northwest Ohio, was active in sports, was a friend to all he met, and was aware of a spiritual path in his teens, he would discover decades later. "Walking the Red Road" was its name. As a US marine, his spiritual growth took off with a set of principles and values beyond reproach, which would strengthen his foundation and see him through a few dark times, including some that were long after he no longer wore the uniform.

With his warped sense of humor, he acknowledges he is not perfect but jokes that he is better than most. He owns his story—from hellish to heavenly and all points in between. Life is not the same for everyone, but it is not a spectator sport. He strives to live it, not merely exist in it. He does not compare his path to another. The only person he is trying to be better than is who he was yesterday.

His spiritual journey as a human being continues. By sharing his experiences, lessons learned, he hopes others will find strength, courage, and resolve to rise like a phoenix in pursuit of living their best life. He has always put others first, but his time in the sun is coming. And I will continue to watch over my dad and the love that awaits him from just north of the rainbow bridge.

Learn more at NitkisDad.com.

Nitki

CPSIA information can be obtained
at www.ICGtesting.com
Printed in the USA
JSHW041818171222
35057JS00002B/17/J

9 781662 476495